Destination
Canada

*A Genealogical Guide
to Immigration Records*

Dave Obee

Front cover:
• The landing stage, Liverpool. From a stereoscopic card, author's collection.
• Arrival document, Halifax. From the author's collection.

Title page:
• Quebec *Mercury*, 1865.

Back cover:
• Harbour, Vancouver. From the author's collection.
• Pier 21 Museum, Halifax. Courtesy Pier 21 Museum.

Edited by Lucinda Chodan.

Published by Dave Obee.
Distributed by Interlink Bookshop,
4687 Falaise Drive, Victoria, B.C. V8Y 1B4 Canada.

Printed in Canada by Friesens Corporation, Altona, Manitoba.

Library and Archives Canada Cataloguing in Publication

Obee, Dave, 1953-
Destination Canada : a genealogical guide to immigration records / Dave Obee.

Includes bibliographical references and index.
ISBN 978-0-9735143-3-9

1. Canada--Emigration and immigration--Archival resources.
2. Canada--Emigration and immigration--History--Sources. 3. Archival resources--Canada. 4. Canada--Genealogy--Handbooks, manuals, etc.
I. Title.

JV7220.O24 2010   929'.371   C2010-900398-5

Destination Canada

A Genealogical Guide to Immigration Records

An introduction

This guide to Canadian immigration records has roots of its own. In 1999 I produced a small guide entitled *Naturalization and Citizenship Indexes in the Canada Gazette 1915-1951*. It was based on material from the University of Victoria library, and inspired by Laura Hanowski of the Saskatchewan Genealogical Society.

Two years later that book was incorporated into the first edition of *Destination Canada: A Guide to 20th Century Immigration Records*. The first *Destination Canada* had just 44 pages, but included information on every type of record available at the time. Researchers had one major Internet source – the index to 1925-1935 arrivals on the website of what was then known as the National Archives of Canada.

In 2004 I produced a new edition of *Destination Canada*. It added, among other things, a bibliography and comprehensive information on the Immigration Branch records. This edition had 78 pages, and again, the major Internet source listed was the 1925-1935 index.

Oh, how things have changed in the past six years. Today, family historians have easy access to sources we did not dare to imagine in 2004. It is time, then, for a book that reflects this new reality, and will help researchers work through the many websites of interest. Updating *Destination Canada*, and expanding its reach to cover the full history of Canadian migration, has resulted in a book that is twice the size of the previous edition.

This work would not have been possible without the help of Lucinda Chodan, the editor-in-chief of the *Times Colonist* newspaper in Victoria, B.C. She served as the editor of *Destination Canada* as well. Many of the photographs in this book were taken, with her permission, from the collection at the *Times Colonist*.

The manuscript was also read by Melanie Arscott, Jutta Missal, Ann Leeson, and Dixie Obee. All of them caught errors and offered suggestions for improvements. (It should be noted, though, that if any errors remain, they are mine, and mine alone.)

Technical advice came from Adrian Raeside, Rob Struthers, Marc Furney, and Jessica Veinot. Thanks also to Jacqueline van Dyk for her words of encouragement.

I have also received help from two notable people – Sylvie Tremblay of Library and Archives Canada and Suzanne Russo Adams of Ancestry.com. Both are true friends to the entire genealogical community.

Dave Obee
Victoria, B.C.
February 2010

Chapter 1
The immigration experience

They came from the urban slums of London, from the estates in the English countryside, and from the islands in the north of Scotland. They came from the Russian steppes, the industrial areas of Germany, and from the Scandinavian lands. They came from the shores of the Mediterranean Sea, the Balkan mountains, and from Africa. They came across the Pacific Ocean, from countries such as China, Japan, and India. They came from the United States as well, crossing the border in search of opportunities and the promise of a better future.

They were your ancestors and mine. They were the immigrants who helped shape Canada, bringing their dreams and ideas and traditions to this country with the hope that Canada would offer more than what they had at home.

There have been millions of immigrants over the decades, and every one had a unique story. The immigrant experience varied for too many reasons to count – including the family's financial status and religion. Perhaps their homeland was in turmoil or they had legal problems. Perhaps their landlord or their parents were forcing them to leave, or perhaps the family did not have enough land for the youngest children. Perhaps friends or relatives had already come to Canada, and had sent word home that the streets here were paved with gold. Perhaps they did not even plan to come to Canada; it could be that they simply set out for America, oblivious to the fact that America had more than one country.

The time frame matters, too. Immigrants in the 17th century faced conditions that were radically different from those in the 20th. Between 1830 and 1930, a century when millions of people came to North America, every decade brought innovation and change. In the early years, ships relied on wind power, but new ones used coal-fired steam engines. Where travel inland had relied on stage coaches, railways were built to cover the distance more reliably. Where the early immigrants had to fend for themselves as soon as they left the ship, the later ones could stay in immigration halls, and were

Passengers were inspected before they were allowed to board

offered help by churches and by colonization societies. Where the first arrivals on the Prairies were greeted by miles and miles of nothing but miles and miles, later arrivals found thriving communities and plenty of support.

Family historians should try to find out everything they can about the immigration of their ancestors. The decision to move from one country to another is one of the most important decisions an individual can make – and one that will forever change the course of a family history. Most Canadians are in this country because their ancestors made the conscious decision to come here.

Along with learning the concrete details about a person's arrival – the date, the place, the name of the ship and so on – genealogists should try to understand the forces that prompted their ancestors to immigrate. Were they lured here by the promise of religious freedom, financial security or some other factor? Or did they feel compelled to leave their former country because of problems there? Hints might be found in local or regional histories.

Many migrants had their choice of destination – they could have picked the United States, Australia, New Zealand, South Africa, South America, or even the Russian Empire, but they opted for Canada. Why did they come here? Were they welcomed to Canada? Were they coming to live next to people from their ancestral area – something known as chain migration – or were they strangers in a strange land? Had they tried other countries, and been turned away?

People were desperate to flee the Irish famine

The earliest immigrants came from France or the British Isles, using sailing ships for the perilous journey across the North Atlantic Ocean. They landed at small harbours and settled nearby, carving out a meagre existence on the land. Later arrivals included many Loyalists, driven north by the revolution that created the United States. And as the decades passed, Canada saw more arrivals from continental Europe and Asia.

There were many organized immigration schemes in the early days, including the Red River settlement in what is now Manitoba, the Peter Robinson settlers in the Peterborough area of Ontario, as well as bride ships carrying "les filles du roi" (the king's daughters) to New France in the 1600s and, two centuries later, willing women to eager men on Vancouver Island.

There were moves made of necessity as well. The potato famine in Ireland in the 1840s drove many people from the island nation. An unknown number died on the emigrant ships or soon after arrival, in quarantine stations or in the poorest areas of cities such as Halifax, Quebec City, and Montreal.

By the time of Confederation in 1867, steamships were starting to replace sails, although most shipbuilders continued to install sails for a few years, just in case. No matter what kind of power these vessels used, there was no guarantee that the voyage would be without incident; catastrophic sinkings took place from time to time.

Your ancestors might have heard of Canada through official sources. The Canadian government opened its first immigration

office in England in 1868, just a year after Canada was established. Over the years it advertised heavily, at various times concentrating on the British Isles, the United States, and to a lesser extent Continental Europe.

A ship departs from England in the 1850s

They might also have been lured to Canada by private settlement or colonization companies – or they might have heard of Canada from friends or relatives. In the 19th century many books were published to help emigrants make the right choices, in the opinions of the authors at least. With titles such as *A Practical Guide for Emigrants to the United States and Canada*, they included information on available work, distances between cities, the cost of living, principal seaports, and what to take on the voyage.

Emigrants obtained passage to Canada in a variety of ways. Many would have gone to an agent who represented numerous shipping lines, and selected a crossing based on its departure date, destination port, and cost. The port of departure was often not close to where they lived, so they needed to get to the port by railway or other means.

While Canada had only a handful of arrival ports, people came here through dozens of ports in Europe and Asia. An emigrant might not have used the port closest, or even one in the same country. Some people went through a couple of other countries, and passed ports that would seem perfectly acceptable, to reach their chosen departure point.

Once at the departure port, they would spend a day or two – or sometimes several weeks or months – waiting for their chance to board a ship to their destination. In later years, Canadian immigration authorities worked in ports overseas, effectively pre-clearing prospective immigrants to ensure they were of good health and good character. The port cities were often busy, teeming with prospective immigrants, with a dozen or more languages heard in the crowds.

Finally, the moment would arrive. The immigrants would board the ship bound for Canada. There still might be a few hours of waiting, because it took time to get everyone on board and ensure that the vessel was ready. Still, most immigrants were eager to go, and did not want to risk missing the sailing.

The immigrants were normally in steerage. This was the large space below the deck, deep within the ship, lined with wooden bunks. Sometimes there were rows of wooden bunks in the middle of the cabin as well as the ones on the sides. In some ships, passengers were expected to bring their own bedding and food, and stoves were provided for them to cook.

A couple of levels above the immigrants were the tourists, travelling in style in first and second class. These are the people who had the time and money to move about in comfort, while the immigrants were usually desperate to preserve what money they had as they sailed into the great unknown.

The departure of a vessel marked a turning point in terms of genealogical research. To that point, records of the immigrant had been found in the home country; now, with the exception of probate documents and obituaries of other family members, their names would be in Canadian records instead.

A researcher's chances of finding a person before his or her arrival in Canada will often depend on the country of origin. From Scotland, England, or Wales? Odds are good. From Eastern Europe? Then it will be less likely that you will find much about the person. Name changes and transcription errors, coupled with a lack of records and difficult access to those which have survived, will work against many genealogical researchers.

The port would be, for many immigrants, the last time they stood on the soil of their native continent. It would have been an emotional moment for them as they recognized that their lives were about to be transformed. Today, standing at the same spot can be emotional for a genealogist. A visit to the departure port is as important to family history research as is a visit to the ancestral village.

The Olympic was one of the White Star passenger liners

The crossing itself could have taken a month or two, in the days of sail, or as little as five or six days after the arrival of steamships. Most immigrants came to Canada in the summer, because that is when more vessels were sailing. Just as well, too. The North Atlantic could be miserable and rough in the winter.

The ships were in constant use, shuttling back and forth across the oceans as quickly as possible in order to do as

much business as possible.

And there was plenty of demand, because it seemed that Canada was the land of opportunities. David Davidson Hay, an immigration agent working for the government of Ontario, reported in 1874 that there was plenty of room for anyone who chose to come. "We can absorb thousands more without any trouble," he said in a letter to London. "Abundance of work for the year round can be got for all who come, the demand being four to one to the supply."

Hay's letter did not say it, but part of the problem was that many people were choosing to leave Canada in those years, lured by the cities and growing factories of the United States. Others stayed in Canada, but headed west from their homes in Ontario or the Maritimes in pursuit of free land or jobs on the Prairies.

In December 1872, the *New York Times* reported that in spite of the best efforts of Canadian immigration authorities, "the great stream of immigration which comes by way of the St. Lawrence has steadily flowed into the western states through Detroit." The government was offering free land in Ontario, but that land represented "hardship and distress" for "the poor unfortunates" who took it, the newspaper said.

Ships became larger and larger as the immigration rush continued. By the early 20th century a ship arriving in Quebec could be carrying more than 1,000 passengers, resulting in long delays as the new arrivals were processed.

Conditions on the ships improved dramatically over the years. Steerage class, as uncomfortable and impersonal as it was, was a step up from the accommodations offered in the early 19th century. Newspaper reports of the time told of people wearing little more than rags on arrival, and of children who were naked when they stepped foot on Canadian soil for the first time.

Newspapers also said that while cargo was protected, the immigrants had to make do on the exposed upper deck of the vessels. The conditions on the ships drew the attention of many humanitarians and social reformers. One of them was Vere Foster, who travelled on the ships with emigrants to see the conditions for himself, and was reported to have paid the fares for 25,000 people. Foster said, in a letter published in *Freeman's Journal and Daily Commercial Advertiser* in Dublin in 1852, that emigrants faced great suffering because of the lack of accommodations. "While horses are most carefully protected on all sides and overhead from the inclemency of the weather, men, women, and children are exposed, perfectly shelterless, in all seasons and all weather."

Shiploads of immigrants often brought an unwelcome cargo – disease. As a result, people who might be sick with something such as cholera – and anyone who had been in contact with those unfortunate people – were kept in quarantine on arrival in Canada until it was determined that the danger had passed.

The quarantined passengers were given a kerosene shower, followed by a hot water shower to wash away the oil, and their belongings were cleaned. They were not allowed to leave quarantine until they were given a clean bill of health.

Most of the time, these quarantine stations were relatively quiet, because ship after ship were considered to be free of disease. Sometimes, though, the stations had far more people than they could handle.

Steerage class

In truth, there was not much class to steerage. Immigrants travelling in steerage class paid the lowest price and were in the lowest decks of a ship, with only the most basic amenities. Still, that was an improvement from the early days of sailing ships, when immigrants were forced to remain on the deck at all times.

Quarantine stations had to be isolated from the population of the port to ensure that any diseases would not be spread. As a result, most were on islands.

Some ships were stopped by disease before they even left the British Isles. One example was the ship Transit, which sailed on April 15, 1832, from Warrenpoint, Ireland, with 100 passengers seeking to go to Quebec City. The next day, the Transit put in to Bangor, near Belfast, reporting that three passengers had died of cholera-like symptoms since leaving Warrenpoint. Another passenger and the captain were also ill.

Many of the Canada-bound ships were boarded by people already sick with cholera or smallpox, and the diseases could spread rapidly in the confined spaces on board. Deaths on the ships were a daily occurrence, but there is no accurate count of those who did not make it. Thousands of people who survived the journey died during the quarantine period, and are buried on the quarantine islands.

The Atlantic quarantine stations – Grosse Île near Quebec City, Partridge Island near Saint John, and Lawlor's Island near Halifax – were busiest during the Irish famine in the 1840s. There is no comprehensive source of information on the people who faced quarantine. Later passenger lists may indicate, however, that arrivals were detained for medical reasons, so they should be checked carefully.

The stations were not perfect; some people hid their symptoms so they could head directly to the port, and some passengers were healthy when they arrived but fell ill while waiting in quarantine. In the late 19th century, all of the Canadian quarantine stations were roundly condemned for being ineffective. Regulations were tightened in 1892 in response to yet another outbreak of cholera.

After being cleared by the health authorities, the immigrants were sent on their way. After the 1880s, many took trains to their final destinations in Ontario or Western Canada.

Adequate land connections were vital to the process, and the completion of the Canadian Pacific Railway in 1885 opened huge areas of the country for settlement. Canadian Pacific launched a fleet of ships on the Pacific Ocean in 1887, and

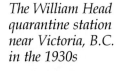

The William Head quarantine station near Victoria, B.C. in the 1930s

Immigrant railway cars had only the basic necessities of life

on the Atlantic Ocean four years later. That made it possible for a person to travel from Liverpool, England, to Japan – 14,000 miles – using the services of one company. It also meant that immigrants from across two oceans could have quick, easy passage to Canada.

Several other shipping companies were lining up to serve the immigrants as well. They included the Allan Line, White Star, Hamburg America, Holland America, and more.

Once you have found an immigrant's ocean arrival, the next step is to find out how long it took to get to the final destination. Schedules for Canadian Pacific and other railways were published by the rail companies and in private publications such as *Waghorn's Guide* – and even in daily newspapers.

In 1900, westbound Canadian Pacific passenger trains travelled overnight from Quebec City to Montreal, and trains travelled between Halifax and Montreal in about 24 hours. Passengers bound for Toronto on the 9:45 a.m. train from Montreal would reach their destination the same day. They could be in Winnipeg in two days, Regina in three, Calgary in four, and Vancouver 36 hours after Calgary.

The eastbound express left Vancouver seven days a week at 2 p.m. One that

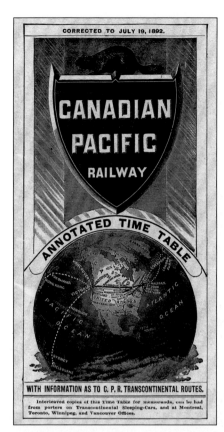

CORRECTED TO JULY 19, 1892.

CANADIAN PACIFIC RAILWAY

ANNOTATED TIME TABLE

WITH INFORMATION AS TO C. P. R. TRANSCONTINENTAL ROUTES.

Interleaved copies of this Time Table for memoranda, can be had from porters on Transcontinental Sleeping-Cars, and at Montreal, Toronto, Winnipeg, and Vancouver Offices.

Railway timetables provide information on travel across the country

left on a Wednesday would have passengers in Calgary early Friday morning, in Regina Friday evening, and in Winnipeg on Saturday afternoon.

Immigrants travelling by train from the port at San Francisco to Vancouver would spend about 36 hours en route.

Winnipeg was a key destination for many arrivals from Eastern Canada in the late 19th century and early 20th century. The "Gateway to the Canadian West" was the base for several immigration and colonization societies. A five-storey immigration hall provided a place for the immigrants to stay while waiting for confirmation of employment and a permanent address. The federal government opened similar halls in other cities because of the success of the Winnipeg one.

After arriving in their new homes, most of the immigrants would settle into jobs, raise their children, and adjust to life in Canada. In time they would appear in record sources known to genealogical researchers – including the census, directories, newspapers, church records, and more.

Not everyone stayed in Canada. In the latter half of the 19th century, the number of people leaving for the United States was almost the same as the number arriving from Europe. Others simply went back to where they had come from – sometimes because they had made enough money here, sometimes because their Canadian dream had failed.

And everyone had different dreams, of course. The Home Children, juveniles sent from the British Isles between 1869 and the 1930s, had little choice about making the journey.

Some people came from Europe for the promise of free land on the Canadian Prairies. One of those people was Rev. George Exton Lloyd, who was one of the leaders of the Barr group of colonists from England, Scotland, and Wales who came to Canada in 1903. He was optimistic about what lay ahead.

"The mother country is being stirred to its centre by the wonderful possibilities afforded in Canada, and in the next few years the greatest exodus ever seen in British history will commence here," he told a reporter soon after the first colonists arrived on the Lake Michigan steamship at Saint John, New Brunswick.

Before long, the colonists discovered that the possibilities on the bald prairie were not quite as wonderful as Lloyd had claimed. Still, they put Lloyd in charge when they deposed their original leader, Isaac M. Barr, and then named the city of Lloydminster – on the Alberta-Saskatchewan border – in his honour.

Contrast Lloyd's optimism with the words of J. Obed Smith, the commissioner of immigration based in Winnipeg, who said in 1908:

"You know what a homestead looks like? It's a piece of ground just the way the Almighty left it. There's no house on it until you build one; no water unless you carry a flask; no food unless you take it in your pockets; nothing on it but a piece of sky, and that's too far away to keep you warm in winter."

Despite his cautionary words, the immigrants continued to pour into Canada, just as they had for more than 300 years.

Chapter 2
Four centuries of immigration

Canada could be considered a nation of immigrants and their descendants. Even the First Nations came from elsewhere – across a land bridge from Asia, if the scientific theories can be believed. In the early 17th century, people started arriving from France, leading the way for European settlers. These settlers survived off the land, and through trade with the local native population.

Although there were some notable exceptions, such as the arrival of foreign Protestants – the Palatine Germans – in Nova Scotia in 1750 to 1752 and the landing of the Hector, with Scottish settlers, at Pictou, Nova Scotia, in 1773, the early years of immigration to Canada were generally quiet. Much more attention was being given to the other British possessions in North America, in the area known as New England.

The American Declaration of Independence in 1776 drove about 70,000 Loyalists north. That spurred development in what became Canada, and helped make this land a destination of choice for further arrivals from the British Isles. It was one of the most important events in the history of Canadian immigration, even though it did not happen here.

The United Empire Loyalists changed the maps through the creation of new colonies. The arrival of thousands of Loyalists in Nova Scotia prompted the sep-

Emigrants wait at Cork, Ireland, for their ship to leave

Irish villagers gather as a priest gives his blessing to a departing family

aration of New Brunswick, Cape Breton, and the Island of St. John (since 1799, Prince Edward Island). The arrival of thousands of Loyalists in Quebec resulted in the splitting of that colony into Upper and Lower Canada – later Canada West and Canada East, and then Ontario and Quebec.

Emigration from the British Isles started in earnest after the end of the Napoleonic wars in 1815. The United States was the first choice for most of the emigrants, but Canada received its fair share of the rising tide.

In the 1830s, churches, charities, and individuals saw emigration as a way to solve Britain's social ills, such as poverty, unemployment, and overcrowding in slums. One example was the Petworth Emigration Scheme, sponsored by the Earl of Egremont and promoted by Thomas Sockett, Anglican rector of Petworth, West Sussex, which sent about 1,800 working-class people from the south of England to Upper Canada between 1832 and 1837.

Most British immigrants went to Upper Canada. The new arrivals included Scots who had been forced from the land in the Highland Clearances, and poor Irish who were escaping the famine of 1847 to 1852.

In the West, the Fraser River gold rush in 1858 caused a flurry of activity on Vancouver Island. Victoria saw thousands of new arrivals, including plenty of people from the United States, Eastern Canada, and elsewhere. The immigrants included blacks, Chinese, Hawaiians, and Jews, all coming up from San Francisco. Many of these original immigrants went back to the United States over the next few years.

Vancouver Island's population growth was given another boost in 1862, when "bride ships" carrying single women put smiles on the faces of a community that was mostly male.

The Dominion of Canada was created in 1867, with the passage in London of the British North America Act. The country started with just four provinces – Ontario, Quebec, New Brunswick, and Nova Scotia – but added Prince Edward Island, Manitoba, and British Columbia in the early 1870s.

Manitoba and the Northwest Territories – including what became the provinces of Alberta and Saskatchewan – saw a rush of people wanting the free land that was made available after the Hudson's Bay Company turned control of the region over to the federal government. In 1885, the Canadian Pacific Railway was completed and it became possible to cross the country by rail.

The railway had been built from Ontario to British Columbia to satisfy the terms of Confederation with British Columbia, and its financial viability required settlement across the vast expanse of the Prairies. So for the next three decades, the government did everything it could to encourage settlers in that area.

It was not easy; the lure of the United States was strong, and as many people were leaving Canada as were arriving. From 1861 through 1901, immigrants were not able to make up for the people who were heading out.

Sir Clifford Sifton, the Minister of the Interior, set the tone for Canada's growth in 1898 when he launched a policy designed to bring in more immigrants from the British Isles, Continental Europe, and the United States. The government worked with the railway companies, which were building new lines in Western Canada and needed settlers along those lines to help make their investments pay off.

Sifton specifically appealed to a previously untapped source – East-Central Europe. This created a stir because of concerns that the new arrivals would not blend in. There was still a belief that much of Canada should be populated with English-speaking white people.

The arrival of about 7,000 Doukhobors from Russia in 1898 and 1899 did not help matters. Their religious beliefs and customs meant the Doukhobors would not swear allegiance to the King, and were reluctant to take part in the 1901 census. The federal government gave them land upon arrival, but took half of it back a few years later.

The train station in Libau, Russia, was adjacent to the dock

Canadians were more comfortable with the crofter colonies, established in Saskatchewan in the 1880s by Scots who had been forced out in the Highland Clearances.

In 1901, Canada had almost 5.4 million people. Only one in 20 was not "British-born" – referring to Canada, England, and the other countries of the British Commonwealth. Ten years later, a wave of immigration from Continental Europe and the United States changed the face of the nation; now, one in 10 residents was from non-Commonwealth countries, with many of the non-"British-born" living on the Prairies. Immigration from Asia in that decade resulted in riots in Vancouver, spurred on by people opposed to the arrival of Chinese and Japanese immigrants.

No industrialized country experienced a population boom to match that of Canada in the 20th century. New arrivals transformed the nation, opening new farmland and causing cities, towns, and villages to swell in size. The number of immigrants was higher, relative to the size of the population, than in the United States.

People were still leaving Canada – one estimate is that 1.1 million moved to the United States between 1911 and 1921 – but Canada saw unprecedented numbers of immigrants during that period. While many people were heading from Quebec to New England, for example, many others were heading north from the Great Plains to the Prairie provinces in order to take up homesteads.

The numbers tell the tale of the nation's remarkable growth. Canada's population, not quite 5.4 million in 1901, hit 7.2 million a decade later, and reached 8.8 million in 1921.

Immigration was a key factor in this explosive growth. In a single three-year period, 1911 to 1914, more than one million people arrived in Canada by ocean or by land. That was a population increase of 13.8 per cent in just 36 months, primarily as a result of immigration. Some areas in Western Canada saw a fourfold increase in population in less than five years as a result of new arrivals.

In those years, immigrants from the British Isles accounted for 38 per cent of the total. Immigrants from the United States were close behind at 35 per cent, with immigrants from all other countries accounting for the remaining 27 per cent.

Immigration peaked in the 12-month period ending March 31, 1914, when there were 402,432 new arrivals. Federal officials at the time were confident that the rate of immigration was likely to remain at that level, or even increase in the years to come.

Advertisements in English newspapers, such as this one for the Royal George, drew more immigrants to Canada

CANADIAN NORTHERN

RAILWAYS   LANDS   STEAMSHIPS

The Royal Line Turbine Twin Screw Steamer "ROYAL GEORGE" (12,000 tons, 18,000 horse-power).

For several months the numbers stayed high, but the outbreak of the Great War in the summer of 1914 brought a sudden end to the immigration boom. Few people came from Europe during the war; there were other priorities at the time. Immigration levels from the United States remained high. Many "British-born" men in Canada returned to the British Isles to sign up for service.

In the mid-1920s, after the end of

the war, immigration levels rose – but not to the high numbers recorded between 1911 and 1914.

In 1922, the British government enacted the Empire Settlement Act, which helped persuade 130,000 British to move to Canada. A wide variety of settlement schemes were developed as a result of this act, including one designed to bring 3,000 families to Canada to settle in rural areas.

Canada's immigration policies in the 1920s still had a strong bias toward arrivals from the United Kingdom, or failing that, English-speaking white people from the United States. In the 1920s, for example, immigrants from England, Ireland, Scotland, and Wales were offered a special rate for passage, and did not need a passport to gain entry. People from the United States could simply cross the border, as long as they stopped at one of the entry stations that the Canadian government had set up along the boundary.

Arrivals from Northern Europe – countries such as Germany and the Netherlands – were welcomed as long as they had a passport and could pay the regular rate for passage.

People coming from Central and Eastern Europe – countries such as Poland – were accepted only if they were agricultural workers or domestic servants, or had close relationships to people already legally in Canada. (This is why immigrants who were definitely not farmers – church ministers, for example – listed themselves as agricultural workers when they applied to enter Canada.) Like the Northern Europeans, arrivals from Central and Eastern Europe also needed a passport, and were not granted a special passage rate.

Many people came to Canada under programs set up by religious organizations. In 1928-1929, for example, 441 people arrived with the help of the Mennonites, 1,516 through the Lutheran Immigration Board, 1,066 through the Association of German Canadian Catholics, and 448 through the German Baptist Board.

In the 1920s, two provinces took most of the new arrivals. The 12-month period ending March 31, 1929, was typical: of 137,162 immigrants, 56,259 said they were going to Manitoba, and 35,192 said they were going to Ontario. That didn't necessarily mean that Manitoba's population grew by that much; for many of the immigrants, Winnipeg was simply the stated destination. Within days or weeks they moved farther west.

The Great Depression, a worldwide economic downturn which started with a stock market crash in 1929, effectively shut off the flow of immigrants. With hundreds of thousands of men unemployed, the public had no appetite for more people needing jobs, and most people in other countries saw no point in coming here. Exceptions were often expatriate Canadians; many people who had moved to the United States returned to Canada during those years. Immigration did not pick up again until after the end of the Second World War in 1945.

For decades, Canada became a new home for tens of thousands of children from the British Isles. Life was not always pleasant for these children, known as Home Children; many lived in near-slavery conditions until they could leave the homes of their sponsors.

Immigrant or emigrant?

One person can be both an emigrant and an immigrant at the same time.

An emigrant is someone leaving one country to live in another.

An immigrant is someone who arrives in a country from another.

After 1914, the busiest year for immigration came in 1957, when 282,164 people arrived. Most were bound for Ontario, Quebec, or British Columbia. In 1958, the boom ended when an economic downturn caused a sharp drop in the number of people admitted.

Canada has welcomed many refugees over the years. They included the people who fled the Soviet Union in the 1920s, near the start of Josef Stalin's reign of terror; people fleeing war-torn Europe in the early 1950s; and refugees from Communist crackdowns in Hungary in 1956 and Czechoslovakia in 1968. In later years Canada opened its doors to "boat people" from Vietnam and others who were fleeing problems in their home countries.

For decades, however, entry to Canada depended on the race of the applicant. There was a strong preference for people from the British Isles, the United States, and Western Europe. Blacks, Asians, and people from Eastern and Southern Europe and the Middle East were discouraged.

In 1914, the ship Komagata Maru, with immigrants from India, was denied permission to land at Vancouver. And in 1939, Canada refused to allow the St. Louis, a ship loaded with Jewish refugees from Germany, to land on our shores. Restrictions based on race and religion were eliminated in 1967.

At the end of the 20th century, the rate of new arrivals was about 200,000 a year, with the nation's population at about 30 million.

The story of immigration to Canada has been told in many books over the years. One of the best sources is a set of two textbooks, *History of the Canadian Peoples*, by Margaret Conrad and Alvin Finkel. Volume One covers the years before Confederation in 1867; Volume Two covers the years since 1867. *Strangers at Our Gates*, by Valerie Knowles, is a history of Canadian immigration and immigration policy from 1540 to 2006.

Researchers can also consult annual reports by the government departments responsible for immigration and naturalization, the microfilmed records of the Immigration Department (see chapter 11) as well as reports by the North West Mounted Police.

Library and Archives Canada has an excellent online exhibition about immigration, entitled Moving Here, Staying Here. The site is designed to make it easier to find information about your immigrant ancestors, using the collections at Library and Archives Canada, and also to make it easier to understand the immigration experience.

ON THE INTERNET:

<www.collectionscanada.gc.ca/immigrants/index-e.html>

Citizenship and Immigration Canada has a comprehensive history of 20th century immigration on its website. Entitled Forging Our Legacy: Canadian Citizenship and Immigration, 1900–1977, it examines the way that immigration helped to shape the Canada of today.

ON THE INTERNET:

<www.cic.gc.ca/english/resources/publications/legacy/preface.asp>

Finding an ancestor on a passenger list is just one step toward understanding the immigration experience. To get the full story, a researcher should find out

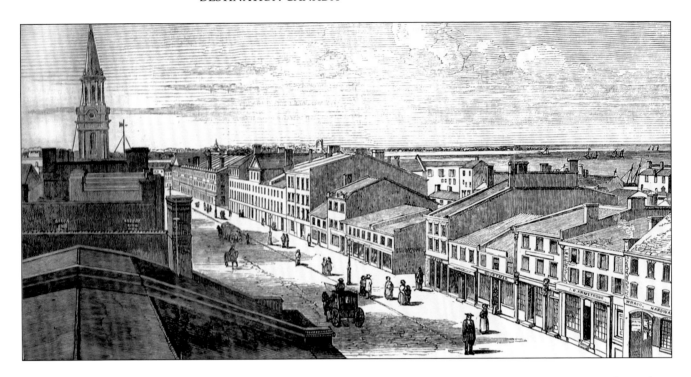

more – including the possible reasons for the decision to emigrate, the logistics of making the journey and the process faced on arrival in Canada, for example. This kind of information is included in several books as well as on websites.

Two sites are noteworthy.

The Maritime Archives and Library at Merseyside Maritime Museum in Liverpool has a collection of books and documents spanning three centuries. This collection includes merchant shipping records from throughout the United Kingdom. The primary focus is Liverpool from the early 18th century, but the coverage is international in scope.

The website includes 70 information guides that deal with almost every aspect of migration. These guides cover, for example, emigration to Canada, child emigration, shipwrecks, and many shipping companies. There is something there for everyone – even if your ancestors never stepped foot in Liverpool.

ON THE INTERNET:

<www.liverpoolmuseums.org.uk/maritime/archive>

Another excellent source is Norway Heritage – and again, you don't need to actually have Norwegian heritage to benefit from the site. Among the topics covered are what it was like in steerage class, daily life at sea, provisions on board sailing ships, health and sickness among the immigrants, the transition from sail to steam, and the arrival of the giant express steamships.

ON THE INTERNET:

<www.norwayheritage.com>

Several maritime atlases have been published over the years. These provide information on the location of ports and on the routes taken by the ships. One to look for is *Lloyd's Maritime Atlas of World Ports and Shipping Places*, which has appeared in about two dozen editions since 1951.

Toronto – shown here in 1847 – was a destination for many immigrants

Ten who made a difference

People who choose to move from one country to another might cite a variety of influences. Sometimes their decisions were made easier because of the actions of others. There have been influential people over the years; here are 10 who helped convince many people to move to Canada.

- **George Exton Lloyd, 1861-1940.** Led the Barr colonists on the Prairies after the group's original leader, Isaac Montgomery Barr, was deposed. In gratitude, the name of the community at the centre of the colony, along the Alberta-Saskatchewan border, was given the name Lloydminster.

- **Sir Clifford Sifton, 1861-1929.** Served as Canadian Minister of the Interior, responsible for immigration, from 1896 through 1905. Encouraged settlers from the United States, the British Isles, and – controversially – East-Central Europe.

- **Frank Oliver, 1853-1933.** Served as Canadian Minister of the Interior from 1905 through 1911, after Sifton, and had a radically different approach. Encouraged immigration from the British Isles and the United States, but tried to bar anyone from Eastern Europe.

- **Leo Tolstoy, 1828-1910.** Russian writer, helped pay the cost of getting the Doukhobors to Canada in 1898 and 1899. His most famous novels are *War and Peace* and *Anna Karenina*.

- **James Douglas, 1803-1877.** Governor of the colonies of Vancouver Island and British Columbia, paved the way for the growth that followed the 1858 Fraser River gold rush.

- **Peter Robinson, 1785-1838.** Organized two migrations of Irish to Upper Canada in 1823 and 1825. The community of Scott's Plains was renamed Peterborough in his honour.

- **John Galt, 1779-1839.** Scottish novelist who served as secretary to the Canada Company, which organized colonization efforts in Upper Canada. He was later involved in the British American Land Company, which sought to develop land in the Eastern Townships of Quebec.

- **Thomas Douglas, the Earl of Selkirk, 1771-1820.** Settled poor Scottish farmers in Prince Edward Island in 1803, Upper Canada in 1804, and the Red River Valley in Manitoba in 1812.

- **Thomas Jefferson, 1743-1826.** Drafted the Declaration of Independence, early in the American Revolution, which prompted a flow of United Empire Loyalists into what is now Canada.

- **Samuel de Champlain, 1567-1635.** Responsible for settlements in Quebec in the early 1600s. He founded Quebec City in 1608.

Chapter 3
A timeline of migration to Canada

1492: First voyage of Christopher Columbus to the Americas

1497: John Cabot arrives in Newfoundland from England

1534, 1535, 1541: Jacques Cartier's ship travels along the St. Lawrence

1541-43: First (and unsuccessful) colonization attempts in New France

1600: First fur trading post in Canada established at Tadoussac, Quebec

1605: Samuel de Champlain tries to establish colonies

1608: First settlement established at Quebec

1610: John Guy makes the first efforts to settle Newfoundland

1611: Jesuits set up a mission in Acadia (now Nova Scotia)

1627: "One Hundred Associates" sends settlers to Canada

1641: Paul de Chomedey, sieur de Maisonneuve, settles island of Montreal

1663: "Les filles du roi" arrive, with a dowry of money and free transport

1665: Jean Talon arrives in New France

1670: Hudson's Bay Company is established in England

1713: Treaty of Utrecht awards Newfoundland, Acadia, and Hudson Bay territory to England

1713: One hundred and sixty French, displaced from Newfoundland, found Louisbourg

1749: Military port established at Halifax

1753: Swiss and Germans settle at Lunenburg

1755-64: Acadians deported from Annapolis Valley

1758: Halifax dockyard enters service

1759-67: New England Planters arrive in Nova Scotia

1763: Treaty of Paris gives Britain all French lands east of the Mississippi

1769: Island of St. John (now Prince Edward Island) declared a colony

1773: Ship Hector arrives from Scotland at Pictou

1774: Quebec Act, passed by the British Parliament, sets up a system of government

1775-85: Thousands of Loyalists come north to Canada

1776: American Declaration of Independence

1778: Captain James Cook visits the Pacific coast

1780: Settlement begins on Ontario's Niagara Peninsula

1783: Treaty of Paris establishes border between the United States and British North America

1784: New Brunswick removed from Nova Scotia and established as a colony

1791: British system of land tenure established in Upper Canada

1791: Quebec divided into Lower Canada (now Quebec) and Upper Canada (now Ontario)

1793: Alexander Mackenzie reaches the Pacific Ocean by land

1793: Probate records start in Upper Canada

1794: An Act Respecting Aliens passed by the Parliament of Lower Canada

1798: Nova Scotia passes act dealing with aliens

1799: Island of St. John renamed Prince Edward Island

1812: Lord Selkirk attempts an agricultural settlement in southern Manitoba

1812-14: War with the United States

1818: The 49th parallel becomes the international boundary between Lake of the Woods and the Strait of Georgia

1823: Experimental colony of Irish established in Bathurst district of Ontario

1826: John Galt organizes the Canada Company, bringing settlers to Ontario

1826: Lachine Canal opens, bypassing rapids upstream from Montreal

1828: Act in Nova Scotia specifies that immigrants could not burden the public

1830s: Directories – lists of residents – launched in major cities

1832: First cholera outbreak reported in what is now Canada

1833: A peak year for immigration, with 66,339 arrivals

1833: Welland Canal opens between Lake Ontario and Lake Erie

1833: Wooden sidewheeler Royal William, powered by steam, crosses the Atlantic

1834: John Galt organizes the British American Land Company

1834: York is incorporated as the city of Toronto

1834: Slavery is abolished in the British Empire

1836: Samuel Cunard, founder of Cunard Lines, starts a steamboat ferry service between Halifax and Dartmouth

1836: First railway line opens in Canada

1837-38: Rebellions in Upper Canada and Lower Canada

1840: Cunard Line's Britannia completes the firm's first trans-Atlantic voyage to provide mail service between Britain and North America

1840: Act of Union brings together Upper and Lower Canada

1842: Census taken in combined Upper and Lower Canada

1846: Irish potato famine causes rush of emigration

1846: 49th parallel becomes the international border in western North America

1848: European rebellions prompt many to emigrate

1849: Vancouver Island becomes a British colony

1854: Cholera epidemic in Saint John, New Brunswick, kills 1,500 people

1856: Montreal Ocean Steamship Company starts regular service between Montreal and Liverpool

1856: Grand Trunk Railway opens between Montreal and Sarnia

1857: Ottawa named the capital of the province of Canada

1858: Fraser River gold rush in British Columbia

1858: British Columbia (the mainland) becomes a colony

1861-65: American Civil War is fought between North and South

1865: Quebec passenger lists record names of arrivals

1866: Trans-Atlantic telegraph cable is laid

1867: Dominion of Canada created with the passing of the British North America Act

Many early settlers tried farming – but later gave it up

18

1868: Federal government opens immigration office in London

1869: First federal immigration act passed

1869: Civil registration begins in Ontario

1869-70: Red River Rebellion in Manitoba

1870: Manitoba becomes a Canadian province

1870: Federal government assumes control of Hudson's Bay Company land on the Prairies

1870: Thomas John Barnardo starts his child emigration system in England

1871: First census of the new Dominion

1871: British Columbia joins Confederation

1872: Dominion Lands Act provides free homesteads on the Prairies

1872: Public Archives of Canada is founded

1873: Prince Edward Island joins Confederation

1873: North West Mounted Police established

1876: Intercolonial Railway connects Halifax with the Great Lakes

1876: First long-distance telephone call is made

1881: Halifax passenger lists start

1885: Northwest Rebellion breaks out on the Prairies

1885: Canadian Pacific Railway completed across Canada

1885: Head tax imposed on Chinese immigrants

1885: Banff National Park and Rocky Mountain National Park are established

1887: Charles Ora Card brings eight Mormon families to Southern Alberta

The driving of the last spike marked the completion of the Canadian Pacific Railway in 1885

1893: Lord Stanley donates a cup for hockey supremacy

1895: Start of records of people entering United States from Canada

1897: Klondike gold rush begins in the Yukon

1898: Sir Clifford Sifton launches major immigration programs

1899-1902: Canada sends troops to the South African (Boer) War

1900: Start of passenger lists for arrivals in Saint John, New Brunswick

1901: First trans-Atlantic wireless signal received at St. John's, Newfoundland

1905: Start of Vancouver and Victoria passenger lists

1905: Saskatchewan and Alberta become provinces

1906: Start of North Sydney, Nova Scotia, passenger lists

1907: Anti-Asian riots occur in Vancouver

1908: Severe restrictions on immigration from Asia

1908: Start of records of people entering Canada by land

1908: Lucy Maud Montgomery publishes Anne of Green Gables

1909: John McCurdy becomes the first person to fly an airplane in the British Empire

1912: Halifax launches a rescue mission after the sinking of the Titanic

1913: All-time peak year of immigration to Canada

1914: The ship Komagata Maru with its Indian immigrants is turned away

1914-18: First World War; 66,000 Canadians are killed

1916: Women in Alberta, Manitoba, and Saskatchewan are granted the right to vote

1917-23: Canadian National Railways is established

1918-19: Canadian troops sent to help quell the Russian revolution

1919: General strikes in Winnipeg and elsewhere in Canada

1922: Empire Settlement Act is passed in Great Britain

1923: Chinese Immigration Act virtually halts arrivals from China

1925: Immigrants from Eastern and Southern Europe considered equal to Western Europeans, as long as they are farmers

1925: United Church of Canada is formed in a merger of three denominations – the Presbyterians, the Methodists and the Congregationalists.

1928: Pier 21 immigration centre opens in Halifax

1928: Peak year of immigration between the wars

1929: "Persons case" determines that women are, in fact, persons

1935: First federal lists of voters are published

1930-39: Great Depression results in immigration restrictions

1937: Trans-Canada Air Lines (now Air Canada) is started

1937: Grosse Île quarantine station closes after 105 years

1939: SS St. Louis is not allowed to bring Jewish refugees to North America

Promotional material stressed the value of the land found in all parts of Canada

1939-1945: Second World War; 38,000 Canadians are killed

1940: Every adult in Canada is required to register with the federal government

1940: Federal unemployment insurance program established

1941: Bombing of Pearl Harbor in Hawaii prompts removal of Japanese-Canadians from the West Coast

1944: First war brides arrive in Canada from England

1946: Displaced persons start arriving from Europe

1946: Canadian Citizenship Act is passed; in effect on Jan. 1, 1947

1947: Oil is discovered near Leduc, Alberta

1949: Newfoundland becomes the 10th province

1949: North Atlantic Treaty Organization is established

1951: Universal old-age pension is established

1952: First Canadian television stations start broadcasting

1956: Refugees arrive from Hungary

1957: Post-war peak year of immigration

1962: Rogers Pass section of the Trans-Canada Highway opens

1962: Immigration Act is made more liberal

1965: Canada's flag is introduced

1967: Immigration Act eliminates racial and religious restrictions

1968: Refugees arrive from Czechoslovakia

1968: Acts of Parliament are no longer needed for divorces

1969: Official Languages Act is passed

1971: Pier 21 in Halifax closes after greeting more than one million immigrants

1973: Asian refugees arrive after being expelled from Uganda

1980: "Boat people" arrive from Vietnam

1992: North American Free Trade Agreement is signed

1999: Nunavut becomes a territory

In the early 20th century, the automobile replaced the horse on Canadian roads

Chapter 4
The key resources

The first choice for family historians looking for information about the arrivals of their ancestors will often be ship passenger lists, which are the most comprehensive source available. Most people came to Canada by crossing the Atlantic or Pacific oceans – and even the ones who came north from the United States would have had an ocean crossing in their family history.

But first, a note of caution. Effective family history research involves working back from the present, generation by generation, and confirming details as you go. Resist the temptation to leap across the water. Research your Canadian ancestry first. Do not simply accept a family legend about roots in Yorkshire, or Loyalist ancestors, or anything else without doing proper research back to that point. Too many family stories turn out to be based on wishful thinking, and too much time is wasted chasing them.

Your research in this country will make your research into immigrant ancestors that much easier. Besides, it helps to learn genealogical research techniques before diving into records in foreign countries.

Ideally, a researcher would try to tell the full story of the migration, using sources on both sides of the water, or the border. That helps to give context to the decision to make the move, as well as the conditions encountered on the journey.

A view of Montreal from Mount Royal in about 1900

Several sources can be consulted. They should be checked even when passenger arrival information has been found, because they can confirm or complement what has been found.

These sources include:

• Passenger lists, which are usually the most important source of information. They are available for arrivals in Quebec from 1865. It took 40 years before they were used consistently at the major ports. As a result, they might not be available for all of your ancestors.

• Census returns, such as the ones from 1901. They include the year of arrival in Canada for those people who were born elsewhere. This information might be crucial to finding a person's arrival – and in some cases it will be the only reference to an arrival. Be warned that accuracy was not all that important to many of our ancestors. A person who claimed in 1901 that he or she arrived in 1850 might have been, frankly, wrong about that.

Also watch for the birthplaces of the children. If the four oldest were born in Austria and the three youngest in Canada, it might be easy to guess at the year of immigration.

Earlier census returns can also help. If a person is in the 1881 census, but cannot be found in the 1871 census, that might indicate that he or she arrived in Canada between the two census years.

• City directories might show individuals soon after their arrival in Canada. Again, that might be a way to narrow down the arrival date. These directories were not always comprehensive, especially when dealing with people who did not have English as a native language.

• Vital records – civil registrations of marriages and deaths – might contain hints. For several years, for example, British Columbia's death registrations included information on how long the deceased person had been in Canada, in the province, and in the municipality. They often included the place of birth. This information was usually second-hand, however, so there might have been guesswork involved.

• Diaries and other records still in private hands might offer clues and, in some cases, precise details.

• Cemetery records might include the place of birth.

• Local histories often include information on family origins. Use caution, because the details were often provided by relatives who had second-hand information, which creates the possibility of errors. The year of arrival might be a guess, and the place of origin might not be spelled correctly. (Your ancestors might not have been literate, or they might have had a dialect that was difficult to understand. Think of the word phonetically.)

• Land records might help narrow the time frame of a person's arrival.

• Church records might have information on when a person or family arrived in the community. You might even find the name of a church official at their point of origin, as membership was transferred from one jurisdiction to another. Do not forget to check for church histories as well – they might include information on individuals, as well as on families that came as a group from other countries or regions.

• Newspaper obituaries might include references to the person's arrival in Canada, and feature stories might include details about a person's early years.

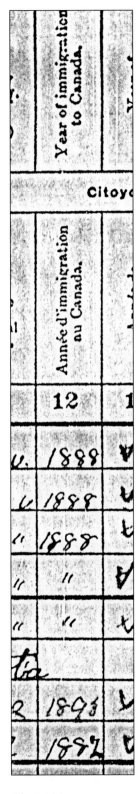

The 1901 census includes the year of arrival in Canada

These references could help focus searches.

A family historian should check as many of these sources as possible. Again, do not be satisfied with only finding a name on a passenger list; look for additional information that will help you tell a more detailed story of your ancestors.

Of all of these sources, as has been mentioned, passenger lists are usually the most important when dealing with immigration since 1865. That does not mean, however, that these lists are perfect – they are not.

The first step in searching through passenger lists should always take you to the Internet.

With so many databases online, it is possible to find an ancestor's arrival within a couple of minutes. In the old days – anytime before 2007, basically – it could have taken weeks to work through dozens of rolls of microfilm in a library. The online databases are not, however, without error, so there will still be times when it makes sense to use the microfilms. Comprehensive lists of film numbers are in this book.

This book includes many references to Internet sites. They are also listed on the "Immigration" page of the CanGenealogy.com site.

ON THE INTERNET:

<www.cangenealogy.com>

If you choose to use the World Wide Web, focus your attention on three major Internet sources.

• Library and Archives Canada contains the most extensive collection of the country's historical documents. It has a comprehensive array of databases on its website.

ON THE INTERNET:

<www.collectionscanada.gc.ca/databases/index-e.html>

• Ancestry.ca, part of the Ancestry.com family of websites, has worked extensively with Library and Archives Canada. All federal government records appearing on the Ancestry site are supposed to eventually be on the Library and Archives Canada website as well.

ON THE INTERNET:

<www.ancestry.ca>

Ancestry.ca website

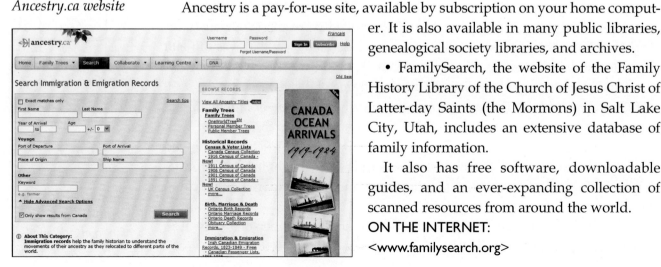

Ancestry is a pay-for-use site, available by subscription on your home computer. It is also available in many public libraries, genealogical society libraries, and archives.

• FamilySearch, the website of the Family History Library of the Church of Jesus Christ of Latter-day Saints (the Mormons) in Salt Lake City, Utah, includes an extensive database of family information.

It also has free software, downloadable guides, and an ever-expanding collection of scanned resources from around the world.

ON THE INTERNET:

Database strategies

An online database is not likely to be perfect. Errors and omissions happen for a variety of reasons. If you cannot find the person you are looking for, you might need to try searching with other parameters – and ultimately, your search might still come up empty. In the end, you might need to consult the original documents on the microfilms back at the library. And yes, that could take weeks.

Here are some search strategies to use:

• Enter a lot of information about a person, and if you do not find him or her, leave some of the fields blank and try again. This is most effective when dealing with a common name, such as John Smith. Be careful, though, because sometimes the first hit you find is not the one that you need.

• Enter a little, then focus. The opposite to the approach above. Enter John Smith, and when you see far too many hits, narrow the date range, or specify the port, and so on.

• Be flexible. The person's age might be wrong. The year of entry might be different from what the family has believed all these years.

• Don't be hung up on the precise spelling of a name. Names will appear differently for many reasons, with errors at the top of the list. Also, some people wanted their names to be anglicized, or were pressured by others to get rid of a foreign-sounding name. And remember that a person might have used a different first name, or the document might not have included full first names. If your relative Fred was listed on the document by his first initial only, you could have a false hit.

• If you have an option for exact matches, try it. If you have an option for a Soundex search, which assigns alphanumeric codes to names, try that too. The idea is to search the database in a variety of ways, because every search could bring different results.

• Use wildcards, those special characters that take the place of letters. On the Ancestry.ca website a "*" symbol will take the place of up to six characters, and a "?" can be used instead of a single character. If you are not sure, for example, whether the name might appear as Mallandaine or Mallandane, search for Malland*ne.

• Search beyond the obvious. Don't just look for the person's arrival record; check for other references to the person in the database. It could be that he or she returned to the old country for a visit a few years after coming to Canada.

• Read the documentation. It might offer more clues that could increase your chances of success.

• The passenger lists include people who were not immigrants. They will show, for example, the names of soldiers returning from the First World War, as well as Canadians returning from vacation in Europe.

Still haven't found your people? There are several reasons why they might not be listed.

Perhaps they came to Canada before 1865, and the passenger list no longer exists. If they came to Canada from Europe after 1865 – the start of passenger lists for Quebec – then perhaps they came through another Canadian port, one that did not yet have passenger lists. Or perhaps they came through the United States.

It is also possible that they are on a passenger list, but not in the database. Sometimes there were mistakes, possibly because the original documents were too difficult to read. Search a database by a first name only, with no family name, and you will see how many family names could not be read or were not included for another reason.

Humans are not perfect. Always bear in mind that a name might have been omitted or mistranscribed. A wise family historian will check every source available, even after a likely ancestor has been found. There are differences between records. In the 20th century, for example, the English outbound ship lists did not necessarily match the inbound Canadian ones.

The online databases should lead you to the passenger lists themselves. Always check the original document; never be satisfied with the information from the database. And always cross-check the information from the original document with what is in the database. In some cases, the databases refer to boats coming from the wrong ports – and the confusion can be quickly cleared up by checking the original passenger lists.

If you do not find your ancestor in the online databases, take a deep breath and dive into the microfilms. Sometimes that will be the only way to find your missing relative.

Passenger lists

Canadian passenger lists date from 1865, although the roots of the documents can be traced back to 1803. In that year, the British Parliament passed the Passenger Act, the first of a series of government initiatives designed to force shipping companies to improve the conditions faced by emigrants.

Ships were required to deposit a list of the passengers on board at the points of departure and arrival. The ships had to carry enough food and water, and provide enough space, to ensure the comfort and safety (within reason, of course) of the passengers on board.

The information collected served other purposes as well. The entry could have been the evidence needed when a person applied for naturalization or citizenship. It also could have given the government some help when a person was being deported, because the shipping line that brought the person to Canada was responsible for the return journey. The passenger list might also have provided the proof needed so an immigration agent could qualify for a bonus for his efforts.

In using the lists, always be sure to gather all of the information available to you. The first page of the list might include general information on the voyage itself, including its length, the number of people on board, and the name of the ship's master. Ports visited in transit might be shown. Check the lists of passenger names for any additional notations, including references to events on board such as births or deaths, as well as notable people. If a name is on the list but

No. of Railroad Order	Names of Passengers	Adults Age Male	Adults Age Female	Children 1 and 12 Age Male	Children 1 and 12 Age Female	Number of Infants not over 1 year	Profession, Occupation or Calling of Passengers	Nation or Country of Birth	Counties in British Isles from which Passengers came	Births at Sea	Deaths	Places of ultimate destination of passengers, excepting "Tourists" and "Returning Canadians" who are to be so described.
							Second Cabin					
	Anderson Miss Kate		25				Machinist	Lanarkshire				Vancouver City
	Armstrong Adam	27					Coml. Traveller	Roxburghshire				Calgary
O.B	Bain Mrs E.		31				Housewife	Midlothian				Brandon
	Batchelor D.W.	29					Poulterer	Forfarshire				Toronto
O.B	Bowie John	28					Baker	Morayshire				Winnipeg
	Boe G.G.	24					Engineer	Norway				Toronto
	Brown Alex	49					Sheet Iron Works	Lanarkshire				Milwaukee
do	Mrs Agnes L.		49				Housewife	do				-
do	Agnes S.		27				nil	do				-
do	Isabel L.				11		Child	do				-
do	John			9			do	do				-
	Carter Chas D.	26					Lithographer	Aberdeenshire				Montreal
	Cochrane Mary		33				Weaver	Lanarkshire				London Ont.
	Craig Mrs Wm		30				Housewife	do				Montreal
do	John			6			Child	do				-
do	Wm					inf.	do	do				-
do	Lily				3		do	do				-
	Colquhoun E.B.	26					Accountant	do				-
O.B	Dorward R.J.	21					Student	Forfarshire				Wapella N.W.J.
	Davidson Jas	a					Carriage Hirer	Lanarkshire				Toronto
do	Mrs		a				Housewife	do				do
O.B	do Thos	28					Grocer	Fifeshire				Winnipeg
O.B	do Mrs Isabella		22				Housewife	do				do
O.B	Duncan Mrs		26				do	Banffshire				Moose Jaw
O.B	do Robt					inf	Child	Midlothian				do
	Enslie David	23					Engraver	Midlothian				Montreal
O.O	Edmiston Mrs J.		46				Housewife	Berwickshire				Balmoral

crossed out, that usually means the person did not make the voyage. Check other vessels and later sailings for that person – and also consider that the person might have died.

Passenger lists are available starting in 1865 for the port of Quebec. Records for Halifax, Nova Scotia, begin in 1881, and Saint John, New Brunswick, in 1900. Records for Vancouver and Victoria, the two British Columbia ports, start in 1905. Lists for North Sydney, Nova Scotia, were started in 1906.

All of the lists that have been opened to the public are available on microfilm from Library and Archives Canada. Microfilms up to 1935 are available in several large libraries in Canada, although coverage varies with each collection. Microfilms up to 1908 are available through the Family History Library and the Family History Centers run by the Church of Jesus Christ of Latter-day Saints.

Most lists have also been digitized and placed on the websites of Library and Archives Canada and Ancestry.ca. The plan is to have all of the lists accessible through the Web. The images were copied from microfilms, and quality varies. Some pages are too dark to read, and others too light.

Most films contain the passenger lists for about 100 ships, although many of the vessels had a relatively small number of passengers – as few as a half-dozen in some cases.

Two Library and Archives Canada microfilms provide lists of the ships that arrived, including the date and the ports of embarkation and arrival. Microfilm T-976 covers Quebec, Halifax, Saint John, North Sydney, Vancouver, and Victoria

A passenger list from a 1903 crossing of the Atlantic

from 1900 through 1908. Microfilm T-5460 includes the information for Atlantic ports, covering Quebec 1865-1920, Halifax 1881-1920, and Saint John 1895-1920. Yarmouth, Nova Scotia, was included with Halifax in 1920.

Quebec was by far the busiest port, even though its season was only from May to November, throughout the era of immigration by ship. In the peak 12-month period, in 1913-1914, Quebec was busier than Halifax, the second-busiest port, by a ratio of almost three to one.

For most years, ship passenger lists were arranged by port and date of arrival. If you are tackling the microfilm, gather as much information as possible – for example, the year and month of the arrival, and the name of the port and the ship, if known.

The quantity of information included in passenger lists varied over the years as the forms evolved. There were also minor differences in the structure of the forms being used by different lines. There was no consistency about the introduction of many of the changes to the forms, so information about individuals might not be consistent – even for arrivals in the same year.

Starting in 1865, lists generally provided the name of the ship, the port of embarkation and the date, as well as the following information for each passenger:

- Name
- Age
- Gender
- Profession
- English, Scotch, Irish, or alien
- Destination port

There were variations as the years passed. From the mid-1870s, some lists show final destination instead of destination port. In 1894, the questions about English, Scotch, or Irish were replaced with a general question about the passenger's nation of birth.

By 1900, lists generally provided the name of the ship, the port of embarkation, the date, and the following information for each passenger:

- Name
- Age
- Gender
- Whether the head of a family was on board
- Number of persons in the family

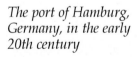

The port of Hamburg, Germany, in the early 20th century

- Profession, calling, or occupation
- Nation or country of birth
- Births at sea
- Deaths
- Places of ultimate destination – details not required for tourists or returning Canadians (identified as RC on some lists)

The questions about families were

eventually replaced with one dealing with marital status.

From 1909 through 1921, the forms generally included for each passenger:

- Amount of money in hand
- Name
- Age
- Gender
- Marital status
- Previous time in Canada, and details
- Intention to settle
- Ability to read and write
- Country of birth
- Race of people
- Destination (post office and province)
- Occupation in old country
- Intended occupation in Canada
- Past work as a farmer, farm labourer, gardener, stableman, carter, railway surfaceman, miner, or "navvy" (a term for labourer)
- Religious denomination
- Means to travel inland

In the first half of the 1920s, the government required individual forms for each person that were then filed, and later microfilmed, in rough alphabetical order. The forms included the same basic information that is found on passenger lists.

An individual manifest, known as Form 30A, was completed and submitted to immigration officers at the ports of arrival. This form, which replaced the large sheet passenger manifests, was introduced in some immigration offices in 1919, while other offices continued to use the sheet manifests as late as 1922.

Officially, the individual manifests were in use from June 1, 1921, to Dec. 31, 1924, when the Department of Immigration and Colonization dropped them in favour of an expanded version of the old large sheet manifests.

A copy of Form 30A had to be submitted for each passenger, including children, except those in transit to the United States. In the early version of the form used in 1919, the names of accompanying dependents were usually included with the head of household. In time, though, the dependents were recorded on separate forms – and as a result, researchers may face a challenge trying to track down and sort out all the members of one family.

Researchers also have to cope with the way the

Form 30A

records were microfilmed – in quasi-alphabetical order. For each letter of the alphabet, surnames are arranged in groupings based on the initial letters of each name. For example, surnames starting with Ada, Adc and Add are grouped together, then sorted alphabetically by given name.

It is much easier to use the database on the Ancestry.ca website, which is linked to digitized versions of the original Form 30A records.

These records include people who worked on ships as well as passengers. Note that passengers who arrived from 1919 through 1922 might appear in this series or in regular passenger lists, so both sets of films may need to be checked.

Each Form 30A usually included:
- Name of ship
- Date of sailing
- Port and date of arrival
- Name
- Age
- Gender
- Marital status
- Occupation
- Birthplace
- Race
- Citizenship
- Religion
- Previous residence in Canada
- Money in hand
- Ability to read and write
- Destination
- Nearest relative in the country from which the immigrant came
- Basic health questions pertaining to tuberculosis and mental and physical condition

Passenger lists took two pages in 1925-1935

If your ancestors arrived between 1925 and 1935, you are in luck. Not only are there databases on the Library and Archives Canada and Ancestry.ca websites, the forms themselves contain a wealth of information.

The database shows the name of the immigrant, as well as the port of arrival, age, country of origin, and the page and film number of the passenger list that contains more information.

The database is not complete; some entries from the original passenger lists were missed. It also does not include the names of returning Canadians, tourists, visitors, and passengers in transit to the United States. To locate those names, you will have to search the actual passenger lists for the relevant port and period.

The 1925-1935 microfilmed lists are arranged by port and date of arrival. They contain more information than any previous Canadian lists, including:

- Name
- Relationship to others on the ship
- Age
- Gender
- Marital status
- Country and place of birth
- Nationality, race, or people
- Previous time in Canada, and details
- Intention to settle
- Literacy and language
- Name of person who paid the passage
- Occupation
- Destination, with name of a person there
- Name and address of nearest relative in country of origin
- Health details
- Passport number
- Means of travel inland
- Action taken by examiner

Valuable clues about the person's life can be found in the names of the contact

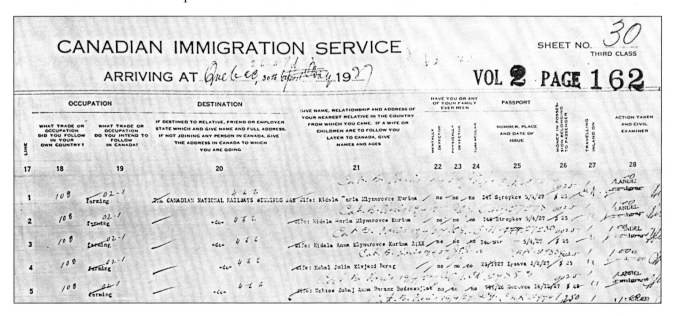

people in Canada and in the previous country of residence. These people are often close relatives, with the nature of the relationship shown.

The microfilms listed in this book are available through inter-library loan. Also, collections of passenger lists (generally to 1919), border entry lists, or both, are in the permanent collections at the following institutions:

• British Columbia Archives and Records Office, Victoria, British Columbia (B.C. ports only)

• Greater Victoria Public Library, Victoria, British Columbia (passenger lists)

• Cloverdale Branch, Surrey Public Library, Surrey, British Columbia (both series)

• Calgary Public Library, Calgary, Alberta (both series)

• Lethbridge Public Library (Lethbridge and District Branch of the Alberta Genealogical Society), Lethbridge, Alberta (both series)

• Saskatchewan Archives Board, Regina and Saskatoon, Saskatchewan (both series)

• Regina Public Library, Prairie History Room, Regina, Saskatchewan (passenger lists and Prairie border entry ports)

• Provincial Archives of Manitoba, Winnipeg, Manitoba (both series)

• Archives of Ontario, Toronto, Ontario (both series)

• North York Central Branch of the Toronto Public Library, Toronto, Ontario (most records to 1935)

• Montreal Municipal Library, Central Branch, Montreal, Quebec (both series)

• Archives nationales du Québec, Quebec City, Quebec (passenger lists – Quebec ports only)

• Public Archives of Nova Scotia, Halifax, Nova Scotia (passenger lists – Nova Scotia ports only)

Library and Archives Canada will provide photocopies by mail. Be sure to provide as much information as possible, including the series number, type of record, microfilm number if known, and approximate location on the reel if known. If you are requesting a copy from a passenger list, include the name and age of the immigrant, the name of the ship, and the date of sailing.

Requests for photocopies are payable by credit card. At the time of printing, copies cost 40 cents per page plus GST and applicable provincial sales tax.

ON THE INTERNET:

<www.collectionscanada.gc.ca/copies/005010-5021-e.html>

Orders may be submitted online.

They can also be sent by fax to: (613) 995-6274

Or send orders by mail to:

Library and Archives Canada

Services Branch

Consultation Services

395 Wellington St.

Ottawa, Ontario K1A 0N4

Chapter 5
The early years

I mmigrants started finding their way to Canada in the 1600s, but comprehensive passenger lists were not started until 1865. That creates a challenge for family historians, because many people managed to arrive on these shores without being noticed, apparently, by anyone with a quill and a piece of paper.

In 1803, the British Parliament enacted legislation to regulate vessels carrying emigrants to North America. The master of the vessel was required to prepare a list of passengers. Unfortunately, few such lists have survived. We should not give up, however, without searching those records that still exist.

There are dozens of sources of information, and many old arrival records have been transcribed. Lists from individual ships have survived for some ports in Canada, and some other records, such as church registers, sometimes contain information on origins.

The scene as a ship prepares to leave Portsmouth, England

Many books have been compiled on early immigration to Canada. An example is Donald Whyte's *Dictionary of Scottish Emigration to Canada Before Confederation*. It is in four volumes published over 20 years by the Ontario Genealogical Society, which has also put all four books onto one CD-ROM. Check for similar books for your area of research.

What was arguably the most important group of early immigrants – the

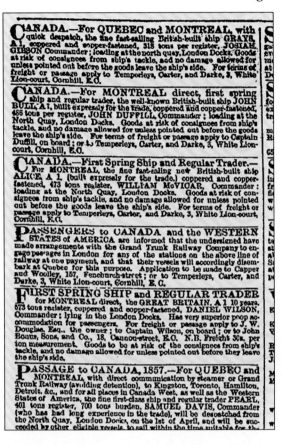

The London Times had advertisements for Canada-bound ships

United Empire Loyalists – did not necessarily arrive by ship. The Loyalists were people who had been in the 13 original U.S. colonies at the outbreak of the American Revolution, but remained loyal to the British crown. Many simply headed north into what remained of British territory after the Declaration of Independence in 1776.

The ocean crossings in the days of sail power were long and uncomfortable. The ships often carried only a handful of passengers – sometimes half a dozen, sometimes as many as 30. There are no accurate records of the number of people who boarded the ships, how many made it to these shores, or even how many ships were lost. The lack of records compounds the issues faced by today's family historians; we cannot be sure how much we are missing.

Several small ports, such as Pictou and Shelburne, Nova Scotia, were used in the early years, but Quebec City, on the St. Lawrence River, soon became the dominant port of entry and exit for ocean-going vessels. It was a key point for the transfer of goods as well as of people – including immigrants to North America.

In 1872, the *New York Times* said dismissively that when the St. Lawrence River was iced over in winter, making access to and from Quebec City impossible, Canadians had no choice but to use ports in the United States. Canada's two most important ports on the Atlantic Ocean, Halifax and Saint John, were not deemed worthy of note; the major port developments there were still to come.

Quebec City was hampered, however, by its lack of a rail link to the west, and suffered greatly when river dredging and improvements in ship design meant that ships could steam past Quebec City and head to Montreal. By the middle of the 19th century, Quebec City lost its role as the most important city in the province.

The most famous quarantine station in Canada was at Grosse Île, an island in the St. Lawrence River downstream from Quebec City. This station was established in 1832, at a time when about 30,000 immigrants were moving through Quebec City every year. It remained in use until 1937.

The port was busy. In his report for 1854, Dr. George M. Douglas, the medical superintendent of the quarantine station, said that 227 vessels had arrived at Quebec, carrying 52,991 passengers. Of those, 512 people, including two women in childbirth, died on the voyage, and 112 children were born.

Vessels departing from the English port of Liverpool had the highest mortality rate, and Douglas said that was likely because many emigrants waiting for a ship in Liverpool stayed in overcrowded, unclean lodging houses, and became "enfeebled and diseased." Douglas reported that passengers from Hamburg and other German ports were far healthier than Germans who had spent time in Liverpool before crossing the Atlantic.

Halifax, Nova Scotia, was founded in 1749, and within a decade had the first naval dockyard in North America. In 1818 it became a free port, allowing foreign ships to move cargo in and out. It did not assume a key role in immigration until the 1870s, when the Intercolonial Railway made it possible to get to the Great Lakes area. Halifax also had a shipbuilding industry that thrived in the age of sail, but went into serious decline when steam power replaced wind power.

Arrivals at Halifax were processed at a quarantine station at Lawlor's Island as well as at onshore facilities.

The city of Saint John, New Brunswick, was established in 1785 after an influx of Loyalists brought a population boom to the region. The Loyalists established a shipbuilding industry at the port, which flourished with trade.

In the early 1800s Saint John was the largest shipbuilding city in Canada and the fourth largest in the British Empire. It also witnessed an immigration boom, largely from the British Isles, and by 1840 there were more immigrants than Loyalist descendants in the Saint John area. In the 1850s a wharf was built to serve passenger steamships.

Saint John was home to the first quarantine station in Canada – Partridge Island. It opened in 1785 and remained in use until 1942.

Several Internet sites serve as entry points for researching early passenger arrivals.

The website of Library and Archives Canada has some material taken from its extensive collection of immigration records, including:

• Immigrants to Canada. Lists of immigrants from before 1865, taken from a variety of sources, have been transcribed for this database. There are 23,482 references to immigration records held by Library and Archives Canada. Many records relate to immigrants coming from the British Isles to Quebec and Ontario, but references to settlers in other provinces are included. The database also has other records such as declarations of aliens and names of some Irish orphans.

• Montreal Emigrant Society Passage Book, 1832. This database has references to 1,945 people who received aid from the society between May 12 and Nov. 5, 1832.

• Immigrants at Grosse Île 1832-1937. This database, provided by Parks Canada, includes information on 33,026 immigrants whose names appear in surviving records of the Grosse Île quarantine station.

• Thematic guide to sources relating to Grosse Île. This guide includes a history, some specific archival sources, as well as selected references relating to quarantine and to Grosse Île.

• Lower Canada Land Petitions 1764-1841. After it became a British colony in 1763, many early settlers, both military and civilian, submitted petitions to the governor to obtain Crown land. This database provides access to more than 95,000 references to individuals who lived in present-day Quebec.

ON THE INTERNET:

<www.collectionscanada.gc.ca/databases/index-e.html>

Ancestry.ca has a couple of databases that might help. They include:

• Passenger and Immigration Lists Index 1500s-1900s. This database has references to about five million individuals who arrived in ports in the United States and Canada. Many early immigrants to Canada came through U.S. ports, so they should be checked as a matter of course. Comprehensive lists were started for American ports in 1820, but lists survive for hundreds of crossings before that year. This database includes references from a comprehensive series of books compiled by P. William Filby and others over the past quarter-century.

• Canadian Immigrant Records 1780-1906, Part One. A collection of more than 193,000 records, including the name of the immigrant, and year and source of the original record. The entries in this database are not complete transcriptions of the original records.

• Canadian Immigrant Records 1780-1906, Part Two. More than 29,000 records, including the name of the immigrant, and year and source of the original record.

• Ship Passenger Lists to Nova Scotia 1750-1752. Listings of more than 2,000 foreign Protestants.

• Irish Canadian Emigration Records 1823-1849. This database contains records and reports of Canadian emigration agents James Allison and A.J. Buchanan. Among the records are emigration and orphan lists. These lists have been indexed and are searchable by name.

• New Brunswick Passenger Lists 1834. Transcripts of ship manifests for 20 ships arriving in New Brunswick.

ON THE INTERNET:

<www.ancestry.ca/search/rectype/default.aspx?rt=40>

Another website worth checking is World Vital Records, which offers some of the same resources available on Ancestry. One of them is Filby's Passenger and Immigration Lists Index, with its references to about five million individuals who arrived in ports in the United States and Canada.

ON THE INTERNET:

<www.worldvitalrecords.com/indexinfo.aspx?ix=pili>

The Provincial Archives of New Brunswick has two important databases dealing with immigration. One of them, with 23,318 records, covers Irish famine migration between 1845 and 1852. It deals with arrivals in Saint John as well as the hardships faced by the immigrants. The other, with 10,412 entries, includes records of immigrants at Saint John, St. Andrews, and Bathurst between 1816 and 1838. The database covers only a fraction of the ship arrivals.

ON THE INTERNET:

<archives.gnb.ca/APPS/PrivRecs/IrishFamine/Default.aspx?culture=en-CA>

<archives.gnb.ca/APPS/GovRecs/RS23E/Default.aspx?culture=en-CA>

Marjorie Kohli's Young Immigrants to Canada site has an extensive collection

of material about emigration in the 19th century. Information was extracted from various government records as well as shipping records, mostly from the Allan Line. It includes voyage accounts, emigration information, lists of ships sailing to Canada, as well as information on the ports and the people.

The ship Westernland of the Red Star line

ON THE INTERNET:

<retirees.uwaterloo.ca/~marj/genealogy/thevoyage.html>

Kohli and Sue Swiggum have also developed The Ships List website, which is designed to be international in scope. There is extensive background information as well as dozens of extracted passenger lists from the 19th century. The entire site is searchable, but be sure to check for a variety of spellings.

ON THE INTERNET:

<www.theshipslist.com>

Olive Tree Genealogy, created by Lorine McGinnis Schulze, also has extracted lists, as well as links to other sites that offer immigration information. It is a comprehensive site well worth exploring.

ON THE INTERNET:

<www.olivetreegenealogy.com/ships/canada>

The inGeneas Genealogical Resources Directory has a free database of about 15,000 references to passenger lists and immigration records. It is based on documents held at Library and Archives Canada.

ON THE INTERNET:

<www.ingeneas.com>

A site devoted to New France – Bits and Pieces for the Descendants of the French Colonists of North America – has passenger lists from the 16th and 17th centuries.

ON THE INTERNET:

<www3.telus.net/michel_robert>

A Lunenburg County, Nova Scotia, website includes information on hundreds of foreign Protestants who arrived by ship in 1750, 1751, and 1752.

ON THE INTERNET:

<www.rootsweb.ancestry.com/~canns/lunenburg/shiplists.html>

Another source for this Palatine immigration is on the Pro Genealogists website.

ON THE INTERNET:

<progenealogists.com/palproject/ns/index.html>

The Immigrant Ships Transcribers Guild has indexed lists from ships arriving in several ports, including Fort Cumberland, Halifax, Newport, Pictou, and Shelburne, Nova Scotia; Montreal and Quebec City; Prince Edward Island; Saint John, New Brunswick; and St. John's, Newfoundland.

ON THE INTERNET:

<www.immigrantships.net/arrivals/canada.html>

<www.immigrantships.net/v2/arrivalsv2/canadav2.html>

The Petworth Emigration Scheme, which saw working-class people from southern England sent to Upper Canada in the 1830s, is the subject of several books and websites. The Petworth Emigration Project is the best place to start your research.

ON THE INTERNET:

<www.petworthemigrations.com>

Dave Hunter's Island Register has early passenger lists dealing with Prince Edward Island. Remember, however, that the island was not a prime destination for trans-Atlantic crossings.

ON THE INTERNET:

<www.islandregister.com/ships.html>

And, of course, there are search engines such as Google and Bing. Search for relevant terms such as "emigrant ships canada" to see what is available.

Some newspapers in port cities published partial lists of new arrivals, although these lists generally included prominent business people, not settlers. Other possible sources for early arrivals could be church records, the census, and directories.

Information on their backgrounds might appear in local histories or on tombstones. If they were still alive in 1901, their year of arrival will be shown in the census, but this will have to be verified.

Researchers dealing with Loyalist ancestry will find many resources available, including societies across Canada as well as dozens of books. These references include collections of family data such as *Loyalist Lineages of Canada 1783-1983; The Loyalists in Ontario: The Sons and Daughters of the American Loyalists of Upper Canada; The Loyalists of Quebec 1774-1825: A Forgotten History; Loyalists and Land Settlement in Nova Scotia;* and *The Loyalists of New Brunswick.*

Extensive information about the Loyalists will be found on the Internet site of the United Empire Loyalists' Association of Canada. The association is an organization dedicated to enriching the lives of Canadians through knowledge of the past, in particular the history of the United Empire Loyalists and their contribution to the development of Canada.

ON THE INTERNET:

<www.uelac.org>

Library and Archives Canada has a couple of databases with Loyalist information.

• Ward Chipman, Muster Master's Office 1777-1785. The Ward Chipman Papers contain muster rolls of Loyalists, and their families, who were members of demobilized regiments and who settled in Nova Scotia and New Brunswick. This research tool provides access to nearly 19,000 references to Loyalist families.

• Port Roseway Associates. This database provides access to 1,498 references to Black Loyalist refugees who settled in Port Roseway, now Shelburne, Nova Scotia.

ON THE INTERNET:

<www.collectionscanada.gc.ca/databases/index-e.html>

Passengers prepare to board the ship Ganges for their voyage to Canada

Chapter 6
Atlantic ports 1865-1935

O dds are that your ancestor came across the Atlantic in the late spring, summer, or early fall, and landed at Quebec City. That is because the port of Quebec City was the busiest in the country, and was not open in the winter.

But then, perhaps your ancestor really stepped foot on Canadian soil in Montreal, rather than Quebec City. Montreal and Quebec City records are combined in passenger lists.

If not one of the ports in the province of Quebec, the next most likely choice would have been Halifax, Nova Scotia, which recorded the second-highest totals after Quebec City and Montreal. The third choice was Saint John, New Brunswick. Halifax and Saint John were Canada's winter ports, allowing companies to continue to bring immigrants during the coldest months of the year.

There are also records for arrivals at North Sydney, Nova Scotia, although the people on board were coming from Newfoundland – a separate country at the time, but not overseas. Many immigrants went through ports in the United States as well, with New York City the most popular choice. But Quebec City was by far the most important Canadian port, even though it was closed every winter. In 1928-1929, for example, there were 74,653 arrivals through Quebec City and Montreal, 44,936 through Halifax, and 13,046 through Saint John.

Atlantic ports

Statistics from the two major ports, Halifax and Quebec City, reveal a strong correlation between an immigrant's nationality and the port of entry. In 1928-1929, Germans made up 16.9 per cent of the arrivals in Halifax, but only six per cent of the arrivals in Quebec City. Immigrants from the British Isles, on the other hand, made up 52.3 per cent of the people coming through Quebec City, but only 24.1 per cent of those using Halifax. Arrivals from Denmark, Norway, Sweden, and Finland were more likely to go through Halifax, while arrivals from Yugoslavia were more likely to go through Quebec City.

Why did immigrants choose these ports? It was because of the routes served by the shipping companies, and because of the lines represented by

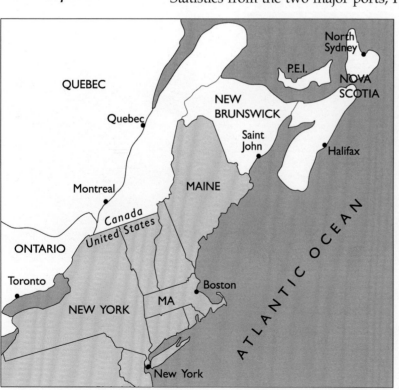

travel agents close to their homes in Europe.

Several sources exist for each port. Other records were compiled inland from the ports, and include people who entered Canada in a variety of ways.

One to check is the Toronto Emigrant Office Assisted Immigration Records Database, an index compiled from four volumes of registers created between 1865 and 1883. The registers are a chronological listing of those new immigrants who were assisted by the government to travel to many destinations in Southern Ontario. More than 29,000 entries have been transcribed from the registers.

ON THE INTERNET:

<www.archives.gov.on.ca/english/db/hawke.aspx>

This database, made available by the Archives of Ontario, is based on a collection known as the Hawke Papers. These records, which date from 1831-1892, were mainly compiled by Anthony Bowden Hawke and his successor, J.A. Donaldson. Hawke was the first specialized emigrant agent assigned to assist immigrants in settling Upper Canada (which became Canada West, and then Ontario).

The Hawke papers, compiled in Toronto and Kingston, include official correspondence and records that document assistance provided to immigrants in the form of transportation, food, and shelter. There are records of assistance provided to widows, orphans, and others who fled to Canada during the Irish famine. More information is on the Archives of Ontario website.

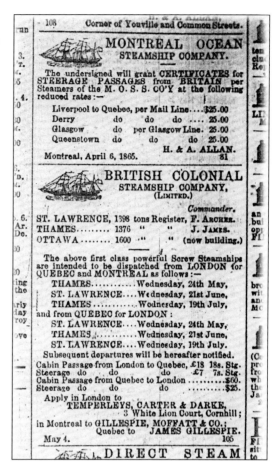

Many companies offered service across the Atlantic

ON THE INTERNET:

<www.archives.gov.on.ca/english/archival-records/interloan/hawke-papers.aspx>

The Archives of Ontario also has, on microfilm, records of the Department of Immigration dating from 1869 to 1901. The provincial government had special bonus and assisted passage schemes to encourage immigration to Ontario. Many of the records are of genealogical interest.

Some of the nominal lists were created by the federal immigration services.

ON THE INTERNET:

<www.archives.gov.on.ca/english/archival-records/interloan/i-immigration-t.aspx>

The inGeneas Genealogical Resources Directory has searchable databases dealing with passenger lists and immigration documents. It includes many early ship arrivals, including thousands of references to passenger lists from Quebec.

ON THE INTERNET:

<www.ingeneas.com>

Not all of the immigrants were adults who had a choice in their destination. Between 1869 and the late 1930s more than 100,000 children were sent to Canada from Great Britain by religious homes run by people such as Thomas Barnardo, Annie Macpherson, and John Middlemore. These children have become known as the Home Children.

Churches and philanthropic organizations believed that orphaned, abandoned, and pauper children would have a better life in Canada. It worked out that way for some children, but others were seen as little more than a source of cheap labour. It has been estimated that two-thirds of the Home Children suffered abuse of some sort.

These children appear in passenger lists. Members of the British Isles Family History Society of Greater Ottawa have been indexing their names, with the databases on the Library and Archives Canada website. The information was drawn from immigration records as well as Boards of Guardians records.

The databases include: Name; age; sex; microfilm reel number; ship name; port and date of departure; port and date of arrival; name of the organization or home that sent the child; and destination.

Several websites and books are devoted to the Home Children, so it is possible to find out more about the organizations involved in an ancestor's young life.

Comprehensive information is also on Marjorie Kohli's Young Immigrants to Canada website.

ON THE INTERNET:

<www.collectionscanada.gc.ca/databases/home-children/index-e.html>

<www.bifhsgo.ca>

<retirees.uwaterloo.ca/~marj/genealogy/homeadd.html>

Quebec City and Montreal, Quebec

Quebec City's port has been a key entry point into Canada since the 17th century. Originally based on the export of fur and lumber to Europe, the port became a major immigration gateway in the early 1800s when ships needed ballast to make their return trips to North America easier. As a result, they offered special fares to people willing to immigrate. It has been estimated that 30,000 immigrants arrived in Quebec each year between 1800 and 1850.

Activity in Quebec City's port declined as a result of dredging in the St. Lawrence River, which enabled ships to reach the port of Montreal. In 1865, the channel was widened to 200 feet and deepened to 20 feet, allowing for ocean-going ships to pass.

Many of the early indexes and databases used by family historians list only Quebec as a ship's destination, so check the passenger list itself. Most carried on to Montreal, but some passengers disembarked at Quebec City.

In 1865, the first year of passenger lists for Quebec City, the records show that 98 vessels arrived at the port. Some of them made five trips across the Atlantic. Some of the busiest ships were owned by the Allan Line – ships such as the Hibernian, Moravian, North American, and Nova Scotian, sailing from Liverpool and Derry (Londonderry), as well as the St. David, St. Patrick, St. Andrew, and St. George, sailing from Glasgow. In 1865, the first arrival at Quebec City was on May 1, and the final one of the season was on Nov. 14.

The 1865 arrivals had departed from a wide variety of ports, including the major ones such as Liverpool, London, and Glasgow, as well as much smaller

ones such as Barcelona, Spain; Gibraltar; Bergen and Haugesund in Norway; Limerick and Youghal in Ireland; and the English ports of Bristol and Plymouth.

By 1900, the emigration business had changed dramatically. That year, 89 vessels arrived at Quebec City and Montreal carrying immigrants. Seventy-three of them came from Liverpool.

Passengers bound for Quebec City or Montreal were subject to inspection at the Grosse Île quarantine station if disease was suspected. The station remained in operation until 1937.

Comprehensive ship passenger lists were started for Quebec City and Montreal in 1865. They are available on microfilm at Library and Archives Canada as well as at the Family History Library and several public libraries in Canada. The microfilms have been digitized and are on the Library and Archives Canada website as well as on Ancestry.ca.

The films have been indexed, with the resulting database available on both the Library and Archives Canada website and the Ancestry website. The entries are linked to images of the original lists.

Both sites also have an index to arrivals from 1925 through 1935, with 418,590 for Quebec City and 4,083 for Montreal – officially, at least.

ON THE INTERNET:

<www.collectionscanada.gc.ca/exploration/index-e.html>

<search.ancestry.ca/iexec/?htx=List&dbid=1263>

Always check the original images to confirm the information. If a person cannot be found in the database, check the original images online, or the microfilms themselves.

Place Viger in Montreal – shown in about 1900 – served as the Canadian Pacific Railway station for points east

Another indexing project is being conducted by FamilySearch, run by the Family History Library of the Church of Jesus Christ of Latter-day Saints (the Mormons). The first material to go live will be from Quebec, 1900 to 1922.

ON THE INTERNET:

<www.familysearch.org>

The Nanaimo Family History Society in British Columbia has launched an ambitious project to index and post Quebec City and Montreal arrival informa-tion on its website. The entries have been transcribed, with sections available as free PDF downloads. The site has more than half a million arrival records from the first decade of the 20th century.

ON THE INTERNET:

<members.shaw.ca/nanaimo.fhs>

The society also hosts a second database, called the Friends of Dave Howard Index. It includes more than 100,000 records of passenger arrivals at Quebec City and Montreal from the 1870s through the 1890s. It is not complete and has many gaps – but it is worth checking in case it has the person you are researching.

ON THE INTERNET:

<members.shaw.ca/nfhs_fodh/>

Arrivals between 1919 and 1925, when Form 30A was used instead of passen-ger lists, are on the Ancestry.ca website, linked to original images.

ON THE INTERNET:

<search.ancestry.ca/iexec/?htx=List&dbid=1588>

A list of Germans from Russia who arrived at Quebec City and Montreal between 1900 and 1914 is on the Odessa website, a collection of online resources dealing with German-Russian ancestry.

ON THE INTERNET:

<odessa3.org/collections/ships>

The Immigrant Ships Transcribers Guild has indexed selected lists from ships arriving in Montreal and Quebec City.

ON THE INTERNET:

<www.immigrantships.net/v3/arrivalsv3/canadav3.html>

Halifax, Nova Scotia

A railway link connected Halifax to the rest of North America in 1872, making it a logical entry point for immigrants. The voyage from Europe to Halifax was not as long as the one from Europe to Montreal, so ships could complete more voyages by using Halifax as their Canadian terminal. In 1880, a dock complex that could house 12 steamers at one time was opened. Halifax also had several small piers, and passengers could have disembarked at any one of them.

Many ships bound for American ports made an interim stop at Halifax. After taking on supplies and dropping off a few passengers, they would continue on to New York or other destinations in the United States such as Portland, Maine. Some vessels stopped at both Halifax and at Saint John, New Brunswick.

Halifax was used year-round, and in many years was as busy in the winter as

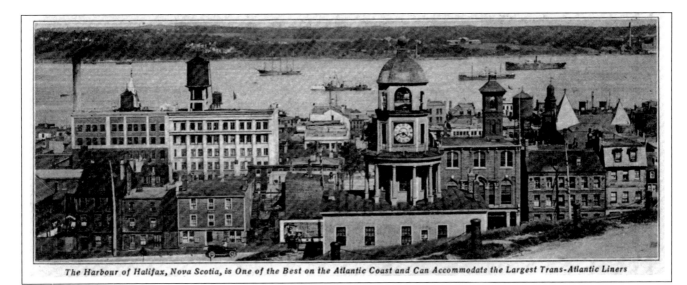

The Harbour of Halifax, Nova Scotia, is One of the Best on the Atlantic Coast and Can Accommodate the Largest Trans-Atlantic Liners

it was in the summer. That helped secure its position as the second most important port in Canada, after Quebec.

Halifax in a 1925 federal government atlas

In 1866, the government established a quarantine station on Lawlor's Island, near the mouth of Halifax Harbour. It was used until 1938. Today, some signs of the old quarantine station can still be seen on the island, which is part of the McNab's Island Provincial Park Reserve.

Halifax played a role in one of the most famous ship disasters of all time. In 1912, a rescue mission after the sinking of the Titanic brought 190 bodies to the city. Some of the victims were buried in Halifax.

The railway was critical to the city's future

In 1928, Shed 21 – on Pier 21 – was opened, combining immigration offices and processing facilities operated by the Department of Immigration and Colonization. The first vessel to use it was the Nieuw Amsterdam of the Holland America line, which carried 51 immigrants in March 1928.

More than one million immigrants passed through the pier by the time it was closed in 1971. It had outlived its usefulness; a drop in immigration and the rise of air travel meant that few people were entering the country by ship.

Comprehensive passenger lists were started for Halifax in 1881, and are on microfilm and on the Internet. The microfilm is at Library and Archives Canada, the Family History Library and several public libraries in Canada. The digitized images are available on the Library and Archives Canada website as well as on Ancestry.ca.

A database of passenger entries is on both the Library and Archives Canada website and the Ancestry website.

Both sites have an index to arrivals from 1925 through 1935, with about 250,000 Halifax arrivals.

ON THE INTERNET:

<www.collectionscanada.gc.ca/exploration/index-e.html>

<search.ancestry.ca/iexec/?htx=List&dbid=1263>

Arrivals between 1919 and 1925, using Form 30A, are on the Ancestry.ca website, linked to original images.

ON THE INTERNET:

<search.ancestry.ca/iexec/?htx=List&dbid=1588>

A list of Germans from Russia who arrived at Halifax between 1900 and 1914 is on the Odessa website.

ON THE INTERNET:

<odessa3.org/collections/ships>

The Immigrant Ships Transcribers Guild has indexed selected lists from ships arriving in Halifax.

ON THE INTERNET:

<www.immigrantships.net/v3/arrivalsv3/canadav3.html>

Saint John, New Brunswick

Saint John has had an active seaport since the 17th century, but it rose to prominence in the 1850s with the construction of a wharf at Reed's Point that was designed to serve passenger steamships.

The ports of Quebec City and Montreal were unable to handle ships during the winter because of ice in the St. Lawrence River. Still, it took the construction of a rail link to Quebec, and intense lobbying by local politicians, for Saint John to be seen as a practical alternative.

Saint John in 1866

In the 1890s ships from several companies, such as Canadian Pacific, started using Saint John as their Canadian terminus, and it became known as Canada's winter port. It saw much less traffic in the summer months. Partridge Island, at the entrance to the harbour, was used as a quarantine station until 1942.

Comprehensive passenger lists were started for Saint John in 1900. They are on microfilm at Library and Archives Canada, the Family History Library and several public libraries in Canada. The microfilms have been digitized and are on the Library and Archives Canada website as well as on Ancestry.ca.

A database of passenger entries is on both the Library and Archives Canada website and the Ancestry website. Both sites also have an index to arrivals from 1925 through 1935, with almost 100,000 people arriving in Saint John.

ON THE INTERNET:

<www.collectionscanada.gc.ca/exploration/index-e.html>

<search.ancestry.ca/iexec/?htx=List&dbid=1263>

Arrivals between 1919 and 1925, when Form 30A was used, are on the Ancestry.ca website.

ON THE INTERNET:

<search.ancestry.ca/iexec/?htx=List&dbid=1588>

A list of Germans from Russia who arrived at Saint John between 1900 and 1914 is on the Odessa website, a collection of resources dealing with German-Russian ancestry.

ON THE INTERNET:

<odessa3.org/collections/ships>

North Sydney, Nova Scotia

North Sydney, on Cape Breton Island, had the fourth-largest port in Canada, by tonnage loaded, by 1900 – but it dealt more with freight than with people. In 1898 a ferry service was launched that linked North Sydney with Port aux Basques, Newfoundland, and most of the entries in the passenger list indexes are based on that route.

Passenger lists were started for North Sydney in 1906. They are on microfilm at Library and Archives Canada, the Family History Library, and several public libraries in Canada. The digitized images are on the Library and Archives Canada website as well as on Ancestry.ca.

A database of passenger entries is on both the Library and Archives Canada website and the Ancestry website. Both sites also have an index to arrivals from 1925 through 1935, including 6,791 references to North Sydney.

ON THE INTERNET:

<www.collectionscanada.gc.ca/exploration/index-e.html>

<search.ancestry.ca/iexec/?htx=List&dbid=1263>

Arrivals between 1919 and 1925, when Form 30A was used, are on the Ancestry.ca website, linked to original images.

ON THE INTERNET:

<search.ancestry.ca/iexec/?htx=List&dbid=1588>

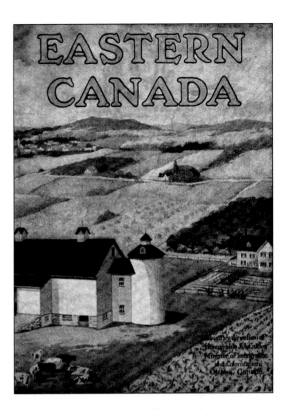

Prospective immigrants were lured with publications promising jobs for all

Arrivals at Quebec City and Montreal 1865-1921 (Passenger lists)

In the province of Quebec. Both ports were closed in winter because of ice in the St. Lawrence River.

Microfilm	Starts with:	Vessel:	Ends with:	Vessel:
C-4520	1865 May 1	Peruvian	1865 Oct.?	Margaret Ann
C-4521	1866 May 1	Hibernian	1867 May 27	Neckar
C-4522	1867 May 27	Neckar	1868 May 26	Germany
C-4523	1868 May 26	Germany	1869 May 12	St. Andrew
C-4524	1869 May 14	Monsoon	1869 Nov. 15	Peruvian
C-4525	1869 Nov. 15	Peruvian	1870 Aug. 8	Avon
C-4526	1870 Aug. 8	Avon	1871 Sept. 10	Thames
C-4527	1871 Sept. 13	Sarmatian	1872 Oct. 27	St. Patrick
C-4528	1872 Oct. 28	Prussian	1874 Aug. 2	Sarmatian
C-4529	1874 Aug. 3	Quebec	1878 July 6	Sardinian
C-4530	1878 July 6	Ontario	1880 Nov. 14	Peruvian
C-4531	1881 Apr. 30	Buenos Ayrean	1882 June 27	Lake Nipigon
C-4532	1882 July 2	Peruvian	1883 July 3	Texas
C-4533	1883 July 3	Lake Winnipeg	1884 July 6	Circassian
C-4534	1884 July 6	Toronto	1886 May 19	Corean
C-4535	1886 May 24	Oregon	1887 Aug. 1	Siberian
C-4536	1887 Aug. 2	Circassian	1889 May 3	Nestorian
C-4537	1889 May 4	Parisian	1890 Nov. 5	Norwegian
C-4538	1890 Nov. 10	Dominion	1892 Sept. 9	Lake Nipigon
C-4539	1892 Sept. 11	Labrador	1893 Oct. 8	Vancouver
C-4540	1893 Oct. 8	Laurentian	1895 Oct. 29	Lake Superior
C-4541	1895 Oct. 31	Christiania	1898 May 28	Scotsman
C-4542	1898 May 28	Numidian	1900 Apr. 24	Lake Megantic
T-479	1900 May 2	Buenos Ayrean	1901 June 24	Numidian
T-480	1901 June 29	Parisian	1902 Aug. 23	Corinthian
T-481	1902 Aug. 25	Sicilian	1903 July 28	Sardinian
T-482	1903 July 31	Parisian	1904 June 11	Bavarian
T-483	1904 June 11	Southwark	1904 Oct. 15	Tunisian
T-484	1904 Oct. 16	Kensington	1905 June 23	Tunisian
T-485	1905 June 25	Montrose	1905 Oct. 7	Lake Michigan
T-486	1905 Oct. 7	Virginian	1906 May 28	Pretorian
T-487	1906 June 1	Virginian	1906 Aug. 6	Pretorian
T-488	1906 Aug. 6	Parthenian	1906 Oct. 21	Sarmatian
T-489	1906 Oct. 21	Lake Champlain	1907 May 29	Mount Royal
T-490	1907 May 29	Ionian	1907 July 8	Montezuma
T-491	1907 July 10	Corinthian	1907 Sept. 6	Canada
T-492	1907 Sept. 6	Victorian	1907 Nov. 10	Southwark
T-493	1907 Nov. 10	Pomeranian	1908 June 28	Hesperian
T-4759	1908 July 3	Empress of Britain	1908 Oct. 2	Victorian
T-4760	1908 Oct. 3	Lake Champlain	1909 June 5	Virginian
T-4761	1909 June 7	Lake Erie	1909 July 24	Sicilian
T-4762	1909 July 25	Corsican	1909 Aug. 30	Grampian
T-4763	1909 Sept. 1	Mount Royal	1909 Oct. 3	Athenia
T-4764	1909 Oct. 3	Montreal	1910 Apr. 26	Athenia
T-4765	1910 Apr. 26	Athenia	1910 May 13	Empress of Ireland
T-4766	1910 May 13	Empress of Ireland	1910 May 27	Empress of Britain
T-4767	1910 May 27	Empress of Britain	1910 June 17	Cairutorr
T-4768	1910 June 18	Montrose	1910 July 7	Lake Erie
T-4769	1910 July 8	Tunisian	1910 Aug. 4	Empress of Ireland
T-4770	1910 Aug. 4	Empress of Ireland	1910 Aug. 27	Laurentic
T-4771	1910 Aug. 27	Laurentic	1910 Sept. 17	Montfort
T-4772	1910 Sept. 17	Montfort	1910 Oct. 13	Empress of Britain

T-4773	1910 Oct. 13	Empress of Britain	1910 Nov. 16	Montezuma
T-4774	1910 Nov. 17	Royal George	1911 May 8	Willehad
T-4775	1911 May 9	Lake Champlain	1911 May 22	Lake Manitoba
T-4776	1911 May 22	Hesperian	1911 June 5	Grampian
T-4777	1911 June 5	Grampian	1911 June 23	Empress of Ireland
T-4778	1911 June 25	Corsican	1911 July 15	Laurentic
T-4779	1911 July 15	Laurentic	1911 Aug. 11	Victorian
T-4780	1911 Aug. 11	Victorian	1911 Sept. 5	Empress of Britain
T-4781	1911 Sept. 5	Empress of Britain	1911 Sept. 24	Mount Temple
T-4782	1911 Sept. 24	Mount Temple	1911 Oct. 21	Willehad
T-4783	1911 Oct. 21	Willehad	1912 May 2	Montezuma
T-4784	1912 May 2	Montezuma	1912 May 13	Letitia
T-4785	1912 May 13	Letitia	1912 May 26	Canada
T-4786	1912 May 27	Montfort	1912 June 9	Scandinavian
T-4787	1912 June 9	Corsican	1912 June 29	Koln
T-4788	1912 June 29	Koln	1912 July 20	Mount Royal
T-4789	1912 July 21	Tunisian	1912 Aug. 12	Lake Manitoba
T-4790	1912 Aug. 12	Lake Manitoba	1912 Sept. 3	Lake Champlain
T-4791	1912 Sept. 3	Lake Champlain	1912 Sept. 22	Hesperian
T-4792	1912 Sept. 22	Hesperian	1912 Oct. 14	Canada
T-4793	1912 Oct. 14	Canada	1912 Nov. 12	Pretorian
T-4794	1912 Nov. 12	Pretorian	1913 May 7	Victorian
T-4795	1913 May 7	Laurentic	1913 May 15	Virginian
T-4796	1913 May 15	Virginian	1913 May 27	Pretorian
T-4797	1913 May 28	Sicilian	1913 June 9	Cassandra
T-4798	1913 June 9	Ausonia	1913 June 23	Ascania
T-4799	1913 June 23	Ascania	1913 July 2	Tyrolia
T-4800	1913 July 2	Manchester	1913 July 18	Tunisian
T-4801	1913 July 18	Tunisian	1913 Aug. 1	Empress of Britain
T-4802	1913 Aug. 1	Empress of Britain	1913 Aug. 18	Canada
T-4803	1913 Aug. 18	Canada	1913 Sept. 3	Virginian
T-4804	1913 Sept. 3	Virginian	1913 Sept. 25	Corsican
T-4805	1913 Sept. 25	Corsican	1913 Oct. 11	Teutonic
T-4806	1913 Oct. 11	Teutonic	1913 Nov. 10	Andania
T-4807	1913 Nov. 10	Andania	1914 May 8	Victorian
T-4808	1914 May 9	Frankfurt	1914 May 24	Alaunia
T-4809	1914 May 25	La Touraine	1914 June 14	Scotian
T-4810	1914 June 14	Laurentic	1914 July 12	Hesperian
T-4811	1914 July 11	Laurentic	1914 Aug. 10	Hesperian
T-4812	1914 Aug. 10	Cassandra	1914 Sept. 6	Laurentic
T-4813	1914 Sept. 7	Cassandra	1914 Nov. 14	Grampian
T-4814	1914 Nov. 15	Corinthian	1915 Oct. 3	Missanabie
T-4815	1915 Oct. 3	Missanabie	1916 Aug. 8	Pretorian
T-4816	1916 Aug. 8	Ascania	1917 May 14	Grampian
T-4817	1917 May 14	Scandinavian	1918 Oct. 7	Tunisian
T-4818	1918 Oct. 7	Cardiganshire	1919 June 11	Melita
T-14700	1919 June 11	Melita	1919 Aug. 3	Scotian
T-14701	1919 Aug. 6	Saturnia	1919 Sept. 13	Scotian
T-14702	1919 Sept. 14	Saturnia	1919 Oct. 20	Saturnia
T-14703	1919 Oct. 20	Saturnia	1919 Nov. 21	Empress of France
T-14704	1919 Nov. 21	Empress of France	1920 May 23	Minnedosa
T-14705	1920 May 23	Minnedosa	1920 June 19	Grampian
T-14706	1920 June 19	Hamilton	1920 July 12	Corsican
T-14707	1920 July 12	Corsican	1920 Aug. 8	Metagama
T-14708	1920 Aug. 8	Metagama	1920 Sept. 4	Minnedosa
T-14709	1920 Sept. 4	Minnedosa	1920 Sept. 26	Lagarfoss

T-14710	1920 Sept. 26	Saturnia	1920 Oct. 24	Corsican
T-14711	1920 Oct. 24	Corsican	1920 Nov. 22	Metagama
T-14712	1920 Nov. 22	Metagama	1921 May 16	Victorian
T-14713	1921 May 16	Victorian	1921 July 13	Minnedosa

Arrivals at Halifax 1881-1922 (Passenger lists)
In Nova Scotia. The primary port during the winter, although not as busy as Quebec City in the summer.

Microfilm	Starts with:	Vessel:	Ends with:	Vessel:
C-4511	1881 Jan.	Moravian	1882 Nov. 9	Polynesian
C-4512	1882 Nov. 16	Polynesian	1886 March 25	Caspian
C-4513	1886 March 25	Parisian	1888 Apr. 11	Sardinian
C-4514	1888 Apr. 11	Sardinian	1891 Aug. 2	Manitoban
C-4515	1891 Aug. 4	Caspian	1893 Dec. 31	Oregon
C-4516	1894 Jan. 1	Carthaganian	1895 Dec. 29	Halifax
C-4517	1896 Jan. 3	Labrador	1897 Apr. 16	Portia
C-4518	1897 Apr. 12	Mongolian	1898 Aug. 31	Corean
C-4519	1898 Sept. 2	London City	1899 Dec. 22	Lake Ontario
T-494	1899 Dec. 19	Pro Patria	1901 Apr. 12	Lusitania
T-495	1901 Apr. 14	Halifax	1902 Apr. 21	Sylvia
T-496	1902 Apr. 21	Glencoe	1903 Apr. 3	Sardinian
T-497	1903 Apr. 5	Armenia	1904 March 18	Barcelona
T-498	1904 March 19	Tunisian	1904 Dec. 30	Oruro
T-499	1905 Jan. 2	Halifax	1905 Oct. 21	Veritas
T-500	1905 Oct. 22	Halifax	1906 Apr. 24	Pretorian
T-501	1906 Apr. 24	Pretorian	1907 March 14	Mongolian
T-502	1907 March 15	Canada	1907 Aug. 29	B.W. Gaspe
T-503	1907 Sept. 2	Rosalind	1908 May 28	Carthaganian
T-4734	1908 June 1	Kanawha	1909 Aug. 9	Boston
T-4735	1909 Aug. 9	Florizel	1910 March 6	Campania
T-4736	1910 March 6	Campania	1910 Apr. 15	Tunisian
T-4737	1910 Apr. 15	Tunisian	1910 Nov. 28	Pretorian
T-4738	1910 Nov. 28	Pretorian	1911 March 12	Canada
T-4739	1911 March 12	Canada	1911 Apr. 10	Hesperian
T-4740	1911 Apr. 10	Hesperian	1911 Aug. 19	Annie E. Banks
T-4741	1911 Aug. 20	Volturno	1912 Feb. 29	Royal George
T-4742	1912 Feb. 29	Royal George	1912 Apr. 1	Canada
T-4743	1912 Apr. 1	Canada	1912 Apr. 24	Volturno
T-4744	1912 Apr. 24	Volturno	1912 Sept. 15	Mongolian
T-4745	1912 Sept. 15	Mongolian	1913 Jan. 13	Canada
T-4746	1913 Jan. 15	Caroline	1913 March 17	Canada
T-4747	1913 March 17	Canada	1913 Apr. 6	Scandinavian
T-4748	1913 Apr. 6	Scandinavian	1913 Apr. 25	Mongolian
T-4749	1913 Apr. 25	Mongolian	1913 June 12	La Plata
T-4750	1913 June 15	Neckar	1913 Oct. 9	Kursk
T-4751	1913 Oct. 9	Kursk	1914 Feb. 10	Tunisian
T-4752	1914 Feb. 13	Shenandoah	1914 Apr. 5	Andania
T-4753	1914 Apr. 5	Andania	1914 May 24	Wilfred M.
T-4754	1914 May 27	Russia	1915 July 25	Seal
T-4755	1915 July 26	Stephano	1917 Feb. 6	Southland
T-4756	1917 Feb. 9	Carpathia	1918 March 16	Orpington
T-4757	1918 March 16	Orpington	1919 Jan. 17	Olympic
T-14794	1919 Jan. 18	Olympic	1919 Mar. 27	Cedric
T-14795	1919 Mar. 31	Cedric	1919 June 9	Lapland
T-14796	1919 June 9	Lapland	1919 Aug. 21	Baltic
T-14797	1919 Aug. 23	Baltic	1919 Nov. 27	Megantic

T-14798	1919 Nov. 28	Megantic	1920 May 15	Caronia
T-14799	1920 May 18	Rosalind	1921 Mar. 25	Canada
T-14800	1921 Mar. 29	Canada	1922 Oct. 2	Rosalind

Arrivals at Saint John 1900-1922 (Passenger lists)

In New Brunswick. Most traffic came in winter, when it was the port for Canadian Pacific ships.

Microfilm	Starts with:	Vessel:	Ends with:	Vessel:
T-504	1900 Jan. 4	Lake Superior	1901 Feb. 11	Degama
T-505	1901 Feb. 16	Lake Superior	1904 March 28	Lake Champlain
T-506	1904 March 28	Ionian	1906 Jan. 26	Lake Erie
T-507	1906 Jan. 26	Corinthian	1907 March 28	Lake Manitoba
T-508	1907 March 28	Lake Manitoba	1908 Apr. 17	Lake Michigan
T-4820	1908 Apr. 17	Lake Michigan	1909 Nov. 28	Montrose
T-4821	1909 Nov. 28	Montrose	1910 Apr. 1	Empress of Britain
T-4822	1910 Apr. 1	Empress of Britain	1911 Jan. 10	Montezuma
T-4823	1911 Jan. 10	Montezuma	1911 March 31	Empress of Ireland
T-4824	1911 March 31	Empress of Ireland	1911 Nov. 25	Empress of Britain
T-4825	1911 Nov. 25	Empress of Britain	1912 March 29	Cassandra
T-4826	1912 March 29	Cassandra	1912 July 5	Ocamo
T-4827	1912 July 5	Ocamo	1913 March 19	Montrose
T-4828	1913 March 19	Montrose	1913 Apr. 25	Empress of Ireland
T-4829	1913 Apr. 30	Kanawha	1914 March 31	Athenia
T-4830	1914 March 31	Athenia	1915 Apr. 17	Corsican
T-4831	1915 Apr. 17	Corsican	1916 Nov. 27	Corsican
T-4832	1916 Nov. 27	Corsican	1917 Oct. 2	Caraquet
T-4833*	1917 Oct. 15	Chaleur	1918 Dec. 30	Sicilian
T-4834*	1918 Jan. 3	Chaudiere	1918 Dec. 1	Scandinavian

* note overlap on these two films

T-14836	1918 Dec. 30	Sicilian	1919 Mar. 6	Melita
T-14837	1919 Mar. 6	Melita	1919 Apr. 25	Corsican
T-14838	1919 Apr. 29	Corsican	1920 Jan. 16	Empress of France
T-14839	1920 Jan. 20	Empress of France	1920 Mar. 28	Melita
T-14840	1920 Mar. 28	Melita	1920 Aug. 30	Caraquet
T-14841	1920 Aug. 30	Grand Manan	1921 Jan. 7/9	Empress of Britain
T-14842	1921 Jan. 7	Cabotia	1921 Mar. 19	Empress of France
T-14843	1921 Mar. 21	Empress of France	1921 Oct. 1	Gov. Dingley
T-14844	1921 Oct. 10	Grand Manan	1922 Sept. 30	Gov. Dingley

Arrivals at North Sydney 1906-1922 (Passenger lists)

In Nova Scotia. Primarily ferry arrivals from Newfoundland and St-Pierre et Miquelon, but includes a few passengers from other countries.

Microfilm	Starts with:	Vessel:	Ends with:	Vessel:
T-520	1906 Nov. 22	Bruce	1908 Aug. 24	Bruce
T-4836	1908 Aug. 27	Bruce	1910 June 11	Bruce
T-4837	1910 June 14	Bruce	1911 May 6	Glencoe
T-4838	1911 May 8	St. Pierre Miquelon	1912 Feb. 28	Bruce
T-4839	1912 Feb. 28	Bruce	1912 Oct. 29	Invermore
T-4840	1912 Oct. 31	Bruce	1913 June 25	Bruce
T-4841	1913 June 26	Lintrose	1913 Dec. 18	Lintrose
T-4842	1913 Dec. 19	Bruce	1914 Aug. 1	Bruce
T-4843	1914 Aug. 2	Sandyford	1915 Apr. 23	Bruce
T-4844	1915 Apr. 25	Bruce	1915 Dec. 13	Pro Patria
T-4845	1915 Dec. 14	Kyle	1916 Sept. 7	Kyle
T-4846	1916 Sept. 9	Kyle	1917 July 5	Kyle

T-4847	1917 July 5	Kyle	1918 May 18	Kyle
T-4848	1918 May 21	Kyle	1918 Oct. 15	Kyle
T-4849	1918 Oct. 16	Glencoe	1919 July 22	Kyle
T-14860	1919 July 23	Glencoe	1920 Jan. 28	Kyle
T-14861	1920 Feb. 3	Meigle	1920 Oct. 7	Kyle
T-14862	1920 Oct. 9	Kyle	1921 Sept. 10	Kyle
T-14863	1921 Sept. 13	Kyle	1922 Aug. 31	Kyle

Ocean Arrivals 1919-1924 (Form 30A)
Includes ports on the Atlantic and Pacific Oceans. Try Ancestry.ca first!

Microfilm / Immigrants included:

T-14939 Aagard, Bjarre to Adams, Julia
T-14940 Adams, Kate to Aizenberg, Fenta
T-14941 Aitken, Amy to Allan, Agnes
T-14942 Allan, Alexander to Aly, Mohamad Kaddoura
T-14943 Alzinger Nicolas Victor to Anderson, John
T-14944 Anderson, John to Angielczyk, Morris
T-14945 Andriet, Nicolai to Archibald, Archibald
T-14946 Arnott, Archibald to Aschenmühl, Moise
T-14947 Asada, Naosuke to Atkinson, Ronald
T-14948 Atkinson, Samuel James to Bacon, James
T-14949 Bacon, Jeanette Margaret to Bakewell, William Y.
T-14950 Bak, Zalom to Ballantyne, Henrietta Carrill
T-14951 Ballantyne, Hilda to Barber, Thomas Leslie
T-14952 Barber, U. to Barr, Arthur George
T-14953 Barr, Barbara to Barton, Norman Hughes
T-14954 Barton, Olive to Baxter, Julia
T-14955 Baxter, Karl E. to Bechet, Eugene
T-14956 Bechro, Fehime to Bell, Godfrey
T-14957 Bell, Gordon to Bending, William S.
T-14958 Bell, Kate to Bennett, Frank
T-14959 Bennett, Frank to Bergson, Isaac
T-14960 Bergmann, Jacob to Bett, Isabella Murray
T-14961 Bethon, James Edgar to Binder, Bluma
T-14962 Binders, Benorion to Bjerre, M.
T-14963 Bjorn, Jene Magnus to Blakeman, Arthur
T-14964 Blakemore, Beatrice to Bochno, Dmytro
T-14965 Bocla, Dumitrio to Bone, Samuel
T-14966 Bonis, Samuel to Bosnic, Mila
T-14967 Bosovska, Mindel to Bowman, Elizabeth Montgomery
T-14968 Bowman, Ellen to Bradley, Austin W.
T-14969 Bradley, Beatrice to Brazzier, George Thomas
T-14970 Brayley, Harold to Briggs, Alice
T-14971 Briggs, Alice Maud to Brookes, Winifred
T-14972 Brooks, A.W. to Brown, Elizabeth Wilson
T-14973 Brown, Price F. to Brown, Walter Oscar
T-14974 Brown, William to Bryunas Pranas
T-14975 Brymner, R.T. to Bullen, Gladys Lilian
T-14976 Bulley, Harry Albert to Burman, Gustav Birger
T-14977 Burling, Helen to Bush, Rose Hannah
T-14978 Bush, Sadie Evelyn to Byrtus, Jozef
T-14979 Byszkiewicz, Katarzyna to Calway, William Roland
T-14980 Camarta, Agostino to Campbell, James
T-14981 Campbell, James to Capon, Sydney
T-14982 Capodagli, Temistocle to Carrier, Evelyn May
T-14983 Carrick, Florence to Casper, Frederick
T-14984 Caspersen, Henrik to Cesal, Zdenka
T-14985 Chacksfield, A. to Charlebois, Eva
T-14986 Charles, Fannie to Chinnock, Walter George
T-14987 Chipman, Warwick Fielding to Churchill, Zachius
T-14988 Ciancone, Alessio to Clark, Sylvia
T-14989 Clark, Thomas to Clemas, Winifred
T-14990 Cleman, Yvonne to Cocking, Gwendoline
T-14991 Cockton, Harold to Coles, Edward Samuel
T-14992 Coles, Edwin Albert to Compagnon, Xavier
T-14993 Compton, Ada to Cook, Ivy Violet
T-14994 Cook, J.F. to Cope, Winifred Mary
T-14995 Copple, A. to Costana, Zoi
T-14996 Costello, Agnes to Cowie, Eveline Marry
T-14997 Cowell, Florence to Crandall, Stephen Harry
T-14998 Cramp, Vernon to Crispin, Muriel Gladys
T-14999 Cristopoli, Nella to Crutcher, Isabella Park
T-15000 Crusham, James E. to Cunningham, Rose
T-15001 Cunningham, Samuel to Czaczkes, Zygmunt
T-15002 D'Achille, Adolfo to Daneliuk, Katerina
T-15003 Danforth, Leola Frances to Davidson, Jessie
T-15004 Davidson, Jessie to Davis, Isabella French Smith
T-15005 Davis, Henry to De Busschere, Zoe
T-15006 De Clercq, Achilla to De Wit, Zweitse
T-15007 Deakin, Agnes to Delves, William George
T-15008 Demirdjian, Adria to Deviney, Gladys
T-15009 Devine, Harry T. to Dickson, Fredrick J.
T-15010 Dickson, Mrs. G. to Dlugary, Zudik
T-15011 Dixon, A. St. John to Domaille, Nora
T-15012 Domenico, Papeto to Doughty, Robert
T-15013 Dougher, Sadie to Drabble, Violet
T-15014 Draycott, Walter to Dueck, Hedwig
T-15015 Duffus, Helen to Dunlap, Ruth Iva
T-15016 Dunlop, Sadie to Dyer, Leslie
T-15017 Dyer, Lilian May to Ediger, Wladimir
T-15018 Edgar, Ada Mary to Ekstrom, Gustaf Georg
T-15019 Ekengren, Helge to Eloranta, Otto
T-15020 Eloquin, Paul to Eriksen Alfhital
T-15021 Erman, Abram to Evans, Owen Elias
T-15022 Evans, Patricia to Falkner, Muriel Joy
T-15023 Falcioni, Nazzareno to Fawdry, Lydia

T-15024	Fawcett, Margaret Jane to Ferguson, Jane
T-15025	Ferguson, Janet to Findlay, Isabella W.
T-15026	Findlay, Jack to Fitch, K.B.
T-15027	Fitt, Lancelot R. to Fliegel, Ruth
T-15028	Fligel, Sholim to Ford, William
T-15029	Ford, William Albert to Foster, Muriel Bernice
T-15030	Foster, Nan to Frank, Barbara
T-15031	Frank, Carl to Frejdman, Sura
T-15032	Freimuth, Wilhelm to Frymet, Zysser
T-15033	Fukuda, Asa to Galandij, Wasyl
T-15034	Galbraith, Aggie to Gardiner, Peter
T-15035	Gardiner, Rachel to Gaunt, Lydia
T-15036	Gauthier, J.M. to Gerigt T. George
T-15037	Gerhardi, Victor to Gibson, Julia L.
T-15038	Gibson, Kathleen G. to Gillett, Earnest G.
T-15039	Gillett, Florence to Gleaves-Doyle, Freda
T-15040	Gleboff, G.A. to Goldenberg, Tysia
T-15041	Goldenberg, Ucher to Goodwin, Winifred
T-15042	Gorbatow, Awrum to Gout, May
T-15043	Goutz, Moishe to Grant, Duncan Campbell
T-15044	Grant, E.C. to Gray, Winnie
T-15045	Greaves, Ada to Greer, Archibald
T-15046	Greer, Cecil to Griffiths, Sidney
T-15047	Griffiths, Stanley to Grycan, Zofja
T-15048	Gualazza, Adolfo to Gyolaji, Anton
T-15049	Gvora, Antonin to Hakansson, Sven Johan
T-15050	Hakkinen, Tilda to Halliday, Ophelia
T-15051	Halliday, Peter to Hammond, Julia
T-15052	Hammond, Kathleen to Hansen, Yorgen C.
T-15053	Hanson, Agnes Mary to Harmanmaa, Kustaa Wihtori
T-15054	Harmon, Leo to Harrison, Frederick William
T-15055	Harrison, G.F. to Harvey, Lucy Helen
T-15056	Harvey, Mary Florence to Hawthorn, Winifred Joan
T-15057	Haworth, Ada to Healy, Kate
T-15058	Healy, Laurence to Helle, Peter
T-15059	Heller, Ronald to Henry, Minnie
T-15060	Henry, Norman to Hewitt, Monica
T-15061	Hewitt, Pearl to Hill, Dykers Campbell
T-15062	Hill, E.B. to Hislop, Cornelius
T-15063	Hisanaga, Daisaburo to Hoff, Mikal
T-15064	Hoff, Peter to Holm, Axel
T-15065	Holm, Bjarne to Hooper, Winifred, Margaret
T-15066	Hooydonk, A. to Hothersall, Elizabeth
T-15067	Hotson, Frederick to Howson, William John
T-15068	Hoyle, Ada to Hughes, William
T-15069	Hughes, William to Hunter, Muriel
T-15070	Hunter, Nellie to Huziuk, Paraskewan
T-15071	Huxley, Patricia to Inman, Ivy Mary
T-15072	Innerst, Jacob Stuart to Ivens, Grace Mabel
T-15073	Izukawa, Hei-Ichi to Jacobs, Phyllis
T-15074	Jacobs, Richard Henry to Jantsen, Iwan
T-15075	Janzen, Jakob to Jenner, Kathleen Emily
T-15076	Jennet, Leon to Johansson, Mathilda Linnea
T-15077	Johannesen, Nils to Johnston, Iza
T-15078	Johnston, J. G. to Jones, Ellen Mary
T-15079	Jones, Ellen Rose to Jones, William Arthur
T-15080	Jones, William Aubery to Jzbinska, Dwoira
T-15081	Juteau, Edgar to Karasewsky, Wladislaw
T-15082	Kariya, Yasuye to Kearney, Joseph
T-15083	Kearney, Laura H. to Kelly, Timothy
T-15084	Kelly, Vernon to Keresztes, Friderik
T-15085	Kerkoulas, George to Kiezerman, Tojba
T-15086	Kieman, V. to Kinney, Minnie L.
T-15087	Kinoshita, Nao to Klaver Van Bueren, J.
T-15088	Klabbers, Karel to Knudsen, Niels
T-15089	Knudsen, Niels Ivar Krause to Koskimies, August
T-15090	Kosovic, Barisa to Kristoffersen, Nilo
T-15091	Kristiansen, Olaf to Kyle, Mary Jane
T-15092	Kyle, Mary Jane to Lalonde, Stella
T-15093	Lamb, Agnes to Langslow, Harry R
T-15094	Langmuir, Helen to Laughton, Minnie
T-15095	Laukkonen, Nikolaj to Lazdan, B.
T-15096	Lazdan, Brasia to Lee, William
T-15097	Lee, William to Lemon, Alma
T-15098	Lemoine, Amélia to Levette, Alice
T-15099	Lever, Annie to Liebing, Hedwig
T-15100	Liebman, Henry to Link, Maude
T-15101	Linka, Miklos to Lloyd, Ruth
T-15102	Lloyd, Sarah to Lonvik, Elizabeth
T-15103	Longton, Elizabeth to Lowe, Bertram
T-15104	Lowe, Beatrice to Luoma, Wilho
T-15105	Lunney, William to MacBride, Mary
T-15106	MacCallum, Mary to Machin, Winifred M.
T-15107	Machalek, Janka to Mackie, John Roy
T-15108	Mackie, James to MacPherson, Hume
T-15109	MacPherson, Ian James to Maitland, Jeanie
T-15110	Maitland, Jeanie to Manabe, Yoshita
T-15111	Mandara to Marcioz, Primo
T-15112	Marewutski, Rachel to Marshall, George William
T-15113	Marshall, H.A.C. to Martin, Sylvia Grace
T-15114	Martin, T. to Matalamaki, Ivari
T-15115	Matcham, Jame to Mauroshat, Gustav
T-15116	Maurin, A to McArthur, William H.
T-15117	McArdle, Adele to McClean, William
T-15118	McClellan, Agnes to McCullum, Henry William
T-15119	McCulloch, A. Leslie to McEachern, William
T-15120	McElroy, Agnes to McGrath, Roy
T-15121	McGrath, Sara to McKay, Isabella M.
T-15122	McKay, James to McKibbin, Willie
T-15123	McKinley, Adela to McLeod, Duncan Clarence
T-15124	McLeod, E. Audrey to McNeilly, Isobella
T-15125	McNeilly, J.H. to Mead, William James
T-15126	Meadows, Ada to Melville, W.
T-15127	Menard, A. to Miatello, Luigi
T-15128	Miceli, Maria to Millar, W.P.
T-15129	Millard, A to Mills, Winifred Ann
T-15130	Milner, Ada Hannah to Mitchell, George

T-15131	Mitchell, George to Molesworth, Ivy Frederica		Olive
T-15132	Molewyk, Jennecke to Moore, Charles William	T-15183	Saunders, Daisy to Scheerpf, Anna
T-15133	Moore, Charles William to Morgan, Sydney	T-15184	Schechter, Beila to Schlesinger, Violet
T-15134	Morgan, T.H. to Morrison, Grace Campbell	T-15185	Schlissel, Abraham to Schroder, Christian
T-15135	Morrison, Grace Walker to Mottram, Thomas Frank	T-15186	Schroder, Daisy Ethel to Scott, Lady Margaret
T-15136	Mottishaw, Walter Bud to Muller, Willi	T-15187	Scott, Margaret to Sellen, Cyril Arthur
T-15137	Mulock, Adele to Murphy, Rowland	T-15188	Sellers, David Harry to Shapero, James
T-15138	Murphy, Sadie to Myles, Charles	T-15189	Shapcott, James to Sheldon, Lucy Ann
T-15139	Myron, David McKenzie to Naylor, William Henry	T-15190	Sheldon, Mabel to Shiraye, Shinzo
T-15140	Neakes, Ada to Neufeld, Kornelius	T-15191	Shihara, Sen to Sim, William Massie
T-15141	Neubaer, Leo to Nichols, Norman	T-15192	Simmard to Sinclair, Archie
T-15142	Nichols, Pery to Nimoy, Motel	T-15193	Sinclair, Barbara to Skintey, Ivan
T-15143	Nimoy, Motel to Nordahl, Petter	T-15194	Skillen, James to Small, Ruth E.
T-15144	Nordal, Ragnhild to Nyburg, Constance	T-15195	Small, Sadie to Smith, Daisy M.
T-15145	Nygaard, D. to Ogjbowski, Gladyslaw	T-15196	Smith, Daisy M. to Smith, Jane
T-15146	Ogden, Alan Whittaker to Olscher, Isak	T-15197	Smith, Jane to Smith, Volera
T-15147	Olmsted, Jeff D. to Ormerod, Kathleen Mary	T-15198	Smith, William to Sodo, Gosta Valfird
T-15148	Orme, Laura Uppercu to Overland, Robert F.	T-15199	Socovan, Hana to Spalding, Dolly R.
T-15149	Ovenden, Thomas to Palin, Gwynedd Marion	T-15200	Spalding, Edith to Sprackles, Thomas
T-15150	Palliser, Harry Cecil to Parker, Audrey Isabel	T-15201	Sprague, Walter to Starcevie, Stephan
T-15151	Parker, Baden Powell to Parton, W.	T-15202	Stares, Walter to Stephan, Charles
T-15152	Partridge, Charles to Patterson, Lydia	T-15203	Stephen, Charles to Steward, Daisy Marion
T-15153	Patterson, M. to Pearce, Stuart	T-15204	Steward, Ellen to Stobbe, Cornelius
T-15154	Pearce, Thomas to Pelton, Ross D.	T-15205	Stock, David to Stragier, I.
T-15155	Peltzer, Rudolf to Perry, Evelyn	T-15206	Strachan, Jack to Sturdzik, Josef
T-15156	Perry, F.S. to Petker, Rudolf	T-15207	Sturm, Kremens to Sutherland, Evelyn
T-15157	Petrovich, S. to Picard, Mélanie	T-15208	Sutherland, Findlay Ross to Swift, Gladys Mary
T-15158	Pickard, A.H. to Piot, Charles	T-15209	Swift, Harold to Tadman, Monica
T-15159	Piper, Charles to Pobjanen, Arvo Vilhelm	T-15210	Tabara, Noboru to Taradasz, Szejwa
T-15160	Point, Beatrice to Porteous, Robert Williamson	T-15211	Teramura, Tohichi to Taylor, John
T-15161	Porte, Sadie to Poyser, Jos. Revill	T-15212	Taylor, John to Tenenvurzel, Lipa
T-15162	Powlton, Kate to Priestland, Grace	T-15213	Tenma, Masuichi to Thomas, Ivor
T-15163	Priestley, Hannah to Purcell, Bertha	T-15214	Thomas, J. to Thomson, A.
T-15164	Purdie, Catherine to Rach, Ludwig	T-15215	Thomson, Baden L. to Threadgold, Ethel P.
T-15165	Raboy, Malca to Ramsay, Josephine	T-15216	Thrun, Florence Idello to Tocher, Francis S.
T-15166	Ramsay, Kate to Ray, Gladys Amelia	T-15217	Tobler, George to Topazzini, Luigi
T-15167	Ray, Hannah to Redford, Victor	T-15218	Topolovec, Magda to Trethewey, Betty
T-15168	Redhead, Thomas to Reid, Rush B.	T-15219	Trewin, Catherine to Tucker, Thomas H.H.
T-15169	Reid, Saada to Reynaurt, Courtandt	T-15220	Tucker, Verna to Turtle, Evelyn Betty
T-15170	Rezniroff, David to Richardson, Annie Elizabeth	T-15221	Turnham, Fanny to Urman, Dvoira
		T-15222	Urano, Eikichi to Vanderspek, Izaak
T-15171	Richardson, Annie Elizabeth to Riley, Rose M.	T-15223	Vanderree, Jacob to Vaughan, Myrtle
T-15172	Riley, Rupert George to Robbins, Ethel	T-15224	Vaughan, Nellie to Vidler, William Thomas
T-15173	Robbins, Ethel Adelaide to Robertson, John	T-15225	Vilutis, A. to Vyberal, Rosie
T-15174	Robertson, J. to Robinson, W.	T-15226	Vujovic, Save to Walker, Aubrey Francis
T-15175	Robinson, William George to Rojtman, Szewa	T-15227	Walker, Alec to Wallace, Julia
T-15176	Rojtman, Szlama to Rosenkranz, Markus	T-15228	Wallace, James to Warburton, May
T-15177	Rosenstien, M. to Roudi, Zima	T-15229	Warburton, Nellie to Wasberg, Isak
T-15178	Rourke, Allan to Ruddock, Evelyn Annie	T-15230	Washer, James to Watson, Winonia
T-15179	Russell, Winifred Maud to Russo, Adolfa di Carmine	T-15231	Watson, Yvonne Beatrice to Weber, Frans
		T-15232	Weber, Georg to Wellburn, Clifford
T-15180	Rudawec, Fedor to Sairanen, Otto Vilhelm	T-15233	Weller, Daisy to Weston, Constance L.
T-15181	Sakuda, Bunzaburo to Sande, Petron	T-15234	Weston, Dacre Leslie to White, John W.
T-15182	Sanborn, Rachel Rice to Saunders, Constance	T-15235	White, Kate to Whyard, Fredrick
		T-15236	Whitton, George to Wilkes, David

T-15237   Wilkes, E. to Williams, Freeman
T-15238   Williams, Florence to Wills, Cuthbert E. T.
T-15239   Wills, Daisy D. to Wilson, James
T-15240   Wilson, Jane to Winstanley, Arthur Reginald
T-15241   Winsor, Bens J. to Wonfor, Herbert
T-15242   Wolverson, Herbert John to Woodall, Jane

T-15243   Woodburn, Jennie to Worton, Harry
T-15244   Wotherspoon, Harry to Wuschke August
T-15245   Wuschke, Berta to Ylinen, Anne
T-15246   Ylitalo, Anna to Yuchtman, Avrum
T-15247   Yule, Barbara to Zic, Vinko
T-15248   Zierold, Walter to Zyromska, Z.

Arrivals at Quebec City 1925-1935 (Passenger lists)

In the province of Quebec. Port was closed in winter because of ice in the St. Lawrence River.

Microfilm	Starts with:		Ends with:	
T-14714	1925 Apr. 25	(vol. 1, p. 1)	1925 May 1	(vol. 1, p. 196)
T-14715	1925 May 2	(vol. 2, p. 1)	1925 May 31	(vol. 4, p. 166)
T-14716	1925 May 31	(vol. 4, p. 166)	1925 July 10	(vol. 7, p. 116)
T-14717	1925 July 10	(vol. 7, p. 116)	1925 Aug. 14	(vol. 10, p. 32)
T-14718	1925 Aug. 14	(vol. 10, p. 32)	1925 Sept. 12	(vol. 12, p. 192)
T-14719	1925 Sept. 12	(vol. 12, p. 192)	1925 Oct. 4	(vol. 14, p. 144)
T-14720	1925 Oct. 14	(vol. 14, p. 144)	1925 Nov. 21	(vol. 17, p. 102)
T-14721	1925 Nov. 21	(vol. 17, p. 103)	1926 May 10	(vol. 3, p. 88)
T-14722	1926 May 10	(vol. 3, p. 89)	1926 June 5	(vol. 5, p. 257)
T-14723	1926 June 7	(vol. 6, p. 1)	1926 July 4	(vol. 8, p. 203)
T-14724	1926 July 4	(vol. 8, p. 204)	1926 July 31	(vol. 11, p. 157)
T-14725	1926 July 31	(vol. 11, p. 158)	1926 Aug. 20	(vol. 14, p. 67)
T-14726	1926 Aug. 20	(vol. 14, p. 68)	1926 Sept. 11	(vol. 17, p. 77)
T-14727	1926 Sept. 10/11	(vol. 17, p. 78)	1926 Oct. 2	(vol. 20, p. 70)
T-14728	1926 Oct. 2	(vol. 20, p. 71)	1926 Oct. 29	(vol. 23, p. 43)
T-14729	1926 Oct. 29	(vol. 23, p. 44)	1927 Apr. 25	(vol. 2, p. 43)
T-14730	1927 Apr. 25	(vol. 2, p. 44)	1927 Apr. 30	(vol. 2, p. 150)
T-14731	1927 Apr. 30	(vol. 2, p. 150)	1927 May 7	(vol. 3, p. 163)
T-14732	1927 May 7	(vol. 3, p. 163)	1927 May 26	(vol. 6, p. 195)
T-14733	1927 May 26	(vol. 6, p. 195)	1927 June 17	(vol. 10, p. 19)
T-14734	1927 June 17	(vol. 10, p. 19)	1927 July 9	(vol. 13, p. 52)
T-14735	1927 July 9	(vol. 13, p. 53)	1927 July 23	(vol. 14, p. 202)
T-14736	1927 July 23	(vol. 14, p. 203)	1927 Aug. 19	(vol. 17, p. 179)
T-14737	1927 Aug. 19	(vol. 17, p. 178)	1927 Sept. 10	(vol. 20, p. 122)
T-14738	1927 Sept. 10	(vol. 20, p. 123)	1927 Oct. 7	(vol. 23, p. 91)
T-14739	1927 Oct. 7	(vol. 23, p. 92)	1927 Nov. 6	(vol. 26, p. 28)
T-14740	1927 Nov. 6	(vol. 26, p. 29)	1928 Apr. 29	(vol. 2, p. 100)
T-14741	1928 Apr. 29	(vol. 2, p. 101)	1928 May 15	(vol. 5, p. 24)
T-14742	1928 May 15	(vol. 5, p. 25)	1928 June 3	(vol. 7, p. 219)
T-14743	1928 June 3	(vol. 8, p. 1)	1928 June 21	(vol. 10, p. 155)
T-14744	1928 June 21	(vol. 10, p. 156)	1928 July 8	(vol. 13, p. 189)
T-14745	1928 July 8	(vol. 13, p. 190)	1928 July 29	(vol. 16, p. 153)
T-14746	1928 July 29	(vol. 16, p. 154)	1928 Aug. 17	(vol. 19, p. 109)
T-14747	1928 Aug. 17	(vol. 19, p. 110)	1928 Sept. 1	(vol. 22, p. 95)
T-14748	1928 Sept. 1	(vol. 22, p. 95)	1928 Sept. 15	(vol. 25, p. 68)
T-14749	1928 Sept. 15	(vol. 25, p. 68)	1928 Oct. 13	(vol. 28, p. 11)
T-14750	1928 Oct. 13	(vol. 28, p. 11)	1928 Nov. 16	(vol. 30, p. 211)
T-14751	1928 Nov. 17	(vol. 30, p. 211)	1929 May 4	(vol. 3, p. 110)
T-14752	1929 May 4	(vol. 3, p. 110)	1929 May 20	(vol. 6, p. 50)
T-14753	1929 May 20	(vol. 6, p. 51)	1929 June 8	(vol. 9, p. 27)
T-14754	1929 June 8	(vol. 9, p. 27)	1929 June 23	(vol. 11, p. 242)
T-14755	1929 June 23	(vol. 11, p. 243)	1929 July 14	(vol. 14, p. 170)
T-14756	1929 July 14	(vol. 14, p. 171)	1929 Aug. 3	(vol. 17, p. 150)
T-14757	1929 Aug. 3	(vol. 17, p. 150)	1929 Aug. 22	(vol. 20, p. 165)
T-14758	1929 Aug. 22	(vol. 20, p. 165)	1929 Sept. 7	(vol. 23, p. 62)

T-14759	1929 Sept. 7	(vol. 23, p. 62)	1929 Sept. 22	(vol. 25, p.230)
T-14760	1929 Sept. 22	(vol. 25, p. 230)	1929 Oct. 19	(vol. 28, p. 131)
T-14761	1929 Oct. 19	(vol. 28, p. 131)	1929 Nov. 22	(vol. 31, p. 124)
T-14762	1929 Nov. 22	(vol. 31, p. 124)	1930 May 9	(vol. 3, p. 138)
T-14763	1930 May 9	(vol. 3, p. 138)	1930 May 25	(vol. 6, p. 111)
T-14764	1930 May 25	(vol. 6, p. 111)	1930 June 16	(vol. 9, p. 75)
T-14765	1930 June 16	(vol. 9, p. 75)	1930 July 6	(vol. 11, p. 188)
T-14766	1930 July 6	(vol. 11, p. 188)	1930 Aug. 1	(vol. 14, p. 181)
T-14767	1930 Aug. 1	(vol. 14, p. 181)	1930 Aug. 22	(vol. 17, p. 79)
T-14768	1930 Aug. 22	(vol. 17, p. 79)	1930 Sept. 7	(vol. 19, p. 202)
T-14769	1930 Sept. 9	(vol. 20, p. 1)	1930 Sept. 28	(vol. 22, p. 148)
T-14770	1930 Sept. 28	(vol. 22, p. 148)	1930 Nov. 10	(vol. 25, p. 143)
T-14771	1930 Nov. 10	(vol. 25, p. 143)	1931 May 16	(vol. 3, p. 30)
T-14772	1931 May 16	(vol. 3, p. 30)	1931 June 20	(vol. 5, p. 208)
T-14773	1931 June 20	(vol. 5, p. 208)	1931 July 27	(vol. 8, p. 172)
T-14774	1931 July 27	(vol. 8, p. 172)	1931 Aug. 27	(vol. 11, p. 94)
T-14775	1931 Aug. 27	(vol. 11, p. 94)	1931 Oct. 2	(vol. 14, p. 70)
T-14776	1931 Oct. 2	(vol. 14, p. 70)	1931 Nov. 21	(vol. 17, p. 56)
T-14777	1931 Nov. 21	(vol. 17, p. 56)	1932 May 23	(vol. 3, p. 111)
T-14778	1932 May 23	(vol. 3, p. 111)	1932 July 8	(vol. 6, p. 45)
T-14779	1932 July 8	(vol. 6, p. 45)	1932 Aug. 12	(vol. 8, p. 124)
T-14780	1932 Aug. 12	(vol. 8, p. 124)	1932 Sept. 11	(vol. 11, p. 74)
T-14781	1932 Sept. 11	(vol. 11, p. 74)	1932 Oct. 23	(vol. 14, p. 33)
T-14782	1932 Oct. 23	(vol. 14, p. 33)	1933 May 8	(vol. 2, p. 45)
T-14783	1933 May 8	(vol. 2, p. 45)	1933 July 8	(vol. 4, p. 204)
T-14784	1933 July 8	(vol. 4, p. 204)	1933 Aug. 31	(vol. 7, p. 152)
T-14785	1933 Aug. 31	(vol. 7, p. 152)	1933 Oct. 29	(vol. 10, p. 95)
T-14786	1933 Oct. 29	(vol. 10, p. 95)	1934 June 18	(vol. 2, p. 218)
T-14787	1934 June 18	(vol. 2, p. 218)	1934 Aug. 19	(vol. 5, p. 132)
T-14788	1934 Aug. 19	(vol. 5, p. 132)	1934 Sept. 27	(vol. 8, p. 71)
T-14789	1934 Sept. 27	(vol. 8, p. 71)	1935 Apr. 26	(vol. 1, p. 96)
T-14790	1935 Apr. 26	(vol. 1, p. 96)	1935 July 7	(vol. 4, p. 37)
T-14791	1935 July 7	(vol. 4, p. 37)	1935 Aug. 25	(vol. 6, p. 233)
T-14792	1935 Aug. 25	(vol. 6, p. 233)	1935 Oct. 5	(vol. 9, p. 164)
T-14793	1935 Oct. 5	(vol. 9, p. 164)	1935 Nov. 24	(vol. 11, p.186)

Arrivals at Montreal 1925-1935 (Passenger lists)
In Quebec. Port was closed in winter because of ice in the St. Lawrence River.

Microfilm	Starts with:		Ends with:	
T-14910	1925 Apr. 22	(vol. 1, p. 1)	1927 Oct. 20	(vol. 1, p. 158)
T-14911	1927 Oct. 21	(vol. 1, p. 159)	1930 Sept. 8	(vol. 1, p. 149)
T-14912	1930 Sept. 14	(vol. 1, p. 150)	1933 Oct. 29	(vol. 1, p. 169)
T-14913	1933 Nov. 1	(vol. 1, p. 170)	1935 Nov. 21	(vol. 1, p. 230)

Arrivals at Halifax 1925-1935 (Passenger lists)
In Nova Scotia. The primary port during the winter, although not as busy as Quebec City in the summer.

Microfilm	Starts with:		Ends with:	
T-14801	1925 Jan. 5	(vol. 1, p. 1)	1925 Apr. 3	(vol. 3, p. 31)
T-14802	1925 Apr. 3	(vol. 3, p. 31)	1925 Aug. 17	(vol. 5, p. 184)
T-14803	1925 Aug. 17	(vol. 5, p. 184)	1926 Feb. 27	(vol. 2, p. 26)
T-14804	1926 Feb. 27	(vol. 2, p. 27)	1926 Apr. 10	(vol. 4, p. 153)
T-14805	1926 Apr. 11	(vol. 4, p. 154)	1926 July 4	(vol. 7, p. 101)
T-14806	1926 July 4	(vol. 7, p. 102)	1926 Nov. 24	(vol. 10, p. 76)
T-14807	1926 Nov. 24	(vol. 10, p. 77)	1927 Mar. 6	(vol. 2, p. 186)

T-14808	1927 Mar. 6	(vol. 2, p. 187)	1927 Mar. 26	(vol. 4, p. 104)
T-14809	1927 Mar. 26	(vol. 4, p. 104)	1927 Apr. 15	(vol. 7, p. 80)
T-14810	1927 Apr. 15	(vol. 7, p. 80)	1927 June 11	(vol. 10, p. 82)
T-14811	1927 June 11	(vol. 10, p. 81)	1927 Dec. 4	(vol. 13, p. 105)
T-14812	1927 Dec. 4	(vol. 13, p. 106)	1928 Mar. 3	(vol. 3, p. 33)
T-14813	1928 Mar. 3	(vol. 3, p. 33)	1928 Mar. 30	(vol. 5, p. 55)
T-14814	1928 Mar. 30	(vol. 5, p. 55)	1928 Apr. 27	(vol. 8, p. 55)
T-14815	1928 Apr. 27	(vol. 8, p. 56)	1928 July 21	(vol. 11, p. 40)
T-14816	1928 July 21	(vol. 11, p. 40)	1928 Nov. 24	(vol. 14, p. 42)
T-14817	1928 Nov. 24	(vol. 14, p. 42)	1929 Feb. 15	(vol. 2, p. 123)
T-14818	1929 Feb. 15	(vol. 2, p. 124)	1929 Mar. 30	(vol. 5, p. 119)
T-14819	1929 Mar. 30	(vol. 5, p. 120)	1929 Apr. 20	(vol. 8, p. 156)
T-14820	1929 Apr. 20	(vol. 8, p. 156)	1929 June 9	(vol. 11, p. 189)
T-14821	1929 June 11	(vol. 11, p. 193)	1929 Sept. 26	(vol. 14, p. 207)
T-14822	1929 Sept. 26	(vol. 14, p. 207)	1930 Jan. 6	(vol. 1, p. 9)
T-14823	1930 Jan. 6	(vol. 1, p. 9)	1930 Mar. 9	(vol. 3, p. 184)
T-14824	1930 Mar. 9	(vol. 3, p. 184)	1930 Apr. 8	(vol. 6, p. 115)
T-14825	1930 Apr. 8	(vol. 6, p. 115)	1930 May 31	(vol. 9, p. 79)
T-14826	1930 May 31	(vol. 9, p. 79)	1930 Oct. 4	(vol. 12, p. 85)
T-14827	1930 Oct. 4	(vol. 12, p. 85)	1931 Mar. 7	(vol. 2, p. 97)
T-14828	1931 Mar. 7	(vol. 2, p. 98)	1931 Nov. 2	(vol. 5, p. 112)
T-14829	1931 Nov. 2	(vol. 5, p. 113)	1932 Feb. 27	(vol. 2, p. 143)
T-14830	1932 Feb. 27	(vol. 2, p. 144)	1932 Sept. 17	(vol. 5, p. 126)
T-14831	1932 Sept. 20	(vol. 5, p. 127)	1933 Feb. 24	(vol. 2, p. 113)
T-14832	1933 Feb. 24	(vol. 2, p. 114)	1933 Dec. 7	(vol. 5, p. 115)
T-14833	1933 Dec. 7	(vol. 5, p. 116)	1934 Apr. 14	(vol. 3, p. 70)
T-14834	1934 Apr. 14	(vol. 3, p. 71)	1935 Feb. 25	(vol. 1, p. 195)
T-14835	1935 Feb. 25	(vol. 1, p. 196)	1935 Dec. 30	(vol. 3, p. 209)

Arrivals at Saint John 1925-1935 (Passenger lists)

In New Brunswick. Canadian Pacific vessels used this port during the winter.

Microfilm	Starts with:		Ends with:	
T-14845	1925 Jan. 10	(vol. 1, p. 1)	1925 Feb. 1	(vol. 1, p. 69)
T-14846	1925 Feb. 1	(vol. 1, p. 69)	1925 Dec. 6	(vol. 4, p. 88)
T-14847	1925 Dec. 6	(vol. 4, p. 88)	1926 Mar. 28	(vol. 3, p. 42)
T-14848	1926 Mar. 28	(vol. 3, p. 42)	1927 Jan. 18	(vol. 1, p. 67)
T-14849	1927 Jan. 18	(vol. 1, p. 68)	1927 Mar. 27	(vol. 4, p. 76)
T-14850	1927 Mar. 27	(vol. 4, p. 76)	1928 Jan. 8	(vol. 1, p. 19)
T-14851	1928 Jan. 8	(vol. 1, p. 18)	1928 Apr. 1	(vol. 3, p. 158)
T-14852	1928 Apr. 1	(vol. 3, p. 159)	1929 Jan. 21	(vol. 1, p. 78)
T-14853	1929 Jan. 21	(vol. 1, p. 78)	1929 Mar. 30	(vol. 3, p. 235)
T-14854	1929 Mar. 30	(vol. 3, p. 236)	1929 Nov. 30	(vol. 6, p. 168)
T-14855	1929 Nov. 30	(vol. 6, p. 168)	1930 Mar. 17	(vol. 2, p. 190)
T-14856	1930 Mar. 17	(vol. 2, p. 189)	1930 Aug. 25	(vol. 5, p. 129)
T-14857	1930 Aug. 25	(vol. 5, p. 128)	1931 Apr. 5	(vol. 2, p. 199)
T-14858	1931 Apr. 5	(vol. 2, p. 200)	1935 Oct. 7	(vol. 1, p. 94)
T-14859	1935 Oct. 7	(vol. 1, p. 93)	1935 Dec. 16	(vol. 1, p. 181)

Arrivals at North Sydney 1925-1935 (Passenger lists)

In Nova Scotia. Primarily ferry arrivals from Newfoundland and St-Pierre et Miquelon.

Microfilm	Starts with:		Ends with:	
T-14864	1925 Jan. 6	(vol. 1, p. 1)	1926 Sept. 18	(vol. 1, p. 112)
T-14865	1926 Sept. 25	(vol. 1, p. 113)	1935 Apr. 1	(vol. 1, p. 8)
T-14866	1935 April 1	(vol. 1, p. 8)	1935 Dec. 23	(vol. 1, p. 43)

Chapter 7
Pacific ports 1858-1935

On Sunday, April 25, 1858, the people who worked at Victoria – a Hudson's Bay Company fort in the colony of Vancouver Island – were just getting out of church when a boat called the Commodore arrived from San Francisco. It was loaded with miners and entrepreneurs who had been lured north by the promise of gold on the Fraser River.

The Commodore's arrival marked the start of large-scale immigration to the west coast of what was to become Canada. Before the vessel entered Victoria's Inner Harbour, the community was largely made up of men who worked for the Hudson's Bay Company, and who moved from fort to fort as required.

Even after Vancouver Island became a colony in 1849, little had been done to encourage settlement. But that changed with the Fraser River gold rush, which caused a building boom in Victoria as businesses were started to serve the miners heading to and from the gold areas.

The gold rush did not last, but Victoria did, becoming the dominant city on the west coast of British North America for the next three decades.

In 1858, most of the people who arrived in Victoria came by vessel from San Francisco. California's own gold rush had petered out, so there were plenty of men looking for new opportunities. They included Americans and Canadians, both white and black, as well as Hawaiians and Chinese. About five per cent were Jewish, including three members of the famous Sutro family, who later went on to much bigger fame and fortune back in California.

Victoria's strong ties to San Francisco continued for decades. Even immigrants from eastern Canada and the United Kingdom came by way of the California city. Without a rail line across the continent, the quickest route was to go by ship to Panama, cross the narrow strip of land between the Atlantic and Pacific oceans, then take another ship north to San Francisco. From there they could get to Victoria in about four days.

Those patient souls who chose to go around Cape Horn in South America rather than taking the shortcut at Panama spent five months on their journey. Going by way of Panama could cut that time in half.

The late 1880s brought huge changes. The completion of the Canadian Pacific Railway in 1885 gave immigrants from Europe another option: They could go to Quebec City or Montreal by ship, then take the train to the west coast. In 1887, CP launched a fleet of ships to connect Victoria and

Pacific ports

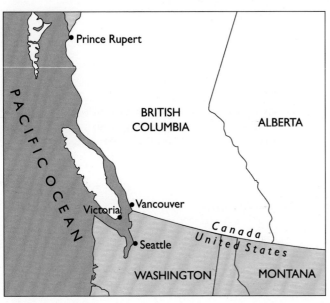

Vancouver with Japan, Hong Kong, Australia, and the Philippines. Mail service between Hong Kong and England went through Canada, thanks to Canadian Pacific ships on the Atlantic and Pacific as well as its rail line across Canada.

The ports of Vancouver and Victoria welcomed immigrants from around the world: The United States at first, then the United Kingdom, and then countries across the Pacific, including China, Japan, India, and the Russian Empire. After the transcontinental rail line opened, the B.C. ports still saw arrivals from the British Isles, because some of them had chosen to try their luck in Australia, New Zealand, India, or Singapore before coming to Canada.

It is not easy to research the early years of migration on the Pacific coast. Passenger lists for Vancouver and Victoria were not started until 1905, almost half a century after the Commodore's arrival.

There are no lists of departures from San Francisco, although passenger arrivals in San Francisco are available from 1893. A series of books entitled *San Francisco Ship Passenger Lists* covers the early 1850s, compiled from newspaper accounts and journals. These books might contain some names of people who later came north to British Columbia.

Early newspapers published lists of the people who arrived on vessels. The lists were not comprehensive and normally included the names of business people and dignitaries rather than immigrants. Still, the lists are worth checking. Digitized copies of the *Daily Colonist*, published in Victoria, from 1858 to 1910 are online.

The railway link through British Columbia's Selkirk Mountains made it easier to move from coast to coast

ON THE INTERNET:

<www.britishcolonist.ca>

Leona Taylor has extracted the names of ship passengers from 19th century issues of the *Daily Colonist*. Her work is on the Victoria's Victoria website, which is run by the University of Victoria.

ON THE INTERNET:

<web.uvic.ca/vv>

A database of arrivals from 1905 to 1922, and from 1925 through 1935, is available on the Ancestry.ca website. The database is linked to images taken from microfilms held by Library and Archives Canada.

ON THE INTERNET:

<search.ancestry.ca/iexec/?htx=List&dbid=1263>

A database covering 1925 through 1935 is also on the Library and Archives Canada website. It has 5,051 passenger arrivals at Victoria and 15,778 at Vancouver.

ON THE INTERNET:

<www.collectionscanada.gc.ca/databases/index-e.html>

Arrivals between 1919 and 1925, when Form 30A was used, are on the Ancestry.ca website, linked to original images.

ON THE INTERNET:

<search.ancestry.ca/iexec/?htx=List&dbid=1588>

Researchers could also check the passenger lists for the American ports of Seattle and San Francisco. Seattle's lists date from 1890; San Francisco's started in 1893. If people destined for Canada stopped at these ports first, then these records provide the only record of their arrival in North America. These lists are available on microfilm from the U.S. National Archives and Records Administration or from the Family History Library, as well as on the Ancestry.com website.

ON THE INTERNET:

<www.ancestry.com/search/rectype/default.aspx?rt=40>

Records of arrivals from China started much earlier than those from other countries, and are available from as recently as 1949. That end date is not as helpful as one might expect, given that the Great Depression, the Second World War and policies designed to discourage Chinese immigrants had effectively closed the door for a quarter of a century.

For many years, immigration from China was actively discouraged. (This was in line with other government policies – Chinese miners, for example, were

*Victoria
in the 1850s*

The harbour at Vancouver in about 1900

required to buy licences at a rate three times higher than that charged to white miners.)

From 1886, following a Royal Commission on Chinese Immigration, a head tax was charged on all Chinese arrivals. The tax started at $50, was increased to $100 in 1900, and to $500 in 1903. The chief controller of Chinese immigration reported to his superior in 1914 that since the tax had been initiated, a period of less than 30 years, a total of $3.5 million had been collected through this tax.

Immigration policies based on racial discrimination were rescinded in 1967.

Library and Archives Canada holds nominal registers of 98,361 Chinese immigrants from 1885 to 1949. The entries are arranged numerically by serial and declaration numbers, in roughly chronological order. They include age, place of birth, occupation, date and port of arrival in Canada, and head tax paid. Library and Archives Canada also has files on most of the immigrants.

These records are available on the Library and Archives website.

ON THE INTERNET:

<www.collectionscanada.gc.ca/databases/chinese-immigrants/index-e.html>

They are also available on microfilm.

Information on Chinese immigrants may also be found in the records of the Immigration Branch – see Chapter 11. Two groups – the bonds of indemnity filed by immigrants (microfilm C-10243) and the orders relating to the landing of immigrants (microfilms C-10266 and C-10267) – contain a high percentage of Chinese arrivals.

Chinese passengers and crew members make up about half of the people who died at the William Head quarantine station, established west of Victoria in 1894. That is where people who might have been carrying a contagious disease – and anyone who had been in contact with those unfortunate people – were kept upon arrival until it was determined that the danger had passed.

Victoria's immigration hall was demolished in 1977

For most of the time, quarantine stations were relatively quiet, because ship after ship could be given a clean bill of health. Sometimes, though, the stations had far more people than they could handle. In July 1911, for example, the Empress of India arrived at William Head with disease on board. The notation on the passenger list says that because of smallpox, all passengers and crew were held at the station. William Head suddenly had to deal with the influx of 513 men, women, and children.

After spending 16 days crossing the Pacific from Yokohama, Japan, it's unlikely the passengers on the Empress of India wanted to wait when they were so close to their destination. Until they could be given a clean bill of health, though, they could not leave.

Before the Second World War, 14 major steamship lines were operating freighters across the Pacific, and their crews had to be checked at the quarantine station. In 1927, its busiest year, 1,068 ships were inspected there.

The station had accommodation for 6,000 people, but was used to house 10,000 at the start of the First World War. That is when Chinese volunteers were en route to France to join the Allied labour battalions. The first Chinese soldier down the gangplank was found to have smallpox, as did many of those who followed. Eventually, the entire contingent was placed in quarantine.

The William Head quarantine station was the second on the Pacific coast. It was set up after the first one, at Albert Head, between William Head and Victoria, proved to be too small to handle the influx of immigrants. The Albert Head station was in service for a decade.

The William Head quarantine station eventually became redundant thanks to improved medical care, better screening techniques at ports overseas, and the drop in the number of people immigrating to Canada by ship.

There is no comprehensive source of information on the people who faced quarantine. Passenger lists may indicate, however, that arrivals were detained for medical reasons, so they should be checked carefully.

The quarantine station was closed in July 1959. The property was converted into a penal institution.

An immigration hall in Victoria, which housed new arrivals, was used until 1952. It was torn down a quarter of a century later.

Arrivals at Vancouver 1905-1922 (Passenger lists)
In British Columbia. The largest city on Canada's Pacific coast.

Microfilm	Starts with:	Vessel:	Ends with:	Vessel:
T-515	1905 Jan. 4	Empress of Japan	1906 Dec. 8	Athenian
T-516	1907 Jan. 7	Empress of Japan	1909 June 12	Empress of India
T-4851	1909 June 12	Empress of India	1910 Aug. 28	Empress of Japan
T-4852	1910 Aug. 28	Empress of Japan	1911 Oct. 9	Crown of Castill
T-4853	1911 Oct. 15	Empress of Japan	1912 Dec. 29	Bellerophon
T-4854	1913 Jan. 5	Monteagle	1914 Jan. 8	Empress of Japan
T-4855	1914 Jan. 8	Empress of Japan	1915 June 28	Azov
T-4856	1915 July 2	Makura	1916 Oct. 2	Monteagle
T-4857	1916 Oct. 14	Empress of Japan	1917 Oct. 15	Empress of Asia
T-4858	1917 Oct. 27	Teesta	1918 Aug. 25	Monteagle
T-4859	1918 Aug. 25	Monteagle	1919 May 30	Empress of Russia
T-14867	1919 June 11	Empress of Russia	1920 Feb. 2	Empress of Asia
T-14868	1920 Feb. 7	Empress of Asia	1920 July 3	Montcalm
T-14869	1920 July 3	Montcalm	1920 Nov. 30	Empress of Japan
T-14870	1920 Dec. 1	Princess Adelaide	1921 July 8	Monteagle
T-14871	1921 July 8	Monteagle	1922 Sept. 28	Princess Charlotte

Arrivals at Victoria and Pacific ports 1905-1922 (Passenger lists)
In British Columbia. Many vessels stopped in Victoria before going to Vancouver or Washington state.

Microfilm	Starts with:	Vessel:	Ends with:	Vessel:
T-509	1905 Apr. 18	Empress of China	1905 July 28	Tartar
T-510	1905 July 28	Princess Victoria	1906 Apr. 18	Umtilla
T-511	1906 Apr. 18	Indianapolis	1907 July 21	Empress of China
T-512	1907 July 21	Empress of China	1908 Sept. 14	Georgia
T-4861	1908 Sept. ?	Aki Maru	1909 June 23	Kaga Maru
T-4862	1909 July 3	Empress of Japan	1910 May 15	Keemun
T-4863	1910 May 24	British Columbia	1911 Jan. 21	Sado Maru
T-4864	1911 Jan. 21	Sado Maru	1911 Aug. 30	Sado Maru

Ships from across the Pacific used the Outer Wharf when they arrived at Victoria

T-4865	1911 Sept. 4	Oanfa	1912 June 6	Sado Maru
T-4866	1912 June 7	Cyclops	1913 Jan. 5	Monteagle
T-4867	1913 Jan. 5	Monteagle	1913 Aug. 19	Niagara
T-4868	1913 Aug. 19	Niagara	1914 May 1	Monteagle
T-4869	1914 May 2	Radnorshire	1915 March 21	Monteagle
T-4870	1915 March 21	Titan	1916 Apr. 8	Empress of Russia
T-4871	1916 Apr. 8	Empress of Russia	1916 Dec. 6	Empress of Japan
T-4872	1916 Dec. 6	Empress of Japan	1917 Oct. 2	Empress of Japan
T-4873	1917 Oct. 2	Empress of Japan	1918 June 11	Empress of Japan
T-4874	1918 June 11	Empress of Japan	1919 Feb. 4	Empress of Japan
T-14872	1919 Feb. 4	Empress of Japan	1919 July 28	Empress of Russia
T-14873	1919 July 29	Mexico Maru	1920 Feb. 19	Manila Maru
T-14874	1920 Feb. 19	Manila Maru	1920 May 22	Arabia Maru
T-14875	1920 May 22	Arabia Maru	1920 Aug. 4	Katori Maru
T-14876	1920 Aug. 4	Katori Maru	1920 Oct. 21	President
T-14877	1920 Oct. 21	President	1921 Jan. 31	Sol Due
T-14878	1921 Feb. 1	Monteagle	1921 May 13	Queen
T-14879	1921 May 13	Katori Maru	1921 Aug. 13	Kashima Maru
T-14880	1921 Aug. 13	President	1922 Sept. 30	Princess Victoria

Ocean arrivals 1919-1924 (Form 30A)
Please see Chapter 6 -- Arrivals at Atlantic ports 1865-1935

Arrivals at Vancouver and Victoria 1925-1935 (Passenger lists)
In British Columbia. Lists for these ports are interfiled.

Microfilm	Starts with:		Ends with:	
T-14881	1925 Jan. 4	(vol. 1, p. 1)	1925 May 28	(vol. 3, p. 157)
T-14882	1925 May 28	(vol. 3, p. 158)	1925 October 6	(vol. 6, p. 14)
T-14883	1925 Oct. 6	(vol. 6, p. 15)	1926 Mar. 22	(vol. 2, p. 60)
T-14884	1926 Mar. 22	(vol. 2, p. 61)	1926 June 14	(vol. 4, p. 176)
T-14885	1926 June 14	(vol. 4, p. 177)	1926 Sept. 23	(vol. 7, p. 127)
T-14886	1926 Sept. 23	(vol. 7, p. 128)	1927 Apr. 1	(vol. 2, p. 114)
T-14887	1927 Apr. 1	(vol. 2, p. 115)	1927 May 29	(vol. 4, p. 73)
T-14888	1927 May 29	(vol. 4, p. 74)	1927 Sept. 11	(vol. 7, p. 35)
T-14889	1927 Sept. 11	(vol. 7, p. 35)	1928 Mar. 25	(vol. 2, p. 21)
T-14890	1928 Mar. 25	(vol. 2, p. 22)	1928 June 18	(vol. 4, p. 183)
T-14891	1928 June 18	(vol. 4, p. 183)	1928 Oct. 20	(vol. 7, p. 148)
T-14892	1928 Oct. 20	(vol. 7, p. 148)	1929 Apr. 6	(vol. 2, p. 156)
T-14893	1929 Apr. 6	(vol. 2, p. 156)	1929 July 12	(vol. 5, p. 129)
T-14894	1929 July 12	(vol. 5, p. 130)	1929 Nov. 18	(vol. 8, p. 94)
T-14895	1929 Nov. 18	(vol. 8, p. 95)	1930 Apr. 25	(vol. 3, p. 33)
T-14896	1930 Apr. 25	(vol. 3, p. 33)	1930 July 25	(vol. 6, p. 17)
T-14897	1930 July 25	(vol. 6, p. 17)	1930 Dec. 26	(vol. 8, p. 204)
T-14898	1930 Dec. 26	(vol. 8, p. 204)	1931 May 24	(vol. 3, p. 137)
T-14899	1931 May 25	(vol. 3, p. 138)	1931 Aug. 30	(vol. 6, p. 120)
T-14900	1931 Aug. 30	(vol. 6, p. 121)	1932 Mar. 14	(vol. 1, p. 167)
T-14901	1932 Mar. 15	(vol. 1, p. 168)	1932 July 19	(vol. 4, p. 150)
T-14902	1932 July 19	(vol. 4, p. 151)	1933 Feb. 20	(vol. 1, p. 91)
T-14903	1933 Feb. 20	(vol. 1, p. 91)	1933 Aug. 2	(vol. 4, p. 25)
T-14904	1933 Aug. 2	(vol. 4, p. 25)	1934 Mar. 11	(vol. 1, p. 159)
T-14905	1934 Mar. 11	(vol. 1, p. 160)	1934 July 15	(vol. 4, p. 60)
T-14906	1934 July 15	(vol. 4, p. 61)	1934 Oct. 7	(vol. 5, p. 202)
T-14907	1934 Oct. 7	(vol. 5, p. 202)	1935 Apr. 18	(vol. 2, p. 77)
T-14908	1935 Apr. 18	(vol. 2, p. 78)	1935 July 30	(vol. 4, p. 220)
T-14909	1935	(vol. 4, p. 220)	1935 Dec. 30	(vol. 6, p. 314)

The Empress of India, a Canadian Pacific ship, linked Vancouver and Victoria with the Orient

Nominal registers of Chinese immigrants
Try the Library and Archives Canada website first!

Microfilm:	Volume:	Register:	From number/date:		To number/date:	
C-9510	694	1	1	14/06/1887	4950	02/08/1889
	695	2	4951	02/08/1889	9975	21/07/1891
	696	3	9976	21/07/1891	13125	26/04/1892
C-9511	696	3	13101	26/04/1892	14950	22/11/1892
	697	4	14951	22/11/1892	18725	26/09/1894
	698	5	18726	26/09/1894	22500	23/09/1896
	699	6	22501	23/09/1896	26275	18/06/1898
	700	7	26276	18/06/1898	27225	21/09/1898
C-9512	700	7	27201	21/09/1898	31225	09/08/1899
	703*	10	41251	25/06/1902	46275	24/06/1903
	702	9	36251	17/10/1900	41250	25/06/1902
C-9513	701*	8	31226	09/08/1899	36250	17/10/1900
T-3484	1061	11	46276	24/06/1903	51275	27/12/1903
	1062	12	51276	27/12/1903	56275	01/05/1911
	1063	13	56276	01/05/1909	63275	18/02/1911
T-3485	1063	13	63276	18/02/1911	63850	14/04/1911
	1064	14	63851	14/04/1911	71150	11/05/1912
	1065	15	71151	11/05/1912	78600	01/05/1913
	1066	16	78601	01/05/1913	83250	09/03/1914
T-3486	1066	16	83226	08/03/1914	86075	12/04/1918
	1067	17	86076	12/04/1918	93600	07/05/1921
T-3486	1068	18	93601	07/05/1921	97114	29/09/1949

* note that the volumes are out of order

Chapter 8
Through the United States

In some of the peak immigration years, more people arrived at our doors than on our shores – through land ports rather than sea ports. They came from the United States, drawn to Canada because of our jobs or our free land for homesteading.

The numbers were significant. In 1913, for example, 139,009 people came from the United States – close to the 150,542 people who came from the British Isles.

Some immigrants from Europe or Asia came through the United States on their way to Canada. They used the U.S. only as a place to set foot on North American soil, and their stay there might have been measured in hours or days.

Even if your ancestors came directly to Canada, it is still worth looking for distant relatives who settled in the U.S. The information they provided to the authorities might provide key clues to the origins of your own ancestors. If you are stuck on your direct line, check for siblings or cousins. Records in the United States are often more comprehensive than those in Canada.

Family historians dealing with immigrant arrivals should look south as well as east or west. Consider the sources for American immigration as well as for Canadian immigration.

Major Atlantic ports in the United States

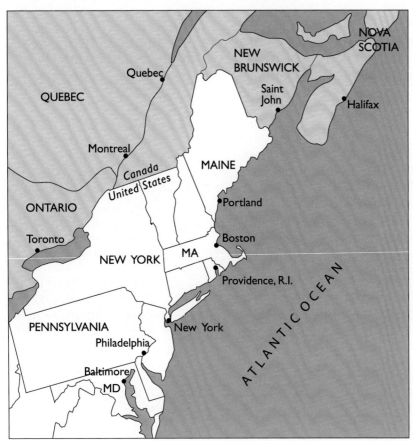

They might also need to look at Canadian border records, which started in 1908. Before that, there were no controls on the border, so there was no need for paperwork.

If your ancestor came to Canada from the United States before 1908, the first reference to his or her presence in this country might be in a census or homestead application.

Some Canadians had to go through the United States to get from one part of Canada to another. The best route from Saint John, New Brunswick, to Southern Ontario, for example, was through Maine. People from Ontario who were heading to homesteads in Manitoba in the 1870s went west into the United States, then north to Winnipeg. Southern Ontario and Manitoba were not linked with a Canadian railway until 1885.

U.S. passenger arrivals

Ellis Island was the first North American stop for many immigrants

Arrivals from Europe were likely to use one of the six busiest U.S. ports: Baltimore, Maryland; Boston, Massachusetts; New York City, New York; Philadelphia, Pennsylvania; Portland, Maine; or Providence, Rhode Island. All provided relatively easy access to major Canadian centres.

Some passengers stated their intention to go to Canada immediately, and their names were recorded on passenger lists separate from the people bound for destinations in the United States. Those lists are available on microfilm from Library and Archives Canada, and have been included in the major indexing projects by Library and Archives Canada and Ancestry.ca.

Two Library and Archives Canada microfilms provide lists of the ships that arrived, including the date and the ports of embarkation and arrival. Microfilm T-976 covers Baltimore, Boston, New York, and Portland from 1900 through 1908. Microfilm T-5460 includes New York from 1905 through 1922, and Baltimore, Boston, Philadelphia, Portland, and Providence from 1905 through 1921.

The best starting point for American immigration is the Ancestry.com website, which has an extensive database of arrivals with links to digitized images. Its database covers many ports with one search, which can help you to find that elusive ancestor quickly and easily. Just remember to follow the basic rules of database searching – and don't give up if you don't find your person right away.

ON THE INTERNET:

<www.ancestry.com>

Ancestry has comprehensive immigration indexes including New York from 1820 to 1957 as well as Boston, Philadelphia, Baltimore, and about 100 other points of entry. More than 100 million names are in the Ancestry collection.

Ancestry includes the Passenger and Immigration List Index, which for several decades has been the most comprehensive source for tracing relatives to the early colonial America period. The database includes about five million people who arrived in ports in the United States and Canada from the 1500s to the 1900s.

The index was started by P. William Filby as a series of books. It was augmented with annual supplements, then made available on CD-ROM, and finally converted to a database and posted online by Ancestry.

ON THE INTERNET:

<www.ancestry.com/search/db.aspx?dbid=7486>

The index is also available on World Vital Records, and is known on that site as Filby's Passenger and Immigration Lists Index.

ON THE INTERNET:

<www.worldvitalrecords.com/indexinfo.aspx?ix=pili>

The busiest American port was at New York, and the name of its immigration gateway, Ellis Island, has become synonymous with the idea of migration to North America in search of a better life. Ellis Island was in use as a processing centre from 1892 to 1954, and records covering most of those years have been opened for research.

A database of passenger arrivals from 1892 through 1924 is available online. That database makes it possible to see images taken from the relevant passenger lists, showing the names of arrivals as well as their ages, occupations, destinations, contact information, and more.

ON THE INTERNET:

<www.ellisisland.org>

Another index to Ellis Island arrivals is available on microfilm through the U.S. National Archives and Records Administration as well as the Family History Library in Salt Lake City and its branches. The microfilmed index extends to 1948, offering 24 more years than the online database.

The microfilmed index, which uses the Soundex system of alphanumeric codes for surnames, is sometimes more accurate than the one online, especially with names from Continental Europe. If a name cannot be found on the website, a researcher should check the microfilms.

Another website is devoted to Castle Garden, on the tip of Manhattan island, which handled New York City arrivals before Ellis Island was opened. Its records date from in 1830.

ON THE INTERNET:

<www.castlegarden.org>

Stephen Morse has devised several different ways to search the Ellis Island and Castle Garden databases, and others.

ON THE INTERNET:

<www.stephenmorse.org>

Microfilmed indexes of passenger arrivals are available for Baltimore (to 1952), Philadelphia (to 1948), Portland (to 1954), Providence (to 1954), and Boston (to 1920). Indexes have also been compiled for San Francisco, Seattle, and other West Coast ports. Along with the indexes, passenger lists are available well into the 1950s for most of these American ports.

These microfilms are available through the U.S. National Archives and Records Administration and the Family History Library. Note, however, that these films have been indexed on the Ancestry website.

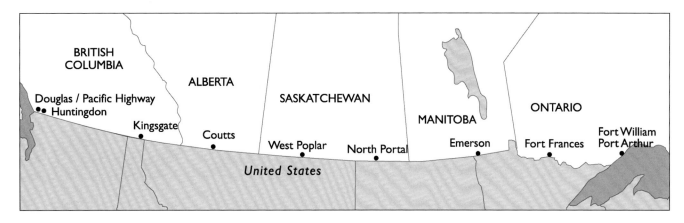

Border entry records – 1908-1935

Busiest border entry points west of Lake Superior

Until 1894, there were no restrictions placed on those crossing the border in either direction. In 1895, the United States started keeping records of people who entered the country. Canada started its own records in April 1908.

Library and Archives Canada has, on microfilm, lists of immigrants crossing the border from 1908 to the end of 1935. These records contain information such as name, age, country of birth, occupation, last place of residence in the United States, and destination in Canada.

These records have been indexed by Ancestry.ca, with an online database linked to original documents. This project represented a great step forward for researchers, because it is time-consuming and frustrating to use the microfilm. If you are dealing with border entry records, start with Ancestry!

ON THE INTERNET:

<search.ancestry.ca/iexec/?htx=List&dbid=1344>

Not everyone who crossed the border was registered. Some crossed when the ports were closed or where no port existed. Many families were not registered because one or both parents had been born in Canada or previously resided here, and they were considered returning Canadians rather than immigrants.

There are three basic groups of border records.

From 1908 through 1918, entries are arranged by border port and date of entry. Unindexed lists of these arrivals are available on a series of 47 microfilms. To use them effectively, a researcher should know the port and month of arrival.

Microfilms on the following pages are listed from west to east. The geographic arrangement makes it easy to search the records if the researcher knows the general area where a person would have entered Canada.

A more comprehensive list is on the Library and Archives Canada website.

ON THE INTERNET:

<www.collectionscanada.gc.ca/genealogy/022-908.005-e.html>

Many of the records were not in order when they were filmed, so be sure to check the entire reel. Be warned that the quality of the microfilming was generally bad, and many pages are quite dark.

From January 1919 to the end of 1924, individual forms (known as Form 30) were used to record immigrants entering Canada from or via the United States.

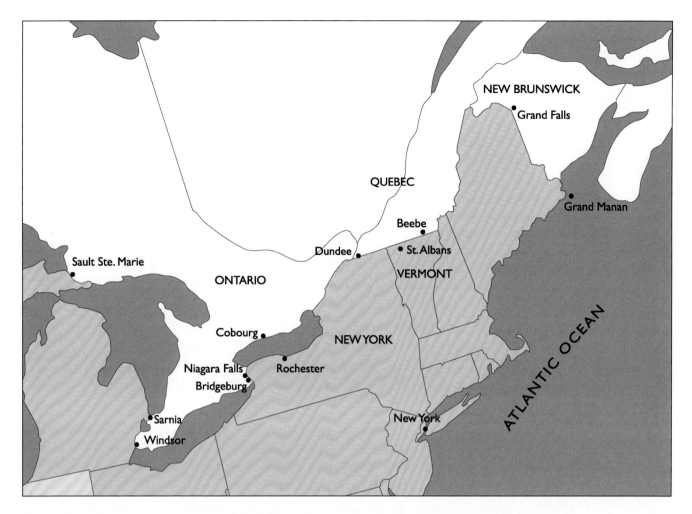

Busiest border entry points east of Lake Superior

The Form 30 records are arranged in a quasi-alphabetical order.

From 1925 through 1935, the use of border entry lists was reinstated. For each month, the records for all ports are filed together. These records contain more information than the earlier lists, including the immigrant's place of birth, the name and address of the relative, friend, or employer to whom they were destined, and the name and address of the nearest relative in the country of origin.

Indexes are available to make research easier for this group. For surnames starting with C, check the immigration records database on the Library and Archives Canada website. For other names, contact the staff at the Genealogy Unit at Library and Archives Canada in Ottawa with enough information, including year of entry, to help them identify the correct individual. The index is not open to searching by the public because it includes post-1935 entries, which are still closed for privacy reasons.

ON THE INTERNET:
<www.collectionscanada.gc.ca/contact/index-e.html>
Mailing address:
Genealogy Unit
Library and Archives Canada
395 Wellington St.
Ottawa, Ontario K1A 0N4

Border entry records 1909-1918 (Lists)

Yukon

Microfilm	Port	Adjacent to	Outside dates
T-5470	Forty Mile	Alaska	April 1909 - Dec. 1917
T-5468	Dawson	Alaska	April 1916 - Aug. 1918

British Columbia (coastal)

Microfilm	Port	Adjacent to	Outside dates
T-5504	White Pass	Alaska	July 1908 - Nov. 1918
T-5499	Stewart	Alaska	Sept. 1910 - Dec. 1912
T-5461	Anyox	Alaska	March 1914 - March 1918
T-5496	Port Simpson	Pacific Ocean	June 1910 - Dec. 1914
T-5496	Prince Rupert	Pacific Ocean	April 1911 - Sept. 1918
T-5489	Ocean Falls	Pacific Ocean	June 1917
T-5495	Powell River	Pacific Ocean	Aug. 1913 - Sept. 1918

British Columbia (Vancouver Island)

Microfilm	Port	Adjacent to	Outside dates
T-5502	Union Bay	Pacific Ocean	June 1911 - Dec. 1911
T-5487	Nanaimo	Pacific Ocean	Jan. 1910 - Dec. 1914
T-5474	Ladysmith	Pacific Ocean	April 1911 - Dec. 1911
T-5463	Bamfield	Pacific Ocean	Oct. 1914 - Dec. 1914
T-5503	Victoria	Pacific Ocean	Dec. 1910

British Columbia (Vancouver and the Fraser Valley)

Microfilm	Port	Adjacent to	Outside dates
T-5499	Steveston	Washington	Feb. 1918
T-5474	Ladner	Washington	April 1915 - March 1917
T-5503	White Rock	Washington	March 1909 - Feb. 1913
T-5504	White Rock	Washington	Jan. 1913 - Dec. 1918
T-5468	Douglas	Washington	April 1908 - Aug. 1918
T-5503	Douglas	Washington	Jan. 1910 - Nov. 1912
T-5504	Douglas	Washington	Feb. 1913 - March 1916
T-5495	Pacific Highway	Washington	March 1913 - Nov. 1918
T-5468	Pacific Highway / Douglas	Washington	April 1913 - June 1913
T-5461	Aldergrove	Washington	Nov. 1911 - Aug. 1918
T-5495	Peardonville	Washington	April 1909 - Oct. 1911
T-5503	Peardonville	Washington	Jan. 1910 - Aug. 1910
T-5472	Huntingdon	Washington	April 1908 - Dec. 1913
T-5473	Huntingdon	Washington	Jan.1914 - Dec. 1918
T-5485	Huntingdon	Washington	Aug. 1908
T-5485	Mission	Washington	Sept. 1913 - April 1915
T-5502	Upper Sumas	Washington	Jan. 1909 - March 1912
T-5466	Chilliwack	Washington	May 1912 - Jan. 1918

British Columbia (Interior – Similkameen to the East Kootenay)

Microfilm	Port	Adjacent to	Outside dates
T-5474	Keremeos	Washington	Feb. 1915
T-5483	Keremeos	Washington	June 1908 - Nov. 1916
T-5499	Similkameen	Washington	July 1918 - Sept. 1918
T-5495	Penticton	Washington	March 1915 - April 1917
T-5489	Osoyoos	Washington	April 1908 - Nov. 1918
T-5463	Bridesville	Washington	April 1908 - Dec. 1918
T-5485	Myncaster	Washington	June 1908 - Dec. 1918
T-5485	Midway	Washington	June 1908 - Oct. 1918

T-5465	Carson	Washington	April 1908 - May 1918
T-5470	Grand Forks	Washington	June 1908 - Oct. 1918
T-5507	Grand Forks	Washington	Dec. 1918
T-5465	Cascade	Washington	April 1908 - July 1918
T-5497	Rossland	Washington	Aug. 1913 - Feb. 1918
T-5495	Paterson	Washington	April 1908 - May 1917
T-5497	Paterson	Washington	March 1916 - Aug. 1917
T-5502	Waneta	Washington	April 1908 - Dec. 1918
T-5503	Waneta	Washington	March 1914 - May 1914
T-5496	Rykerts	Idaho	April 1908 - Sept. 1913
T-5497	Rykerts	Idaho	Oct. 1913 - Dec. 1918
T-5481	Kingsgate	Idaho	April 1908 - Oct. 1911
T-5482	Kingsgate	Idaho	Nov. 1911 - March 1914
T-5483	Kingsgate	Idaho	April 1914 - Dec. 1918
T-5483	Kingsgate	Idaho	May 1917 - Dec. 1917
T-5471	Gateway	Montana	April 1908 - March 1915
T-5487	Newgate	Montana	April 1915 - Dec. 1918
T-5496	Phillips/Roosville	Montana	April 1916 - May 1917
T-5497	Roosville	Montana	Nov. 1917 - June 1918

Alberta

Microfilm	Port	Adjacent to	Outside dates
T-5502	Twin Lakes	Montana	June 1914 - Oct. 1918
T-5466	Coutts	Montana	April 1908 - Dec. 1910
T-5467	Coutts	Montana	Jan. 1911 - June 1917
T-5468	Coutts	Montana	July 1917 - Dec. 1918
T-5495	Pinhorn	Montana	Oct. 1911 - Nov. 1918

Saskatchewan

Microfilm	Port	Adjacent to	Outside dates
T-5502	Willow Creek	Montana	Oct. 1917 - Dec. 1918
T-5462	West Poplar River	Montana	May 1918 - July 1918
T-5496	West Poplar River	Montana	Dec. 1917 - Dec. 1918
T-5502	Wood Mountain	Montana	May 1915 - Nov. 1917
T-5462	East Poplar River	Montana	Sept. 1917
T-5496	East Poplar River	Montana	Sept. 1918 - Dec. 1918
T-5495	East Poplar River	Montana	Oct. 191(?)
T-5462	Big Muddy	Montana	March 1912 or 1913 - Dec. 1918
T-5496	Radville	Montana	July 1917
T-5485	Marienthal	North Dakota	July 1913 - Aug. 1918
T-5496	Marienthal	North Dakota	July 1917
T-5489	North Portal	North Dakota	Dec. 1909 - March 1910
T-5490	North Portal	North Dakota	April 1910 - Jan. 1911
T-5491	North Portal	North Dakota	Feb. 1911 - Nov. 1911
T-5492	North Portal	North Dakota	Nov. 1911 - Jan. 1913
T-5493	North Portal	North Dakota	Feb. 1913 - March 1914
T-5494	North Portal	North Dakota	March 1914 - April 1917
T-5495	North Portal	North Dakota	May 1917 - Dec. 1918
T-5487	Northgate	North Dakota	Jan. 1914 - Dec. 1918

Manitoba

Microfilm	Port	Adjacent to	Outside dates
T-5462	Bannerman	North Dakota	April 1908 - Dec. 1918
T-5499	Snowflake	North Dakota	May 1908 - Dec. 1918
T-5499	Snowflake and Killarney	North Dakota	Aug. 1918 - Nov. 1918
T-5499	Mowbray	North Dakota	April 1908

T-5485	Morden	North Dakota	March 1913 - Dec. 1918
T-5472	Haskett	North Dakota	April 1910 - Oct. 1918
T-5470	Gretna	North Dakota	May 1908 - April 1910
T-5471	Gretna	North Dakota	April 1910 - Dec. 1912
T-5475	Emerson	Minnesota	Dec. 1909 - March 1911
T-5476	Emerson	Minnesota	April 1911 - March 1912
T-5477	Emerson	Minnesota	March 1912 - March 1913
T-5478	Emerson	Minnesota	March 1913 - Dec. 1913
T-5479	Emerson	Minnesota	Dec. 1913 - Nov. 1914
T-5480	Emerson	Minnesota	Dec. 1914 - March 1918
T-5481	Emerson	Minnesota	Jan. 1918 - Dec. 1918
T-5497	Sprague	Minnesota	Feb. 1909 - Dec. 1918

Ontario (Manitoba border to Sault Ste. Marie)

Microfilm	Port	Adjacent to	Outside dates
T-5497	Rainy River	Minnesota	Jan. 1913 - Dec.1918
T-5468	Fort Frances	Minnesota	Jan. 1909 - June 1911
T-5469	Fort Frances	Minnesota	June 1911 - Oct. 1917
T-5470	Fort Frances	Minnesota	Nov. 1917 - Dec. 1918
T-5496	Pigeon River Bridge	Minnesota	Jan. 1918 - Dec. 1918
T-5470	Fort William	Minnesota	Oct. 1908 - Nov. 1918
T-5496	Port Arthur	Minnesota	May 1908 - Nov. 1918
T-5499	Sault Ste. Marie	Michigan	March 1909 - May 1910
T-5500	Sault Ste. Marie	Michigan	June 1910 - April 1917
T-5501	Sault Ste. Marie	Michigan	May 1917 - Dec. 1918

Ontario (Georgian Bay to Windsor)

Microfilm	Port	Adjacent to	Outside dates
T-5463	Bruce Mines	Michigan	Sept. 1909 - May 1914
T-5502	Thessalon	Michigan	July 1909 - Dec. 1913
T-5463	Blind River	Michigan	June 1909 - Jan. 1914
T-5466	Cutler	Michigan	Aug. 1909 - Dec. 1914
T-5471	Gore Bay	Michigan	April 1914 - Aug. 1917
T-5475	Little Current	Michigan	June 1909 - Dec. 1914
T-5468	Depot Harbour	Michigan	July 1909 - Dec. 1914
T-5496	Parry Sound	Michigan	May 1909 - Dec. 1914
T-5466	Collingwood	Michigan	May 1909 - Dec. 1914
T-5472	Goderich	Michigan	Aug. 1909 - Dec. 1914
T-5496	Point Edward	Michigan	March 1909 - Sept. 1918
T-5501	Sarnia	Michigan	May 1909 - Feb. 1916
T-5502	Sarnia	Michigan	March 1916 - Dec. 1918
T-5466	Courtright	Michigan	Oct. 1908 - Sept. 1918
T-5499	Sombra	Michigan	Nov. 1908 - Sept. 1918
T-5496	Port Lambton	Michigan	Nov. 1908 - Dec. 1918
T-5504	Walpole Island	Michigan	Sept. 1910 - May 1917
T-5504	Wallaceburg	Michigan	Dec. 1913 - April 1918

Ontario (Windsor to the Niagara Falls area)

Microfilm	Port	Adjacent to	Outside dates
T-5502	Walkerville	Michigan	Jan. 1912 - Dec. 1918
T-5504	Windsor and Walkerville	Michigan	March 1909 - Sept. 1910
T-5505	Windsor	Michigan	Oct. 1910 - Oct. 1913
T-5506	Windsor	Michigan	Oct. 1913 - June 1917
T-5507	Windsor	Michigan	July 1917 - Dec. 1918
T-5489	Ojibwa	Michigan	April 1911 - Dec. 1911
T-5461	Amherstburg	Michigan	April 1908 - Feb. 1918

T-5496	Port Stanley	Ohio	April 1908 - Oct. 1917
T-5496	Port Burwell	Ohio	Nov. 1908 - Oct. 1915
T-5496	Port Dover	New York	May. 1908 - May 1916
T-5496	Port Colborne	New York	May 1908 - Mar. 1909
T-5504	Windmill Point	New York	Oct. 1912 - Dec. 1913
T-5466	Crystal Beach	New York	June 1909 - June 1918
T-5470	Fort Erie	New York	Dec. 1908 - Dec. 1918
T-5470	Erie Beach (filed with Fort Erie)	New York	July 1910 - June 1918
T-5463	Bridgeburg	New York	May 1908 - Aug. 1911
T-5464	Bridgeburg	New York	Aug. 1911 - April 1918
T-5465	Bridgeburg	New York	May 1918 - Dec. 1918
T-5487	Niagara Falls	New York	June 1908 - March 1912
T-5488	Niagara Falls	New York	April 1912 - Sept. 1915
T-5489	Niagara Falls	New York	Oct. 1915 - Dec. 1918
T-5474	Lewiston, New York	(port in U.S.)	July 1908 - May 1911
T-5475	Lewiston, New York	(port in U.S.)	July 1911 - Oct. 1918
T-5485	Lewiston, New York	(port in U.S.)	Aug. 1908

Ontario (Lake Ontario to the Quebec border)

Microfilm	Port	Adjacent to	Outside dates
T-5496	Port Dalhousie	New York	March 1909 - Dec. 1913
T-5502	Toronto	New York	Sept. 1908 - June 1918
T-5496	Port Hope	New York	Nov. 1908 - Dec. 1914
T-5465	Cobourg	New York	Oct. 1908 - Dec. 1917
T-5466	Cobourg	New York	Jan. 1915 - Dec. 1918
T-5496	Rochester, New York	(port in U.S.)	June 1916 - Sept. 1916
T-5465	Charlotte (Rochester), New York	(port in U.S.)	May 1913 - Sept. 1914
T-5466	Charlotte (Rochester), New York	(port in U.S.)	July 1914 - Sept. 1918
T-5463	Brighton	New York	Oct. 1908 - Dec. 1914
T-5502	Trenton	New York	Feb. 1913 - Aug. 1915
T-5463	Belleville	New York	Oct. 1908 - Dec. 1914
T-5496	Picton	New York	Oct. 1908 - Dec. 1913
T-5468	Deseronto	New York	Oct. 1908 - Dec. 1914
T-5463	Bath	New York	Oct. 1908 - June 1912
T-5483	Kingston	New York	Sept. 1908 - Nov. 1918
T-5504	Wolfe Island	New York	March 1915 - June 1918
T-5472	Gananoque	New York	Oct. 1908 - Feb. 1917
T-5496	Rockport	New York	Oct. 1908 - Dec. 1918
T-5462	Brockville	New York	Sept. 1908 - Dec. 1918
T-5495	Prescott	New York	Jan. 1909 - Dec. 1918
T-5474	Iroquois	New York	Sept. 1908-Aug. 1915
T-5484	Morrisburg	New York	Sept. 1908 - Sept. 1918
T-5461	Aultsville	New York	July 1917 - Oct. 1918
T-5466	Cornwall	New York	Oct. 1908 - Dec. 1918

Quebec

Microfilm	Port	Adjacent to	Outside dates
T-5499	St. Regis	New York	April 1918 - Sept. 1918
T-5468	Dundee	New York	Oct. 1908 - Feb. 1915
T-5486	Dundee	New York	March 1910
T-5472	Huntingdon/St-Agnes	New York	Feb. 1915 - Dec. 1918
T-5486	Malone, New York	(port in U.S.)	June 1908 - Dec. 1918
T-5486	Athelstan	New York	Aug. 1918
T-5472	Hemmingford	New York	April 1913 - Oct. 1917
T-5499	St. John's	New York	April 1914 - Oct. 1917
T-5483	Lacolle Junction	New York	July 1910 - Dec. 1910

T-5484	Lacolle Junction	New York	Jan. 1911 - Dec. 1918
T-5497	Rouses Point, New York	(port in U.S.)	June 1908 - Dec. 1918
T-5486	Alburg, Vermont	(port in U.S.)	Dec. 1910 - June 1914
T-5486	Noyan Junction	Vermont	April 1909 - Oct. 1916
T-5487	Noyan Junction	Vermont	Nov. 1916 - Sept. 1917
T-5498	St. Armand	Vermont	Apr. 1910 - Mar. 1911
T-5497	St. Albans, Vermont	(port in U.S.)	June 1908 - Sept. 1909
T-5498	St. Albans, Vermont	(port in U.S.)	Oct. 1909 - Dec. 1915
T-5499	St. Albans, Vermont	(port in U.S.)	Jan. 1916 - Dec. 1918
T-5470	Frelighsburg	Vermont	April 1908 - May 1918
T-5473	Highwater	Vermont	Mar. 1909 - Mar. 1912
T-5474	Highwater	Vermont	April 1912 - Dec. 1918
T-5486	Highwater	Vermont	March 1910
T-5484	Mansonville	Vermont	June 1913 - Dec. 1918
T-5484	Magog	Vermont	Aug. 1910 - June 1917
T-5471	Georgeville	Vermont	Oct. 1908 - Aug. 1916
T-5461	Beebe Junction	Vermont	April 1909 - April 1914
T-5462	Beebe Junction	Vermont	April 1914 - Dec. 1918
T-5486	Beebe Junction	Vermont	March 1910
T-5502	Stanstead Junction	Vermont	July 1908 - Oct. 1908
T-5499	Stanhope	Vermont	Oct. 1908 - Nov. 1918
T-5465	Coaticook	Vermont	Nov. 1908 - Dec. 1918
T-5486	Coaticook	Vermont	March 1910
T-5472	Hereford	Vermont	Sept. 1917 - Dec. 1918
T-5466	Comins Mills (with Paquetteville)	New Hampshire	Jan. 1909 - Nov. 1918
T-5465	Comins Mills	New Hampshire	Dec. 1917
T-5495	Paquetteville (with Comins Mills) filed with Comins Mills	New Hampshire	Jan. 1911 - March 1911
T-5466	Paquetteville	New Hampshire	April 1911 - Aug. 1912
T-5486	Megantic and Lake Megantic	Maine	April 1910 - Dec. 1918
T-5461	Armstrong	Maine	April 1916 - July 1918

New Brunswick

Microfilm	Port	Location	Outside dates
T-5465	Connors	Maine	Nov. 1917 - April 1918
T-5465	Clair	Maine	Dec. 1908 - July 1918
T-5466	Clair	Maine	Oct. 1910
T-5499	St. Hilaire	Maine	March 1918
T-5468	Edmundston	Maine	March 1911 - Dec. 1918
T-5471	Green River Rivière Verte	Maine	Feb. 1909 - March 1912
T-5499	St. Leonard	Maine	Jan. 1909 - Dec. 1918
T-5472	Grand Falls	Maine	Oct. 1908
T-5471	Grand Falls	Maine	Sept. 1909 - Aug. 1913
T-5472	Grand Falls	Maine	Aug. 1913 - Sept. 1918
T-5461	Aroostook Junction	Maine	Oct. 1908 - Dec. 1918
T-5461	Andover	Maine	Oct. 1908 - Dec. 1918
T-5466	Centreville	Maine	March 1909 - July 1917
T-5465	Centreville	Maine	May 1917
T-5496	Richmond Road/Richmond Corner	Maine	June 1912 - Oct. 1918
T-5504	Woodstock (with Richmond)	Maine	Dec. 1909 - Oct. 1917
T-5468	Debec Junction	Maine	April 1908 - Dec. 1918
T-5470	Fosterville	Maine	Sept. 1911 - Feb. 1912
T-5484	McAdam Junction	Maine	Dec. 1908 - Dec. 1913
T-5485	McAdam Junction	Maine	Jan. 1914 - Dec. 1918
T-5502	Upper Mills	Maine	March 1909 - Nov. 1918
T-5485	Milltown	Maine	Nov. 1908 - Dec. 1918

T-5486	Milltown	Maine	May 1909 - Nov. 1917
T-5499	St. Andrews	Maine	Nov. 1908 - Dec. 1918
T-5499	St. Andrews	Maine	June 1908 - Nov. 1918
T-5470	Fair Haven	Maine	June 1918
T-5504	Wilsons Beach	Maine	Dec. 1909 - Oct. 1917
T-5504	Welshpool	Maine	Jan. 1912 - March 1915
T-5487	North Head	Maine	Jan. 1912 - Nov. 1917
T-5471	Grand Manan	Maine	Aug. 1917 - Feb. 1918
T-5470	Grand Manan	Maine	Sept. 1917
T-5475	Letete	Maine	Aug. 1914 - Sept. 1918

Nova Scotia

Microfilm	Port	Adjacent to	Outside dates
T-5465	Clements Port	Atlantic Ocean	April 1909 - Dec. 1914
T-5507	Yarmouth	Atlantic Ocean	April 1908 - Dec. 1914
T-5475	Liverpool	Atlantic Ocean	Oct. 1917 - Jan. 1918
T-5496	Port Hawkesbury	Atlantic Ocean	July 1909 - Sept. 1909
T-5499	Sydney	Atlantic Ocean	July 1914 - Sept. 1918

United States ports not close to the Canadian border

Microfilm	Port		Outside Dates
T-5495	Portland, Maine	(also ocean port)	May 1910 - Dec. 1913
T-5462	Boston, Massachusetts	(also ocean port)	July 1910 - May 1917
T-5463	Boston, Massachusetts	(also ocean port)	June 1917 - March 1918

Border entry records 1919-1924 (Form 30)

Microfilm: ... Names of immigrants:

T-15249	Aadland, Alf to Altin, Carl	T-15277	Evano, Pauline to Ferguson, Ward
T-15250	Allen, Eltran C. to Anderson, Margaret B.	T-15278	Ferguson, Wesley to Fontaine, Eva
T-15251	Anderson, M. to Ashworth, Arthur	T-15279	Fontaine, Flora to Frazier, J. H.
T-15252	Ashworth, Arthur to Baker, N.A.	T-15280	Frazur, Jean to Gallagher, William
T-15253	Baker, N.A. to Barrette, Siméon	T-15281	Gallan, Andrew to German, Isabel
T-15254	Barrett, Thomas to Becker, Buddy	T-15282	Germain, Jos. Arthur to Godbout, Gervais P.
T-15255	Becker, Carl William Gustav to Bentley, Bessie	T-15283	Gobeille, Henry to Graner, Otis
T-15256	Bent, Caroline to Birbynick, Metro	T-15284	Granum, Ohara to Grussey, F. J.
T-15257	Birdsall, Nellie to Blanton, Ester	T-15285	Grussing, Fred to Hallett, William
T-15258	Bishop, A to Bolstad, Bjarne	T-15286	Hallground, Walter C. to Harper, Blake
T-15259	Bolt, C. to Bowman, Athel	T-15287	Harper, Chas. to Haynes, Stanley
T-15260	Bowman, Carl to Breandler, Carl	T-15288	Haynes, Violet Sylvia to Herring, William Odus
T-15261	Brawdy, Thelma to Brown, Lynn	T-15289	Herrod, Charles William to Hoehne, Clara
T-15262	Brown, Mary to Burley, Fred	T-15290	Hoe, Emma to Housman, Zilpha
T-15263	Burkman, Harold to Cabot, William	T-15291	Houston, Adelaide to Hyatt, William George
T-15264	Caddens, Ann J.K. to Carns, John W.	T-15292	Hyde, Alice to Jenkinson, Robert Edwin
T-15265	Carollo, Joe to Champlin, Edna S.	T-15293	Jenks, Alvah Owen to Johnson, Owdin
T-15266	Champagne, Frank to Clark, Lyle	T-15294	Johnson, Oscar to Kane, William C.
T-15267	Clark, Margaret May to Coleman, Lyman	T-15295	Kantarowitz, Abraham to Kershuer, Opal
T-15268	Coleman, Mabel to Cornelson, A. B.	T-15296	Kershaw, Paul to Knudtzon, Joseph
T-15269	Cornish, Dora M. to Crew, Gertrude	T-15297	Knud, K. Arneldi to Lachapelle, Eva
T-15270	Crews, George to Dale, Anna	T-15298	Lacasse, Flagien to Lanouette, Arthur
T-15271	Dale, Arnold to Dean, Winnie	T-15299	Lannon, Bill to Laxson, Violette
T-15272	Dean, Charles H. to Davine, Kenneth	T-15300	Layman, Alexander to Leshia, Frank
T-15273	DeVincenza, Lucia to Doody, K.	T-15301	Lescallett, George Calvin to Livingston, E. M.
T-15274	Dooley, Laura to Duners, Laurence	T-15302	Livingston, Fred to Luzmoor, Ernest
T-15275	Dumais, Mary to Edwards, Richard M.	T-15303	Lutz, George to Maniscalco, Samuel
T-15276	Edwards, Robert to Evanger, Nels	T-15304	Manion, Thos. B. to Mason, W.

T-15305	Mass, Allan to McClure, Evelyn	T-15326	Sanders, Bernard to Schulman, Bessie
T-15306	McClure, James A. to McGranaghan, Teresa	T-15327	Schuler, C. R. L. to Shanks, Doris
T-15307	McGrath, Allen G. to McMahon, Hugh B.	T-15328	Shanahan, Edward to Simons, Briceis H.
T-15308	McMahon, Jack to Merrick, Wayne	T-15329	Simons, Chancey to Smith, Emil
T-15309	Merrill, Alice to Mills, Gordon	T-15330	Smith, Emil to Sorenson, M.
T-15310	Mills, McHannah to Moorey, Verne B.	T-15331	Sorbo, Adolph to Steggall, Tressie
T-15311	Mooren, William to Mullen, Hernon James	T-15332	Stein, Alexander to Street, Wesley
T-15312	Mullen, L. A. to Nelson, Charlie	T-15333	Stregger, Alvina to Szeyallo, Joseph
T-15313	Nelson, Charlie A. to Nolting, Iber	T-15334	Szmiot, Kerstant to Thompon, John
T-15314	Nolet, Joseph to Olsen, Roy L.	T-15335	Thistle, Le Baron C. to Todd, Harold
T-15315	Olsen, Sarah to Page, W. M. O.	T-15336	Todd, Harriet to Turner, Dora
T-15316	Pageau, Arthur to Paulson, Myrtle	T-15337	Turner, Earl H. to Venning, Clarence
T-15317	Paulson, Nellie to Peterie, Joseph	T-15338	Venes, Dilon to Wallace, Wylie
T-15318	Pester, Lewis to Pittman, F. E.	T-15339	Wallauch, Arthur to Webb, W. L.
T-15319	Pittman, F. E. to Prerley, George E.	T-15340	Webber, Addie to Whisker, William M
T-15320	Prena, Joseph to Randall, Guy Leslie	T-15341	Whitaker, Arthur to Williams, Ivan T.
T-15321	Randall, Harold M. to Renmickson, William	T-15342	Williams, James to Wolbert, Verdie
T-15322	Renner, Selma P. to Rissanen, Ananias	T-15343	Wolf, Adalina to Young, Ewen
T-15323	Rising, Benjamin C. to Rolseth, Mathilda	T-15344	Young, Fadia to Zwietusch, William Y.
T-15324	Rollin, Norman to Rungan, Martha		
T-15325	Rungan, Martha to Sandmoen, Alfred	T-15345	People refused entry at the border

Border entry records 1925-1935 (Lists)

Microfilm:	Start date:		End date:	
T-15346	1925 January	(vol. 1, p.1)	1925 April	(vol. 1, p. 200)
T-15347	1925 April	(vol. 1, p.200)	1925 July	(vol. 2, p. 419)
T-15348	1925 July	(vol. 2, p. 419)	1925 October	(vol. 4, p. 137)
T-15349	1925 October	(vol. 4, p. 137)	1926 March	(vol. 1, p. 374)
T-15350	1926 March	(vol. 1, p. 374)	1926 June	(vol. 3, p. 209)
T-15351	1926 June	(vol. 3, p. 209)	1926 August	(vol. 4, p. 362)
T-15352	1926 September	(vol. 5, p. 1)	1926 December	(vol. 6, p. 183)
T-15353	1926 December	(vol. 6, p. 183)	1927 April	(vol. 2, p. 115)
T-15354	1927 April	(vol. 2, p. 115)	1927 June	(vol. 3, p. 315)
T-15355	1927 June	(vol. 3, p. 315)	1927 August	(vol. 5, p. 351)
T-15356	1927 August	(vol. 5, p. 351)	1927 October	(vol. 7, p. 101)
T-15357	1927 October	(vol. 7, p. 101)	1928 January	(vol. 1, p. 73)
T-15358	1928 January	(vol. 1, p. 73)	1928 April	(vol. 2, p. 462)
T-15359	1928 April	(vol. 2, p. 462)	1928 June	(vol. 4, p. 331)
T-15360	1928 June	(vol. 4, p. 332)	1928 August	(vol. 6, p. 250)
T-15361	1928 August	(vol. 6, p. 251)	1928 September	(vol. 7, p. 352)
T-15362	1928 September	(vol. 7, p. 352)	1928 December	(vol. 9, p. 400)
T-15363	1929 January	(vol.1, p. 1)	1929 April	(vol. 2, p. 429)
T-15364	1929 April	(vol. 2, p. 429)	1929 June	(vol. 4, p. 224)
T-15365	1929 June	(vol. 4, p. 224)	1929 August	(vol. 6, p. 106)
T-15366	1929 August	(vol. 6, p. 106)	1929 October	(vol. 8, p. 79)
T-15367	1929 October	(vol. 8, p. 80)	1930 January	(vol. 1, p. 34)
T-15368	1930 January	(vol. 1, p. 34)	1930 April	(vol. 3, p. 117)
T-15369	1930 April	(vol. 3, p. 117)	1930 June	(vol. 5, p. 27)
T-15370	1930 June	(vol. 5, p. 27)	1930 July	(vol. 6, p. 210)
T-15371	1930 July	(vol. 6, p. 211)	1930 August	(vol. 7, p. 378)
T-15372	1930 August	(vol. 7, p. 378)	1930 October	(vol. 9, p. 168)
T-15373	1930 October	(vol. 9, p. 169)	1931 January	(vol. 1, p. 106)
T-15374	1931 January	(vol. 1, p. 107)	1931 April	(vol. 3, p. 108)
T-15375	1931 April	(vol. 3, p. 109)	1931 June	(vol. 5, p. 124)

T-15376	1931 June	(vol. 5, p. 125)	1931 July	(vol. 6, p. 430)	
T-15377	1931 August	(vol. 7, p. 1)	1931 September	(vol. 8, p. 215)	
T-15378	1931 September	(vol. 8, p. 216)	1931 December	(vol. 10, p. 250)	
T-15379	1931 December	(vol. 10, p. 251)	1932 April	(vol. 2, p. 202)	
T-15380	1932 April	(vol. 2, p. 203)	1932 June	(vol. 4, p. 93)	
T-15381	1932 June	(vol. 4, p. 93)	1932 August	(vol. 6, p. 21)	
T-15382	1932 August	(vol. 6, p. 22)	1932 September	(vol. 7, p. 323)	
T-15383	1932 October	(vol. 8, p. 1)	1933 February	(vol. 1, p. 146)	
T-15384	1933 February	(vol. 1, p. 146)	1933 June	(vol. 3, p. 20)	
T-15385	1933 June	(vol. 3, p. 21)	1933 August	(vol. 5, p. 216)	
T-15386	1933 August	(vol. 5, p. 217)	1933 December	(vol. 7, p. 243)	
T-15387	1933 December	(vol. 7, p. 244)	1934 May	(vol. 2, p. 343)	
T-15388	1934 June	(vol. 3, p. 1)	1934 September	(vol. 4, p. 270)	
T-15389	1934 September	(vol. 4, p. 271)	1935 February	(vol. 1, p. 126)	
T-15390	1935 January	(vol. 1, p. 1)	1935 March	(vol. 1, p. 249)	
T-15391	1935 March	(vol. 1, p. 249)	1935 July	(vol. 3, p. 333)	
T-15392	1935 July	(vol. 3, p. 333)	1935 November	(vol. 5, p. 252)	
T-15393	1935 November	(vol. 5, p. 252)	1935 December	(vol. 5, p. 392)	

Arrivals at New York 1906-1921 (Passenger lists)

Includes only the passengers who stated their intention of proceeding directly to Canada. On some reels, manifests are not in strict chronological order.

Microfilm	Starts with:	Vessel:	Ends with:	Vessel:
T-517	1906 Jan.	Konigin Luise	1906 Feb. 22	United States
T-518	1906 Feb. 22	Sicilia	1907 March 4	Ethiopia
T-519	1907 March 5	Columbia	1908 Feb. 18	Duca Degli Abruzzi
T-4699	1908 Feb. 18	Alice	1910 June 17	Mauretania
T-4700	1910 June 17	Mauretania	1911 Jan. 3	Lapland
T-4701	1911 Jan. 13	Adriatic	1911 Apr. 21	Konig Albert
T-4702	1911 Apr. 21	Konig Albert	1911 June 18	Indiana
T-4703	1911 June 18	Indiana	1911 Sept. 5	Lapland
T-4704	1911 Sept. 22	Cameronia	1911 Nov. 27	Adriatic
T-4705	1911 Nov. 27	Caledonia	1912 March 2	La Savoie
T-4706	1912 March 2	La Savoie	1912 Apr. 23	Rochambeau
T-4707	1912 Apr. 23	Havana	1912 June 11	Noordam
T-4708	1912 June 11	Noordam	1912 Aug. 16	Ivernia
T-4709	1912 Aug. 16	Ivernia	1912 Oct. 17	Carpathia
T-4710	1912 Oct. 17	Carpathia	1912 Dec. 26	Rotterdam
T-4711	1912 Dec. 26	Rotterdam	1913 March 12	Sant Anna
T-4712	1913 March 12	Europa	1913 Apr. 19	Cristobal
T-4713	1913 Apr. 19	Cristobal	1913 May 24	Vestris
T-4714	1913 May 25	La Lorraine	1913 July 9	Hellig Olav
T-4715	1913 July 9	Hellig Olav	1913 Sept. 5	Adriatic
T-4716	1913 Sept. 5	Adriatic	1913 Nov. 6	Kaiser Wilhelm Grosse
T-4717	1913 Nov. 6	Kaiser Wilhelm Grosse	1914 Feb. 3	Martha Washington
T-4718	1914 Feb. 3	Martha Washington	1914 Apr. 10	Imperator
T-4719	1914 Apr. 10	Imperator	1914 May 25	Caledonia
T-4720	1914 May 25	Caledonia	1914 July 29	Prinz Joachim
T-4721	1914 July 29	Prinz Joachim	1914 Nov. 23	Thessaloniki
T-4722	1914 Nov. 23	Thessaloniki	1915 Apr. 20	Tuscani
T-4723	1915 Apr. 20	Tuscania	1915 Aug. 3	Espagna
T-4724	1915 Aug. 3	Espagna	1915 Dec. 4	Marracaibo
T-4725	1915 Dec. 4	Maracaibo	1916 Apr. 17	New York
T-4726	1916 Apr. 17	New York	1916 July 23	Esperenza
T-4727	1916 July 23	Esperanza	1916 Nov. 10	Carrillo

T-4728	1916 Nov. 10	Carrillo	1917 Apr. 6	Chicago
T-4729	1917 Apr. 9	St. Louis	1917 Sept. 22	New York
T-4730	1917 Sept. 23	Lancastrian	1918 May 1	Coamo
T-4731	1918 May 1	Mexico	1918 Oct. 2	Baltic
T-4732	1918 Oct. 2	Baltic	1919 Apr. 8	Mayarro
T-14914	1919 Apr. 8	Mayarro	1919 Aug. 14	Mayarro
T-14915	1919 Aug. 16	Adventuress	1919 Dec. 4	Churybdis
T-14916	1919 Dec. 4	Churybdis	1920 Apr. 9	Columbia
T-14917	1920 Apr. 9	Columbia	1920 June 8	Guiana
T-14918	1920 June 8	Guiana	1920 Sept. 6	France
T-14919	1920 Sept. 6	France	1920 Dec. 13	Kaiser Auguste Victoria
T-14920	1920 Dec. 13	Adriatic	1921 Apr. 9	Carmania
T-14921	1921 Apr. 9	Aquitania	1921 July 18	Rochambeau
T-14922	1921 July 18	Celtic	1921 Dec. 8	Fort Hamilton

Arrivals at Atlantic ports 1905-1921 (Passenger lists)
Including Baltimore, Boston, New York, Portland, Philadelphia, and Providence.

Microfilm	Starts with:	Vessel:	Ends with:	Vessel:
T-513	1905 July 5	Cassel	1906 Sept. 23	Parisian
T-514	1906 Oct. 1	Bohemian	1908 March 23	Dominion
T-4689	1908 no date	Dominion	1910 July 28	Ivernia
T-4690	1910 Aug. 1	Tortoria	1911 Nov. 26	Ascania
T-4691	1911 Nov. 26	Canada	1912 Apr. 9	Megantic
T-4692	1912 Apr. 9	Megantic	1913 Jan. 14	Canada
T-4693	1913 Jan. 14	Canada	1913 Apr. 9	Arabic
T-4694	1913 Apr. 9	Arabic	1914 March 26	Scotian
T-4695	1914 March 26	Scotian	1913 Dec. 31	Sicilian
T-4696	1913 Dec. 31	Sicilian	1916 June 15	Canopic
T-4697	1916 June 15	Canopic	1921 Nov. 4	Asia

Arrivals at New York 1925-1931 (Passenger lists)
Includes only passengers who stated their intention of proceeding directly to Canada.

Microfilm	Starts with:		Ends with:	
T-14923	1925 Jan. 1	(vol. 1, p. 1)	1925 Apr. 21	(vol. 2, p. 195)
T-14924	1925 Apr. 21	(vol. 2, p. 196)	1925 Sept. 5	(vol. 5, p. 30)
T-14925	1925 Sept. 5	(vol. 5, p. 31)	1926 Jan. 19	(vol. 1, p. 64)
T-14926	1926 Jan. 19	(vol. 1, p. 64)	1926 May 5	(vol. 3, p. 34)
T-14927	1926 May 5	(vol. 3, p. 35)	1926 Aug 19	(vol. 5, p. 113)
T-14928	1926 Aug. 19	(vol. 5, p. 113)	1926 Dec. 11	(vol. 9, p. 61)
T-14929	1926 Dec. 11	(vol. 9, p. 61)	1927 Mar. 29	(vol. 3, p. 175)
T-14930	1927 Mar. 29	(vol. 3, p. 176)	1927 July 31	(vol. 6, p. 183)
T-14931	1927 Aug 1	(vol. 7, p. 1)	1927 Dec 7	(vol. 9, p. 125)
T-14932	1927 Dec. 7	(vol. 9, p. 126)	1928 May 1	(vol. 3, p. 108)
T-14933	1928 May 1	(vol. 3, p. 109)	1928 Nov. 1	(vol. 6, p. 86)
T-14934	1928 Nov. 1	(vol. 6, p. 87)	1929 July 29	(vol. 3, p. 58)
T-14935	1929 July 29	(vol. 3, p. 59)	1930 June 17	(vol. 1, p. 336)
T-14936	1930 June 19	(vol. 1, p. 337)	1931 Apr. 23	(vol. 1, p. 177)
T-14937	1931 Apr. 23	(vol. 1, p. 178)	1931 Dec. 20	(vol. 3, p. 206)

Arrivals at other Atlantic ports 1925-1928 (Passenger lists)
Includes only passengers who stated their intention of proceeding directly to Canada.

Microfilm	Starts with:		Ends with:	
T-14938	1925 Jan. 2	(vol. 1, p. 1)	1928 Dec. 30	(vol. 1, p. 78)

The Empress of Canada was one of the Canadian Pacific ships serving the Atlantic routes

Chapter 9

Arrivals since 1935

In the 1930s, immigration to Canada fell sharply, reaching lows that would have been unbelievable a few years earlier. In 1935, for example, only 11,277 immigrants arrived at our shores and border posts. Canadian border guards watched more people leave than arrive in the 1930s. It was the only decade in the 20th century when more people left Canada than arrived.

The low numbers were in stark contrast to the statistics recorded a few years earlier. In 1928, there had been 166,783 immigrants, and in 1913, 400,870 people had arrived.

Immigration to Canada hit such a low level – its lowest since 1867, the year of Confederation – because of the Great Depression. There was little public appetite for newcomers when so many of the people already here were barely getting by. Our doors were effectively closed, for all but a select few, while the country tried to cope with the economic collapse.

Even cases of extreme hardship were turned away. The most notorious rejection of the time was the government's refusal to allow the passenger ship St. Louis, filled with Jewish refugees from Germany, to land in Canada. After their return to Germany, most of the passengers on board were arrested.

Immigration fell further during the Second World War, reaching 7,576 in 1942. When the war ended, immigration picked up again. It was fuelled by war brides – women who had fallen in love with Canadian soldiers posted overseas – as well as people who wanted to escape the mess that was left in Europe. Some of these

Unloading a Canadian Pacific vessel at the harbour in Victoria

people were refugees, displaced from their homes for one reason or another. Since they were already on the move, and had to make a fresh start in unfamiliar territory anyway, the journey to Canada had an appeal.

In 1948, the number of people coming to Canada exceeded 100,000 for the first time since 1930. Between 1951 and 1960, a total of 1,478,611 immigrants arrived, with 282,164 of them in 1957 alone.

Immigration dropped again in the early 1960s, hitting peaks in 1967 (222,876) and 1974 (218,465) and valleys in 1978 (86,313) and 1985 (84,302). Since 1989, the number of immigrants admitted each year has stayed consistently close to the 200,000 mark.

Research into these arrivals might pose problems for researchers, since Canada's privacy laws will keep many of the best records behind locked doors for years. On the other hand, many of the people who arrived since 1935 might still be alive – and might be able or willing to provide the information first-hand.

Passenger lists from most ship arrivals since Jan. 1, 1936, are still closed to researchers. There are, however, ways to obtain more information.

The best source will usually be Citizenship and Immigration Canada, which holds the post-1935 immigration records. To obtain a copy of another person's immigration record, you must be a Canadian citizen or an individual residing in Canada, and you must use an Access to Information Request Form available on the department's website.

ON THE INTERNET:

<www.tbs-sct.gc.ca/tbsf-fsct/350-57-eng.asp>

Your request should include the full name at time of entry into Canada, date of birth, and year of entry. If you also know the country of birth, port of entry, or names of accompanying family members, include that as well.

The request must be accompanied by a signed consent from the person concerned or proof that he or she has been dead for 20 years or more. Proof of death can be a copy of a death record, a newspaper obituary, or a photograph of the gravestone showing name and death date. Proof of death is not required if the person would be over 110 years of age.

Include a cheque or money order for $5.00, payable to the Receiver General for Canada.

Send your request to:

Citizenship and Immigration Canada

Public Rights Administration

360 Laurier Ave. W.

10th Floor

Ottawa, Ontario K1A 1L1

For a copy of your own landing record, submit an Application for a Certified True Copy, Correction, or Replacement of an Immigration Document to Citizenship and Immigration Canada. The form is on the department's website.

ON THE INTERNET:

<www.cic.gc.ca/english/information/applications/certcopy.asp>

Or you can apply for a copy of a Permanent Resident Card. Again, that can be done through the department's website.

ON THE INTERNET:

<www.cic.gc.ca/english/information/pr-card/index.asp>

There are other ways to obtain information about post-1935 arrivals. Information on those sources will be found elsewhere in this book.

Look for outbound records from other countries (Chapter 10), naturalization and citizenship documents (Chapter 12), and records of the federal Immigration Branch (Chapter 11). Records about Chinese arrivals are available up to 1949, but restrictive laws kept the number of arrivals low (see Chapter 7).

Also, you might find information in specific sources. For example, a book about the German Baptist resettlement efforts after the Second World War – *They Came From East and West* by William Sturhahn – includes an extensive list of arrivals, including the names and dates of the ship sailings (and even a few flights).

Chapter 10

Outbound records

W hile Canada has only a handful of immigration seaports, our ancestors could have embarked on their journeys at any one of dozens of places. Of course, it is doubtful that they chose a port; they usually chose a shipping company, then went to the spot where the ships owned by that company would depart.

The list of ports includes some busy, well-known ones such as Liverpool, England, and Hamburg, Germany, as well as many that would be hard to find on a map. Some of the most important ones were Libau, Russia, now Liepaja, Latvia; Boulogne-sur-Mer, France; Le Havre, France; Southampton, England; Bremen, Germany; Glasgow, Scotland; Rotterdam, the Netherlands; and Antwerp, Belgium.

Some of these ports have information that might help you. In genealogical research, there is a theory that if we hit a roadblock, we should step to one side – looking at a sibling, for example – and then try again. The same theory applies in searching for immigration information. If Canadian arrival records do not help, try the records from other countries.

Do not assume that outbound records in other countries will reflect the

Rotterdam's famed Erasmus Bridge is close to the dock where ships left for ports in Canada

Some of Europe's departure ports

inbound ones in Canada, with the same names and information. No record group is perfect. For many different reasons, there are inconsistencies between the documents compiled by authorities on either side of the ocean.

Records have been compiled in several countries. To find them in the Family History Library catalogue, look for the port, then "emigration and immigration."

ON THE INTERNET:

<www.familysearch.org>

It is possible that what you are looking for is included in one of the comprehensive emigration databases that have been placed online. The Association of European Migration Associations maintains a list of the major ones.

ON THE INTERNET:

<www.aemi.dk/home.php>

All the usual rules about using databases apply when using foreign ones – and if the language is not English, take extra care to make sure you try all of the options. Before using the database, check the frequently asked questions (FAQs), search tips, or anything else that might provide clues on how to use it to maximum effectiveness. The documentation for the site might include hints on using wildcards, which will help you deal with letters with accents.

Given names might be spelled differently in the home country – Christian might have been Kristian, Anderson might have been Andersen, and so on. Being flexible will increase your chances of success.

Also, be aware of changes in the names of places. Christiana, Norway, is Oslo today; Danzig, Germany, is now Gdansk, Poland; the Adriatic Sea port of Fiume in the Austro-Hungarian Empire is now Rijeka, Croatia. If you cannot find the port used by your ancestors, you might need to search for other possible names. A good maritime atlas might help with this.

The United Kingdom 1890-1960

The most comprehensive source for outbound records is probably the English website Ancestors on Board. It is part of the findmypast.com family of services.

ON THE INTERNET:

<www.ancestorsonboard.com>

Ancestors on Board has more than 24 million records of people sailing on ships from the United Kingdom to destinations around the world, including Canada, from 1890 to 1960. The database was produced in association with The National Archives.

The outward-bound passenger lists include individuals or groups leaving for destinations including Canada, Australia, India, New Zealand, South Africa, and the United States. Passengers include not only immigrants and emigrants, but also businessmen, entertainers, diplomats, and tourists.

Most of the passengers were British emigrants. An estimated 125,000 British people emigrated to the United States, 50,000 to Canada, and 25,000 to Australia every year between 1890 and 1914. After the lull caused by the First World War, large-scale emigration resumed but did not reach its pre-war numbers.

The database offers departures up to 1960 – a quarter of a century after the end of the Library and Archives Canada passenger lists that are open to researchers. It includes the first decade after the resumption of immigration following the Second World War. In those years, Canada saw the arrival of many war brides – English women who married Canadian servicemen – as well as refugees from a variety of countries.

The database is not limited to people from the British Isles. Your relative might have been from Continental Europe, but could have gone to England to catch a ship bound for North America. If so, he or she would appear in the Ancestors on Board database. It could be the only record available at this time that shows the person crossing the ocean.

Many Europeans who sailed from Britain arrived there through the port of Kingston upon Hull, a port with connections to most of the key ports on the continent. Between 1836 and 1914, an estimated 2.2 million migrants passed through Kingston upon Hull.

From there, most went by train to their next departure point – often Liverpool, London, Southampton, or Glasgow.

The passenger lists on the Ancestors on Board website include information on how the Europeans leaving the United Kingdom had arrived there. You will find the name of their arrival port as well as the name of the ship, or the shipping company, they used for the first part of their journey to Canada.

In the database, references to individuals often have just a first initial, rather than a given name. That can result in checks of several people before the right one is found and confirmed. (If you find a likely hit, be cautious: Look at all the likely hits before deciding which ones to investigate further.)

Also, do not assume that the age listed is exact; the date of birth was calculated by subtracting the age from the year of departure.

That is not always accurate. The database has a default of plus or minus two years when you search by year of birth. It is best to leave it at the default, rather than trying for an exact age. Don't forget to check the people for whom no birthdate is shown.

You can narrow your search of the database to destination ports in Canada, or specific ports of departure.

Remember, however, that the person might not have left from the port closest to their last address in the British Isles. It might be that their local travel agents only sold tickets from certain ports, or that there was a deal on tickets for a ship that sailed from a distant port.

Record for the Liddell family, heading to Canada from England in 1936

What if your person does not appear in the database? The name might have been entered incorrectly, either on the original manifest or in the compilation of

"	"	"	Dorothy	1	"			12	"	"
82907	"	Liddell	Frank	1	"	50			C/o C.P.R. Liverpool	Messenger
"	"	"	Sarah	1	"		39		"	H'wife
"	"	"	Herbert	1	"		14		"	School
"	"	"	Frances	1	"			13	"	"
82908	"	Spence	James	1	"		41		Goff Nook,Barrowford,Nelson	Motorman

the database. If you know the name of the ship and the date it sailed, you can search through the entire manifest to find your person. Choose "ship search" to find and browse through the entire document. You might find a name has been spelled incorrectly, possibly phonetically. You might also find, with some Eastern European names, that the first and last names have been reversed. In other words, Gottlieb Schmidt might be found by looking for Gottlieb as a surname.

After completing a search of the database, you can sort your results by clicking on the column heading. This can make it easier to scan the list of records.

Images of the passenger lists are available to download, view, save, and print. The passenger lists do not follow a set format. They vary in size and in length, they changed over time, and different shipping lines used their own forms. Some are decorative and beautiful historical documents, others are more functional in their appearance. Some are typed, others are handwritten; some record a minimum of detail, others have exact address and ultimate destination.

Passenger lists were generally divided into three parts. The header provides details about the ship and its voyage. The body of the list gives details of the passengers travelling on board. The summary section gives statistical detail on the number of passengers and usually a signature and stamp from the Board of Trade, to which the list was sent by the shipping line.

Some shipping lines produced passenger lists in duplicate or even triplicate for the Board of Trade. As a result, there can be two or even three originals of some of the passenger lists. Such duplicates were written out again by hand. The differences between these copies are usually cosmetic but there are sometimes minor differences in content or in the Board of Trade's annotations or stamps upon them.

These duplicate lists have been included in the database, so you might see two entries for the same individual that correspond to two slightly different original copies of the same list.

Original copies of the lists featured on the Ancestors on Board website are from The National Archives, which has an extensive collection of material relating to emigration from the United Kingdom.

These include Privy Council registers (1540 to 1978), plantation books (1678 to 1806), Treasury Board papers (1557 to 1920), Ministry of Health poor law union papers (1834 to 1890), Foreign Office passport registers (1795 to 1898), passenger lists, registers of passenger lists (1906 to 1951), child emigration and records relating to individual colonies. Comprehensive guides to these records are on the website of The National Archives.

ON THE INTERNET:
<www.nationalarchives.gov.uk/searchthearchives/migration.htm>

Ireland 1800-1860

The Irish Emigration Database is a computerized collection of 33,000 primary source documents on Irish emigration to North America in the 18th and 19th centuries. It is based on emigrant letters, newspaper articles, shipping advertisements, shipping news, passenger lists from 1800 to 1860, official government reports, family papers, records of births, deaths, marriages, and extracts from books and periodicals.

ON THE INTERNET:

<www.dunbrody.com/database2.php>

The database is also available through the Centre for Migration Studies at the Irish American Folk Park in Omagh, Northern Ireland, as well as the Public Record Office of Northern Ireland (PRONI), Northern Ireland libraries through the local studies departments and public access terminals in the branch libraries.

For a fee, the Centre for Migration Studies will perform a search of the database and any relevant books held in its library collection. You should provide the following information about your ancestor: First and last name, where he or she lived in Ireland, where he or she settled in North America, approximate date of emigration, whether he or she was travelling alone or with family (include names and ages of additional family members if relevant), ports of departure and arrival, and dates of birth or death or both.

ON THE INTERNET:

<www.qub.ac.uk/cms/about/Research.html>

Scotland 1890-1960

The Scottish Emigration Database, provided by the University of Aberdeen, has records of 21,090 passengers who embarked at Glasgow and Greenock for non-European ports between Jan. 1 and April 30, 1923, and at other Scottish ports between 1890 and 1960.

The database includes a passengers' table, for use when searching for individuals, or for occupational or regional patterns of emigration. There is also a ships' table for information about vessels.

ON THE INTERNET:

<www.abdn.ac.uk/emigration/>

The Digital Archive, with digitized historic records from Scotland, has a database of people who were assisted by the Highlands and Islands Emigration Society between 1852 and 1857. The society helped almost 5,000 individuals to leave western Scotland for Australia. This is one of the few sources for emigration held by the National Archives of Scotland.

ON THE INTERNET:

<www.scan.org.uk/researchrtools/emigration.htm>

Denmark 1868-1908

The Danish Emigration Archives were established in 1932 in Aalborg, Denmark, to record the history of the Danes who emigrated and to maintain cultural bonds to those who have their roots in Denmark. It has an extensive online resource – the Danish Emigration Database – that will help researchers find ancestors from throughout the Scandinavian countries (Denmark, Norway,

Sweden, and Finland).

The database includes references to 394,000 people who emigrated between 1868 and 1908. It is based on emigration lists compiled by the Copenhagen police between May 1868 and December 1940. These lists give the name, last residence, age, year of emigration, and first destination of the emigrant from Denmark.

The Danish parliament passed stringent regulations in 1868 that called for the Copenhagen chief of police to approve and monitor all emigration agents in Denmark and authorize all overseas tickets made out in Denmark. This was to be done whether an emigrant would be travelling directly from Copenhagen to the United States or indirectly (via another European harbour) for destinations overseas.

All the information from each ticket was copied in ledgers. Ninety volumes were compiled, containing the same type of information for every emigrant. There are two series of ledgers – one for emigrants who had direct passage from Copenhagen and one for those who had indirect passage. In each series, the emigrants are listed year by year in roughly alphabetical order according to the first letter of his or her surname.

In 1990, the Danish Emigration Archives began compiling its database, including all the information provided in the police records for all Danish emigrants.

For each emigrant, the database includes: Surname, first name, occupation, family status, age, place of birth (from 1899), last known residence (for Danish emigrants, for aliens only name of country), name of the emigration agent, ticket number, ticket registration date, name of the ship (only for direct passage from Copenhagen), destination and possible cancellation of the ticket. There are also 11 sets of codes to assist in making searches.

You will see references to Direkte (Direct) and Indirekte (Indirect). Direct tickets were issued for those people going straight from Copenhagen to New York, and the database will provide information about the name of the ship. Indirect tickets were issued by Danish agents for departures from a non-Danish port (often German or English) and give no information about the name of the ship.

The Danish Emigration Archives holds a large collection of private letters, manuscripts, diaries, biographies, newspaper clippings, photographs, and portraits. It has also published several books on emigration to the United States, Canada, Australia, and New Zealand. All of its publications and books, as well as copies of original material, are for sale at the archives.

The Danish Emigration Archives charges a fee of US $50 for a search in the emigration records for 1868-1939. The money should be paid to:

The Danish Emigration Archives

Arkivstraede 1

P.O. Box 1353

9100 Aalborg, Denmark

Money can be transferred directly to the archives' bank account: Danske Bank A/S, Algade 53, postboks 1264, 9100 Aalborg, reg.nr.: 3201 konto: 3402 189096.

The Danish Emigration Archives does not carry out extended genealogical research, but refers genealogists to societies throughout Denmark as well as about 600 local and regional archives.

ON THE INTERNET:

<www.emiarch.dk>

Another Danish emigration database includes 4,109 records from 1879 through 1889.

These emigrants bought their tickets from two emigration agents in Vejle, the Mouritzen brothers, who represented HAPAG (the Hamburg America Line). The records consist of two registers from Vejle Byfogedarkiv and give the following information: Name, place of last residence, succession number in the registers, and date of registration.

The Vejle emigration records are on the Internet thanks to Vejle City Archives and the Danish Emigration Archives.

ON THE INTERNET:

<www.aalborgkommune.dk/borgerportal/applikationer/udvandrer/SoegpostEngelsk.asp>

The North Frisian Emigrant-Archive, or Nordfriisk Instituut, has a databank with information on about 5,000 emigrants from North Frisia and the northwestern part of the former duchy of Schleswig, now a part of Denmark.

ON THE INTERNET:

<www.nordfriiskinstituut.de/eng/indexausw_e.html>

Sweden 1783-1951

The Swedish Emigration Records (Emigranten Populär) 1783-1951 on Ancestry.com include about 1.5 million records of people leaving Sweden. The database is drawn from several sources, and includes departures from Göteborg (1869 to 1951), Hamburg (1850 to 1891), Helsingborg (1929 to 1950), Kalmar (1881 to 1893), Köpenhamn (Copenhagen) (1868-1898), Malmö (1874 to 1928), Norrköping (1859 to 1922), and Stockholm (1869-1940).

The database also includes passengers on the Swedish America Line from 1915 to 1950, both to and from North America.

ON THE INTERNET:

<www.ancestry.com/search/DB.aspx?dbid=1189>

Finland 1890-1950

The Institute of Migration – Siirtolaisuusinstituutti – in Turku, Finland, aims to promote and carry out migration and ethnic research and to encourage the compilation, storage, and documentation of material relating to international and internal migration in Finland. It serves also as a resource site for genealogists.

It maintains an extensive online database, with limited searches available at no charge and more advanced ones available for a fee.

The Institute of Migration established the Emigrant Register in 1989 as a service for genealogists and the descendants of Finnish emigrants. Sources available online include 189,000 passport records (1890 to 1950), 318,000 passenger records of the Finnish Steamship Company (1892 to 1910) and information on Finns who died abroad (1918 to 1950). There are also 19,200 references to books and newspapers, 3,800 references to Australian Finns, 1,100 to New Zealand Finns, and more than 8,000 references to Finnish Russians from 1930 to 1950.

The institute's computerized database is being expanded regularly. The goal is to have about one million entries.

ON THE INTERNET:

<www.migrationinstitute.fi>

The Åland Islands' Emigrant Institute, maintained by the Åland Islands' Emigrant Institute Society, collects, catalogues, and distributes material connected with Ålandic emigration. An online database has references to about 1,500 individuals from the islands, which are between Finland and Sweden.

ON THE INTERNET:

<www.eminst.net/starte.htm>

Norway 1825-1873

The Digitalarkivet, based in Bergen, offers more than 5,000 databases of interest to those researching in Norway. Ninety-one of the databases deal with emigration.

ON THE INTERNET:

<digitalarkivet.uib.no/cgi-win/WebMeta.exe?spraak=e>

The emigration databases include references to people who have moved, or who indicated their intention to move. The word "emigrant" has been given a wider meaning than just those who left the country. Those who left the country can be found in the emigration protocols, the passport registers, or in the ships' lists.

The original sources for these databases were in a variety of archives, most of them in Norway but some overseas.

The Digitalarkivet also has church registers, which might include the names of emigrants. In searching on the website, look under the Church Registers category for the sub-category Migrants.

The website of the Norway Heritage Project has a free database of 70,963 passengers from 453 journeys from 1825 through 1873. The data is mainly transcribed from passenger lists, but in some cases information about Norwegian emigrants was added from sources such as newspaper announcements and voyage accounts. There are also some entries from the Norwegian Police Emigration Records.

ON THE INTERNET:

<www.norwayheritage.com/pasquest.asp>

Germany

Hamburg 1850-1934

A database of Hamburg passenger lists from 1850 to 1934 on the Ancestry.com site has five million names, including about 214,000 people who immigrated to

Canada. Eighty per cent of the people on the lists were bound for the United States.

One-third of the passengers who departed Hamburg were from Germany. The rest were primarily from Eastern Europe, including 1.2 million from the Russian Empire, the Austria-Hungarian Empire, Romania, and other countries of south-eastern Europe. The records include about 750,000 Jewish immigrants from Russia, who were sailing for the United States.

The database is linked to images of the passenger lists digitized from micro-film in partnership with the Staatsarchiv Hamburg, or Hamburg State Archives. Only the years 1885 through 1914 have been included in the database; for depar-tures in other years, you will have to look through the scanned images.

From 1850 to 1854 the lists consisted merely of a roughly alphabetical registra-tion, sometimes with abbreviated first names, later with more detailed informa-tion.

From 1854 to 1910, separate lists were maintained for direct passengers and indirect passengers.

"Direct passengers" were those who arrived at their final destination upon the same ship that they were registered on when they departed Hamburg. These pas-sengers may have had stopovers in other ports on their way to their final desti-nation, but they remained on the same ship.

"Indirect passengers" were those who were registered on one ship in Hamburg, but transferred to another ship before reaching their final destination. Transfers to other ships occurred mostly in English, French, Belgian, and Dutch ports, and usually had to do with reducing travel costs.

Between 1870 and 1892, one-third or more of the passengers travelled via the indirect route, but later this declined to about four per cent of the total.

From 1911, all passengers were included in a single list.

Information contained in this database includes: Name, gender, age, birth date or estimated birth year, birthplace, occupation, residence, nationality, marital sta-tus, relationship to head of family, religion, military service, destination, port of departure, date of departure, port of arrival, ship name, and source information.

ON THE INTERNET:

<search.ancestry.com/iexec/?htx=List&dbid=1068>

Another option on the Ancestry site is the handwritten index to the Hamburg passenger lists from 1855 to 1934. The database includes images digitized from microfilm in partnership with the Staatsarchiv Hamburg.

These handwritten indexes can help you find a person in the original lists, especially from the years that have not yet been electronically indexed. The indexes list all passengers alphabetically by the first letter of the surname for a range of departure dates.

To find a passenger, first choose the appropriate year range, then the volume (in German, Band) with the date range when the ship departed. Then select the letter of the alphabet for the passenger's surname. The alphabetical listing is arranged according to the first letter of the surname. You might need to search the entire alphabetical section in order to find the person you're looking for.

Check both direct and indirect lists unless you are certain that you know the route taken by your ancestor.

ON THE INTERNET:

<search.ancestry.com/iexec/?htx=List&dbid=1166>

Hamburg's port in about 1900, from an old postcard

Bremen 1920-1939

A total of 690,592 people are included in the Bremen passenger list database, a project of the Bremen Chamber of Commerce (Handelskammer) and the Bremen State Archives (Staatsarchiv Bremen).

The database is based on 3,017 passenger lists from the years 1920 to 1939. All other Bremen lists were destroyed because of a lack of storage space, or because of bombing during the Second World War.

Ship owners using the port of Bremen have been required to keep passenger lists since 1832. In 1851 the Bremen Chamber of Commerce established the Nachweisungsbureau für Auswanderer (Information Office for Emigrants), where ship captains had to deliver the lists.

The lists that survived – and form the basis for this database – were part of a collection of archival documents stored in a salt mine at Bernburg an der Saale in 1942. Bernburg was in the Soviet zone at the end of the Second World War, and the lists were taken to archives in Moscow. In 1987 and 1990 they were given to the Bremen Chamber of Commerce.

The Chamber and the Bremen Society for Genealogical Investigation, Die Maus ("the Mouse"), worked together to place the database online.

Information provided includes family name, first name, gender, age, family status, residence, destination, and profession.

ON THE INTERNET:

<www.passengerlists.de>

Bremerhaven 1820-1939

The German Emigrants Database at the Historisches Museum Bremerhaven is a research project dealing with European emigration to the United States. The database includes information on emigrants who left Europe between 1820 and 1939, primarily from German ports.

Much of the data in the database was taken from the ship passenger manifests. Additional information on emigrants has been found in other sources. The aim of the project is to make statistical social evaluations of this data and present them scientifically.

The database is constantly being added to, though it already contains data on 4.4 million emigrants. The current data covers the years 1820 to 1833, 1840 to 1891, 1904, and 1907. Visitors to the Historisches Museum Bremerhaven can do research about emigrants at two terminals.

ON THE INTERNET:

<www.dad-recherche.de/hmb/index.html>

Southwest Germany 1700s-1900s

The database Emigration From Southwest Germany contains about 260,000 family names. The total number of emigrants in the database is much higher than that. The database covers the period between the middle of the 18th and the beginning of the 20th century. It gives an overview of the numbers of emigrants that left the southwestern area.

ON THE INTERNET:

<www.auswanderer-bw.de>

Schleswig-Holstein 1830-1930

About 70,000 emigration records from Schleswig-Holstein have been compiled and posted on a website run by Klaus Struve of Kiel. He estimates that his site contains about one-quarter of the people who emigrated from the province between 1830 and 1930.

ON THE INTERNET:

<www.rootdigger.de/Emi.htm>

The Netherlands 1900-1940

The Family History Library has copies of passenger lists from the Holland America Line (Holland-Amerikalijn), which was a Rotterdam-based shipping company that carried many European immigrants to Canada.

Holland America ships stopped at Halifax before carrying on to New York City.

The Family History Library lists are on a set of more than 1,000 microfiches covering voyages from 1900 to 1940. The lists are also held by the city archives in Rotterdam.

Each passenger list begins with the ship's name, destination, sailing date, the amount paid for first, second, and third class and the amount paid for sea passage, as well as European and North American train passage.

The ship manifests provide, in columnar form, the following information:

- Ship contract and agent contract number
- Passenger's name
- Number of fares divided between full, half, and none
- The price arrangement between different shipping companies
- City where passage was booked and the destination
- Whether rail passage was booked, with booking number, number of tickets, class, and price
- Company agent and place of agency where passage was booked
- Adult fare price
- Commissions paid to agents and place
- Net amount of prepaid fares
- Number and amount, reservation fee
- Subsequent payments in foreign and/or Dutch currency
- Sea and rail passage agents
- Totals for sea, European, and American rail passage
- Remarks

The information is also held by the Gemeentearchief Rotterdam, the Rotterdam city archives.

Italy

The Italian Emigrant Database has information on 2,567 different surnames. It was created to make it easier to research the emigrants of the beginning of the last century. All data was provided by Italian town halls. The database is updated as more information is made available.

ON THE INTERNET:
<www.theitalianheritage.it/?lang=english>

Switzerland

The Swiss Roots website features a database with the family names listed in the Swiss "Family Name Handbook" and the communes where these names originally came from. This can be helpful in determining where people lived before they came to North America.

ON THE INTERNET:
<www.swissroots.org/swissroots/en/stories/heritage/Genealogy.html>

Chapter 11
Immigration Branch (RG76)

One of the greatest resources for Canadian immigration research is a set of 583 microfilms at Library and Archives Canada. It holds information, drawn from several government departments, regarding immigrants who arrived from 1892 to the 1950s. Copies of this set of microfilms were distributed to provincial archives across Canada in the 1980s.

This set of films – known as RG76, records of the Central Registry of the Immigration Branch of the Department of the Interior – might be the only accessible source for many post-1935 arrivals. It also offers additional information about many people who arrived in Canada up to 1935, as well as the organizations that helped bring them to Canada.

There is a problem, however – these microfilms might not be digitized for years, so research will have to be done the old-fashioned way, on a microfilm reader at a library.

The immigration branch existed as part of the Department of the Interior until 1917, when it was transformed into the Department of Immigration and Colonization. In 1936, the department's functions were rolled into the Department of Mines and Resources, and in 1950 a new Department of Citizenship and Immigration took over the function.

The RG76 series includes a wide variety of documents pertaining to the operation of the branch, so a genealogical researcher will have to do a bit of digging to find gems about specific families. As an example, hidden in the files that deal primarily with the supply and distribution of forms – on microfilms C-4663 through C-4667 – is a list of people who arrived at Quebec on the Arosa Kulm on Oct. 2, 1952.

Documents include deputy ministers' files, operational records of federal government immigration agencies in Canada, the United States, Great Britain, and Continental Europe, extracts from passenger lists, and infor-

Prospective settlers in 1908-1910

96

mation on specific immigrants.

While ship passenger lists are straightforward, listing everyone who came by ocean vessel over a specific period of time, the branch files are divided by topic, or by group of people.

Coverage varies considerably. For example, it's likely that these files offer information on virtually every one of the Barr Colonists – a group of settlers in the Lloydminster area of Saskatchewan and Alberta in the early 20th century – but they are much less comprehensive with most other groups of immigrants.

People could appear in a variety of different files, so all possible categories should be checked. Start by identifying specific characteristics about an immigrant.

The files contain extensive information on juvenile immigrants – the Home Children – often including the names of the Canadians to whom the arriving child was assigned. There are also files on overseas agents, the people who collected bonuses based on the number of immigrants they sent to Canada.

There are files on a wide variety of ethnic groups, from both Europe and Asia, as well as files created under the Empire Settlement Act, which encouraged the settlement of Canada by people from the British Isles. There is also plenty of information on post-war refugees.

Why bother checking this series of films? It will enable the researcher to put the immigration experience into context. The supporting documentation will help to reveal the thinking behind government policies of the day, which had an impact on who would be allowed into Canada. Many groups were excluded from this country, or placed under severe restrictions for a variety of reasons.

The series may seem daunting at first, and it might not contain anything that directly relates to your family. Still, it is worth checking. A researcher is likely to learn more about the mass movement of people to Canada in the 20th century, and understand more about the influences felt by individual families.

A comprehensive list of the films that include the names of individuals is included in this chapter. It will be the easiest way to find references of interest, assuming that those references exist.

A database on the Library and Archives website also includes references to the files included in RG76. Go to Government of Canada Files, and search for the keyword of your choice in the record group identified as Immigration – RG76. Your keyword should be based on the category of interest – Home Children, Lithuanians, or Baptists, for example.

ON THE INTERNET:

<www.collectionscanada.gc.ca/archivianet/020105_e.html>

The website of Library and Archives Canada includes a series of guides that might help you determine which films will help you to learn more about the arrival of your ancestor, or the influences of the day.

ON THE INTERNET:

<www.collectionscanada.gc.ca/the-public/005-1142-e.html>

General

C-10443	Agitators and disturbers to be refused admission 1933-1949
C-10443	Agitators and undesirables to be refused admission 1949-1954
C-10243	Bonds of indemnity filed by immigrants 1904-1936
C-10267	Canada - Orders in Council authorizing entry of immigrants 1953-1958
C-10267	Canada - Orders in Council authorizing entry of immigrants 1958
C-10266	Canada - Recommendations to Council relating to landing of immigrants 1944-1948
C-10266	Canada - Recommendations to Council relating to landing of immigrants 1948-1949
C-10266	Canada - Recommendations to Council relating to landing of immigrants 1950
C-10266	Canada - Recommendations to Council relating to landing of immigrants 1950-1952
C-10267	Canada - Recommendations to Council relating to landing of immigrants 1950-1952
C-10266	Canada - Special cases of immigrants admitted by Order in Council 1940-1944
C-10266	Canada - Special cases of immigrants admitted by Order in Council 1949
C-7356	Canadian Catholic Emigration Society 1899-1902
C-7356	Canadian Catholic Emigration Society 1902-1905
C-7309	Canadian Land Settlement Certificates 1897-1907
C-7310	Canadian Land Settlement Certificates 1916-1920
C-7402	Canadian National Railway - Movement of continental families with capital 1925-1935
C-10631	Canadian Pacific Railway - Inspection of steerage passengers on Lake Manitoba at Quebec on 22 Sept. 1908
C-10297	Canadian Pacific Railway and Canadian National Railway admission of track workers (navvies) 1920-1929
C-10297	Canadian Pacific Railway and Canadian National Railway admission of track workers 1929-1957
C-7810	Canadian Pacific Railway, Canadian National Railway and Department agreement relating to immigration 1925
C-7811	Canadian Pacific Railway, Canadian National Railway and Immigration Department agreement relating to immigration 1925
C-7811	Canadian Pacific Railway, Canadian National Railway and Department agreement relating to immigration 1925-1926
C-7811	Canadian Pacific Railway, Canadian National Railway and Department agreement relating to immigration 1926-1927
C-10613	Canadian Residence Certificate 1916-1920
C-10659	Cash bonds for temporary admission 1911-1924
C-10256	Catholic Immigrant Aid Society of Western Canada 1928-1930
C-10684	Deportation of undesirable immigrants 1902-1903
C-10426	Deportation of undesirable women from Pacific coast (also Japanese and East Indians) 1907-1908
C-10286	Deportation of undesirables 1915-1918
C-10287	Deportation of undesirables 1915-1918
C-10287	Deportation of undesirables 1926-1928
C-10287	Deportation of undesirables 1929-1931
C-10288	Deportation of undesirables 1929-1931
C-10288	Deportation of undesirables 1934-1937
C-10288	Deportation of undesirables 1944-1948
C-10417	Deportation of undesirables via United States ports 1908-1923
C-10308	Deportation Reports 1937-1939
C-10309	Deportation Reports 1937-1939
C-10247	Deportations - Railway Agreements and Empire Settlement Act 1926-1932
C-10311	Deportees - Advising Great Britain about return of deportees 1907-1921
C-10653	Diseased persons admitted for treatment 1934-1948
C-7829	Doubtful cases of immigrants with railway certificates 1920-1930
C-7823	Doubtful cases of immigrants with railway certificates 1926
C-7824	Doubtful cases of immigrants with railway certificates 1926
C-7824	Doubtful cases of immigrants with railway certificates 1926-1927

C-7824	Doubtful cases of immigrants with railway certificates 1927
C-7825	Doubtful cases of immigrants with railway certificates 1927
C-7825	Doubtful cases of immigrants with railway certificates 1927-1928
C-7825	Doubtful cases of immigrants with railway certificates 1928
C-7826	Doubtful cases of immigrants with railway certificates 1928
C-7827	Doubtful cases of immigrants with railway certificates 1928
C-7828	Doubtful cases of immigrants with railway certificates 1928
C-7828	Doubtful cases of immigrants with railway certificates 1928-1929
C-7828	Doubtful cases of immigrants with railway certificates 1929
C-7829	Doubtful cases of immigrants with railway certificates 1929
C-7829	Doubtful cases of immigrants with railway certificates 1930
C-7830	Doubtful cases of immigrants with railway certificates 1930
C-7830	Doubtful cases of immigrants with railway certificates 1930-1931
C-10286	Insane immigrants in United States and Canadian asylums (deportation) 1906-1907
C-10654	Inspection of crews of vessels touching Canadian ports 1919
C-10656	Inspection of crews of vessels touching Canadian ports 1940-1941
C-10656	Inspection of crews of vessels touching Canadian ports 1941-1942
C-10677	International Association for Exchange of Students for Technical Experience 1952-1954
C-10677	International Association for Exchange of Students for Technical Experience 1955-1956
C-10678	International Association for Exchange of Students for Technical Experience 1955-1959
C-7379	Lumbermen and Woodworkers 1923-1929, 1946-1952
C-7380	Lumbermen and Woodworkers 1923-1929, 1946-1952
C-10256	Medical inspection 1947-1948
C-10255	Medical inspection at ports of embarkation 1928-1929
C-10255	Medical inspection at ports of embarkation 1929-1930
C-10595	Medical inspection of displaced persons 1947-1953
C-10406	Merchant Seamen order (detainees) 1941-1942
C-10406	Merchant Seamen order (detainees) 1942-1943
C-7373	North Atlantic Trading Company - Continental Arrivals at Ocean Ports 1902-1903
C-7373	North Atlantic Trading Company 1903
C-7373	North Atlantic Trading Company 1905
C-7390	Ottawa Valley Immigration Aid Society 1901-1904
C-10676	Overseas Settlement Service 1950-1954
C-15868	Pauper Immigration 1891-1905
C-10606	Prospective settlers 1908-1910
C-7807	Railway - John Franklin, Ottawa, employed on trains checking immigrants 1902-1905
C-10673	Railway employees exercising seniority rights 1937-1943
C-10628	Railways - Legislation dealing with liability of railroad contractors for employees 1908-1911
C-7811	Railways agreement 1927
C-7812	Railways agreement 1927
C-7812	Railways agreement 1927-1928
C-7812	Railways agreement 1928-1929
C-7813	Railways agreement 1929-1931
C-7813	Railways agreement 1931-1949
C-10318	Refugee immigration 1939-1941
C-10318	Refugee immigration (International Refugee Organization) 1940-1941
C-10319	Refugee immigration (International Refugee Organization) 1940-1941
C-10319	Refugee immigration (International Refugee Organization) 1941-1943
C-10319	Refugee immigration (International Refugee Organization) 1943
C-10319	Refugee immigration (International Refugee Organization) 1943-1944
C-10319	Refugee immigration (International Refugee Organization) 1944-1945
C-10320	Refugee immigration (International Refugee Organization) 1944-1945
C-10320	Refugee immigration (International Refugee Organization) 1945-1946
C-10320	Refugee immigration (International Refugee Organization) 1947
C-10321	Refugee immigration (International Refugee Organization) 1949
C-10321	Refugee immigration (International Refugee Organization) 1949-1950

C-10322	Refugee immigration (International Refugee Organization) 1949-1950
C-10322	Refugee immigration (International Refugee Organization) 1950
C-10322	Refugee immigration (International Refugee Organization) 1950
C-10657	Refunds of deposits for deserters and hospitalization 1942-1949
C-10270	Repatriating Continentals (alien unemployed) 1931-1934
C-10276	Seventh Day Adventists 1932-1961
C-10276	Seventh Day Adventists 1962-1963
C-4696	Steamship Company Bonds 1935-1952
C-10589	Sugar beet workers 1947-1954
C-10269	Technical Engineers 1951-1952
C-10397	Women - Regulations re: women and children entering or leaving during wartime 1942-1943
C-10397	Women - Regulations re: women and children entering or leaving during wartime 1942-1945
C-10397	Women - Regulations re: women and children entering or leaving during wartime 1945-1946
C-10398	Women - Regulations re: women and children entering or leaving during wartime 1945-1946
C-10398	Women - Regulations re: women and children entering or leaving during wartime 1946
C-10434	Women and children going to England (Soldiers' dependants) 1917
C-10306	Women's Canadian Employment Bureau, Montreal 1908-1909
C-10306	Women's Canadian Employment Bureau, Montreal 1909-1912
C-10306	Women's Canadian Employment Bureau, Montreal 1912-1913
C-10307	Women's Canadian Employment Bureau, Montreal 1912-1913
C-10307	Women's Canadian Employment Bureau, Montreal 1913-1917
C-7840	Women's Domestic and Business Guild of Canada, Montreal 1903, 1905-1907
C-7840	Women's Domestic Guild of Canada, Montreal 1907-1911
C-7840	Women's Domestic Guild of Canada, Montreal 1911-1912
C-7841	Women's Domestic Guild of Canada, Montreal 1911-1912
C-7841	Women's Domestic Guild of Canada, Montreal 1912-1913
C-7841	Women's Domestic Guild of Canada, Montreal 1913-1922

Canada

C-10649	Athabasca, Alta. - Immigration Building 1926-1933
C-10650	Athabasca, Alta. - Immigration Building 1933-1938
C-7805	Barr Colony, Lloydminster, Sask. - colonists 1903
C-7403	Barr Colony, Lloydminster, Sask. - settlers 1903
C-7403	Barr Colony, Lloydminster, Sask. 1903-1904
C-7403	Barr Colony, Lloydminster, Sask. 1904-1906
C-7403	Barr Colony, Lloydminster, Sask. 1906-1955
C-7805	Barr Colony, Lloydminster, Sask. 1906-1955
C-10305	Belleville, Ont. - John H. Carr, government employment agent 1910-1912, 1923
C-4705	Brandon, Man. - Hospital - Brandon General 1898-1907
C-10270	Bruce County, Ont. - George H. Mooney of Ripley, government employment agent 1906-1909
C-10270	Bruce County, Ont. - George H. Mooney of Ripley, government employment agent 1909-1913
C-10271	Bruce County, Ont. - George H. Mooney of Ripley, government employment agent 1909-1913
C-10686	Calgary - Hospital 1907-1908
C-10305	Carleton Place, Ont. - Alex Mclean, government agent 1910-1923
C-10305	Chesterville, Ont. - Wesley Hamilton, government employment agent 1907-1923
C-10302	Cobourg, Ont. - James D. Haig, distributor of farm labour 1924-1927
C-10431	Conscription in Canada 1917
C-10431	Conscription in Canada 1918
C-10686	Dauphin, Man. - Hospital 1900, 1903-1908
C-10402	Dependents - Movement to Canada of servicemen's dependants 1951-1954
C-10402	Dependents - Soldiers' dependents repatriated to Canada 1946-1947
C-10425	Deseronto, Ont. - Unemployed immigrants 1907-1908, 1914
C-10404	Distressed Canadian seamen in Great Britain 1933, 1940-1943
C-10403	Distressed Canadians in enemy occupied countries in Europe 1945-1946
C-10404	Distressed Canadians in German occupied territory (and Far East) 1948-1951

C-10403	Distressed Canadians in Germany and enemy occupied territory 1941
C-10403	Distressed Canadians in Germany and enemy occupied territory 1941-1942
C-10403	Distressed Canadians in Germany and enemy occupied territory 1944-1945
C-10404	Distressed Canadians in Germany and enemy occupied territory 1944-1946
C-10306	Dominion Bureau for the Employment of Women 1907-1908
C-9672	Dominion Coal Company, Admission of Help 1921-1923
C-10406	Dominion Textile Company, Montreal - (Immigrants to work in the mill) 1907, 1910-1913
C-10591	Dressmakers Project - 1948-1951
C-10592	Dressmakers Project - 1948-1951
C-10301	Drumbo, Ont. - George Law, government employment agent 1907-1914
C-10267	Eastern Townships - Farm and industrial labourers 1906
C-10268	Eastern Townships - Farm and industrial labourers 1906
C-7323	Edmonton - Edmonton General Hospital, Grant in aid of immigration patients 1896-1919
C-7810	Edmonton - Hospital 1902-1919
C-7862	Edmonton - Immigration Building 1916-1923
C-7862	Edmonton - Immigration Building 1923-1925
C-7863	Edmonton - Immigration Building 1923-1925
C-7863	Edmonton - Immigration Building 1925-1926
C-7863	Edmonton - Immigration Building 1926-1927
C-7863	Edmonton - Immigration Building 1928-1929
C-7385	Farm Help Applicants 1929-1930
C-10447	Fines collected by immigration officer 1919-1921
C-10448	Fines collected by immigration officer 1919-1921
C-10448	Fines collected by immigration officer 1921-1925
C-4761	General Colonization and Repatriation Society, Montreal 1915-1919
C-10612	Grand Forks, B.C. - inspection of immigrants 1908-1936
C-10659	Grande Prairie, Alta. - Immigration Building 1917-1920
C-10649	Grande Prairie, Alta. - Immigration Building 1933-1938
C-7858	Halifax - Medical Inspector of Immigrants 1903-1911
C-7851	Halifax - Medical inspector's record of examination of immigrants 1922-1924
C-7851	Halifax - Medical inspector's record of examination of immigrants 1923-1924
C-7852	Halifax - Medical Inspector's record of examination of immigrants 1923-1924
C-7852	Halifax - Medical inspector's record of examination of immigrants 1924-1926
C-7852	Halifax - Medical inspector's record of examination of immigrants 1927
C-7852	Halifax - Medical inspector's record of examination of immigrants 1928-1930
C-7853	Halifax - Medical Inspector's record of examination of immigrants 1928-1930
C-7851	Halifax - Reports of admissions and rejections 1921-1922
C-10659	High Commissioner for Canada. Relief to distressed Canadians 1930-1940
C-7809	Hudson's Bay Company Overseas Settlement Limited 1928-1929
C-7809	Hudson Bay Settlement Scheme (Hudson's Bay Company Overseas Settlement Limited) 1929-1946, 1949
C-10275	Immigration Branch Annual Reports 1905-1906
C-10583	Imperial Veterans in Canada 1920-1937
C-10584	Imperial Veterans in Canada 1920-1937
C-10595	Jewish - Canadian Jewish Congress 1947-1953
C-7808	Jewish - Federated Jewish Farmers of Ontario - Training Jewish boys in agriculture 1925-1929
C-4749	Jewish Colonization Association, Montreal 1920-1936
C-4749	Jewish Colonization Association, Montreal 1936-1949
C-4749	Jewish Colonization Association, Montreal 1949-1951
C-10313	Jewish families for farm settlement 1938-1940
C-10649	Lac La Biche, Athabaska Landing, Alta - Accommodation for immigrants 1909-1916
C-10268	Lancaster, Ont. - William J. McNaughton, distributor of farm labour 1906-1907
C-10270	Land Settlement Committee, Immigration Department and Canadian Railways 1931-1933
C-10686	Lethbridge, Alta. - Immigration Building 1909-1916
C-7353	Lethbridge, Alta. - Immigration Building 1916-1929
C-10613	Manitoba - Assistance to settlers in unorganized districts 1908

C-7817	Medical inspection of immigrants 1923-1925
C-7370	Medical treatment of immigrants outside of hospital 1928-1938, 1942
C-7371	Medical treatment of immigrants outside of hospital 1928-1938, 1942
C-4797	Medicine Hat, Alta. - Hospital 1892-1908
C-4798	Medicine Hat, Alta. - Hospital 1908-1911
C-4798	Medicine Hat, Alta. - Hospital 1911-1921
C-10312	Millbrook, Ont. - C.V. Pym, government employment agent 1907-1909
C-10239	Montreal - Detention Hospital 1920-1921
C-10238	Montreal - Detention Hospital 1920-1921
C-10671	Montreal - Dorchester House (Canadian Women's Hostel) 1926-1927
C-10672	Montreal - Dorchester House (Canadian Women's Hostel) 1926-1927
C-10639	Montreal - Drs. Lachapelle and E.M.P. Benoit. Examining undesirable immigrants 1909-1910
C-10312	Montreal - E. Marquette, provincial immigration agent 1914-1918, 1935
C-7853	Montreal - Medical Inspector's record of examinations of immigrants 1905-1918
C-7853	Montreal - Medical Inspection 1918-1921
C-7853	Montreal - Medical Inspector's record of immigrants 1920-1922
C-7853	Montreal - Medical Inspector's record of immigrants 1923-1925
C-7854	Montreal - Medical Inspector's record of immigrants 1923-1925
C-7854	Montreal - Medical Inspector's record of immigrants 1925-1928
C-10239	Montreal - Payment of detention expenses 1926-1929
C-10312	Montreal Colonization Society, government employment agent 1907-1909
C-7391	Moose Jaw, Sask. - Immigration Building 1915-1918
C-7861	Moosomin, Sask. - General Hospital 1904-1917
C-7314	Movement of population in the Canadian North West 1899-1911
C-7315	Movement of population in the Canadian North West 1899-1911
C-10297	Muskoka, Ont. - Hospital - National Sanitarium. Foreign born people inmates of Muskoka Free Hospital 1907
C-10269	New Brunswick - Notice of arrivals of families under Family Settlement Quotas 1931-1939
C-7839	New Brunswick - Settlement of British families on unoccupied and agricultural land 1927-1929
C-10665	Newfoundland - Entry of Newfoundlanders prior to Confederation 1946-1949
C-10265	North Sydney, N.S. - Inspection of immigrants 1936-1949
C-10266	North Sydney, N.S. - Inspection of immigrants 1936-1949
C-10412	North Sydney, N.S. - Arrival of deaf, mute and blind persons from Newfoundland 1907
C-7319	North West Mounted Police, Ottawa re: destitute condition of immigrants, applications for seed grain, etc. 1906-1910
C-10294	Northumberland, Ont. - E. Terrill, Wooler, Ont., government employment agent 1906-1910
C-7859	Ontario - Bulk Nominations. Adults Nos. 1-117 1927
C-7859	Ontario - Bulk Nominations. Adults Nos. 543-686 1927
C-7859	Ontario - Bulk Nominations. Adults Nos. 855-1077 1927
C-7860	Ontario - Bulk Nominations. Adults Nos. 855-1077 1927
C-10583	Ontario - government assisted passages for farm labourers and household workers 1926-1928
C-10301	Perth, Ont. - Henry Taylor, government employment agent 1915-1919
C-10307	Peterborough, Ont. - George H. Hawson, government employment agent 1912-1914, 1923
C-10641	Philips, Sask. - Immigration Building 1909-1918
C-10286	Picton, Ont. - Albert G. MacDonald, immigration agent 1906-1909
C-10431	Port Arthur and Fort William, Ont. - Passengers leaving boats 1915-1932
C-7322	Port Arthur, Ont. - Agent - Rev. R.A. Burris 1900-1902
C-7323	Port Arthur, Ont. - Agent - Rev. R.A. Burris 1900-1902
C-7323	Port Arthur, Ont. - Agent - Rev. R.A. Burris 1902-1904
C-7387	Prince Albert, Sask. - Hospital - Victoria Hospital 1901-1907
C-10686	Prince Albert, Sask. - Immigration Shed 1913-1918
C-10267	Quebec - Eastern Townships - E.W. Brewster - Distributor of farm labour 1906-1908
C-10267	Quebec - Eastern Townships - E.W. Brewster - Distributor of farm labour 1908-1913
C-7854	Quebec - Medical Inspection. Record of examinations 1920-1921
C-7854	Quebec - Medical Inspection. Record of examinations 1921-1922
C-7855	Quebec - Medical Inspection. Record of examinations 1922-1927

Winnipeg, Manitoba, was a popular destination for immigrants in the late 1800s

C-7855	Quebec - Medical Inspection. Record of examinations 1928-1929
C-7856	Quebec - Medical Inspection. Record of examinations 1928-1929
C-7854	Quebec - Record of persons detained 1919-1920
C-7854	Quebec - Record of persons detained 1922
C-7855	Quebec - Record of persons detained 1922
C-7856	Quebec - Report Sheets from May 7, 1923 to Nov. 8, 1923
C-10309	Quebec - Tobacco workers 1941-1950
C-10289	Quebec - Undesirables 1908-1941
C-10264	Quebec City - Inspection of personnel of advance party of R 100 (dirigible) 1930
C-10653	Regina - Fines and prosecutions 1912-1943
C-10425	Regina - Hospital - Account for treating immigrants (Grey Nuns Hospital) 1913-1916
C-10425	Regina - Hospital - Account for treating immigrants 1908-1913
C-7856	Saint John, N.B. - Medical inspections of immigrants 1920-1923
C-10276	San Francisco - British Consul General. Distressed Canadians 1906-1907
C-10583	Saskatchewan government assisted passages for farm labourers and household workers 1920-1929
C-10583	Saskatchewan - assisted passages for farm labourers and household workers 1929-1937
C-10399	Saskatoon, Sask. - Grant for St. Paul's Hospital 1907-1910, 1912
C-7386	Saskatoon, Sask. - Immigration Building 1913-1918
C-10400	Soldiers' dependents repatriated to Canada 1940-1943
C-10401	Soldiers' dependents repatriated to Canada 1944
C-10401	Soldiers' dependents repatriated to Canada 1945-1946
C-10401	Soldiers' dependents repatriated to Canada 1946-1947
C-10402	Soldiers' dependents repatriated to Canada 1947-1950
C-10434	Spirit River, Alta. - Immigration building 1916-1933
C-10261	Teulon, Man. - Reverend A.J. Hunter, Teulon Cottage Hospital 1905-1915, 1917
C-10635	Toronto - Agent - Sarah McArthur, Canadian Domestic Guild 1916
C-10635	Toronto - Agent - Sarah McArthur, Canadian Domestic Guild 1916-1917
C-10635	Toronto - Agent - Sarah McArthur, Canadian Domestic Guild 1918-1920
C-10261	United Church of Canada, Board of Home Missions 1952-1958
C-7856	Vancouver - Medical Inspector's record of examination of immigrants 1918-1920
C-7856	Vancouver - Medical Inspector's record of examination of immigrants 1921-1926
C-7857	Vancouver - Medical Inspector's record of examination of immigrants 1921-1926
C-7857	Victoria - Medical Inspection of immigrants 1921-1923

C-10247   Virden, Man. - Alexander McOwen, special immigration agent to Scotland 1904-1906
C-10268   Virden, Man. - Rental of school house as a shelter for immigrants 1906-1919
C-10301   Watford, Ont. - W.S. Fuller, distributor of farm labour 1907-1912
C-10429   White Rock, B.C. - Immigration inspection 1919-1924
C-7857   Winnipeg - Deported immigrants 1910-1922
C-7341   Winnipeg - Hospital - General 1898-1907
C-7341   Winnipeg - Hospital - General 1907-1910
C-7341   Winnipeg - Hospital - General 1910-1914
C-7342   Winnipeg - Hospital - General 1910-1914
C-7342   Winnipeg - Hospital - General 1914-1922
C-7342   Winnipeg - Hospital - St. Boniface - Grant to the Hospital 1906-1912
C-4677   Winnipeg - Immigration Building 1925-1932
C-7822   Winnipeg - Margaret Scott Nursing Mission 1904-1911
C-7823   Winnipeg - Margaret Scott Nursing Mission 1904-1911
C-7823   Winnipeg - Margaret Scott Nursing Mission 1911-1922
C-7395   Women - Lois McCusker, Immigration Conductress, Atlantic Ports 1924-1928
C-10301   Woodstock, Ont. - Piercie Irving, distributor of farm labour 1907-1912

British Isles

C-10627   Aberdeen, Scotland - Agent - H.W.J. Paton, farm hands and domestics 1908-1914
C-10627   Aberdeen, Scotland - Agent - H.W.J. Paton 1914-1921
C-10644   Aberdeen, Scotland - Agent - Mackay Brothers and Company 1910-1919, 1921
C-10261   Ayr, Scotland - Agent - James Scott. Bonus claims 1905-1923
C-10313   Ballymena, Ireland - Agent - William Cameron 1907-1921
C-10303   Banbury, England - Agent - A. Pargeter. Bonus claims 1906-1921
C-10604   Baptist Church. Religion of immigrants 1908-1910
C-10635   Belfast, Ireland - Agent - Sarah McArthur 1908-1913
C-10635   Belfast, Ireland - Agent - Sarah McArthur, Canadian Domestic Guild 1913-1916
C-10260   Birmingham, England - J. Francis Brame, Booking Agent 1913-1915, 1920
C-10325   Blairgourie, Scotland - Agent - Andrew Spalding 1907-1923
C-10263   Bridgewater, England - Agent - Hickman and Company 1912-1921
C-4764   Bristol Emigration Society, England 1896-1906
C-10309   Bristol, England - Agent - Mark Whitwell and Son 1907-1915
C-7838   British Emigration, Tourist and Colonization Society 1903-1907
C-7838   British Emigration, Tourist and Colonization Society 1908-1919
C-4766   British Immigration and Colonization Association, Montreal 1927-1928
C-4766   British Immigration and Colonization Association, Montreal 1928-1929
C-4766   British Immigration and Colonization Association, Montreal 1929-1930
C-4766   British Immigration and Colonization Association, Montreal 1930-1931
C-4767   British Immigration and Colonization Association, Montreal 1930-1931
C-7385   British Reduced Rate Settlers 1928
C-10604   British Welcome League, Toronto 1908-1925
C-10408   British West Indies. Enlistments in Canadian Army 1943-1945
C-10593   Bulk labour from British Isles 1949
C-10268   Carlisle, England - Agent - Fred Telford 1906-1916
C-7833   Catholic Emigration Association (Father Berry's Homes, Liverpool, England) (Crusade of Rescue) (St. George's Home, Hintenburg, Ont.) 1903-1910
C-7834   Catholic Emigration Association (Father Berry's Homes, Liverpool, England) (Crusade of Rescue) (St. George's Home, Hintenburg, Ont.) 1903-1910
C-7834   Catholic Emigration Association (St. George's Home, Ottawa) 1911-1918
C-7836   Catholic Emigration Society, Birmingham, England. St. George's Home, Ottawa 1902-1920
C-7834   Catholic Emigration Society, Birmingham, England. St. George's Home, Ottawa 1918-1923
C-7834   Catholic Emigration Society, Birmingham, England. St. George's Home, Ottawa 1923-1925
C-7835   Catholic Emigration Society, Birmingham, England. St. George's Home, Ottawa 1926-1929
C-7835   Catholic Emigration Society, Birmingham, England. St. George's Home, Ottawa 1929-1932

C-7836	Catholic Emigration Society, Birmingham, England. St. George's Home, Ottawa 1929-1932
C-7836	Catholic Emigration Society, Birmingham, England. St. George's Home, Ottawa 1932-1950
C-10303	Central Unemployed Body of London, England. Copies of Immigration Act 1908
C-10271	Church Army, London, England 1928-1929
C-10604	Church of England. Religion of immigrants 1909-1910
C-10605	Church of England. Religion of immigrants 1909-1910
C-10605	Church of England. Religion of immigrants 1910, 1912
C-10605	Congregational Church - Names and addresses of immigrants 1909-1910
C-10260	Cumnock, Scotland - Agent - J.P. Ballantine. Bonus claims 1911-1932
C-10268	Diss, Norfolk, England - Lusher Brothers. Bonus claims 1906-1921
C-10627	Distress Committee of the Borough of West Ham, England. Further information on deported immigrants from Oshawa and Deseronto, Ontario 1908-1910, 1913
C-10254	Domestics - Benjamin Pipe, Wapella, Assiniboia, proposes bringing from England girls as domestic servants 1905-1908, 1911
C-10293	Domestics - Mrs. Simpson Hayes, Winnipeg, to bring domestics from Great Britain 1906-1916
C-10312	Dudley, Northumberland, England - Agent - William Gibson 1907-1914
C-10264	Edinburgh, Scotland - Agent - Mackay Brothers 1915-1922
C-10315	Elgin, Scotland - Agent - John Sinclair 1907-1923
C-10629	Enniscorthy, County Wexford, Ireland - Agent - John Norman Green 1908-1923
C-10311	Falkirk, Scotland - Agent - Mary J. Farnon 1907-1921
C-10297	Farm Delegates to Great Britain 1906-1908
C-10302	Glasgow, Scotland - Agent - Alexander Wyllie. Bonus claims 1907-1909
C-10309	Glasgow, Scotland - Agent - D. Cumming. Bonus claims 1907-1915, 1918
C-10315	Glasgow, Scotland - Agent - D. McFarlane 1907-1909
C-10315	Glasgow, Scotland - Agent - D. McFarlane 1909-1923
C-7303	Glasgow, Scotland - Agent - H.M. Murray 1897-1909
C-10276	Great Britain and Ireland - Letters from agents re bonus claims 1920-1921
C-10311	Ilkley, Yorkshire, England - Agent - John F. Chapmen, 1907-1914
C-10260	Ipswich, England - Agent - Waters and Son. Bonus claims 1913-1923
C-7303	Ireland - Charles R. Devlin, Commissioner of Immigration 1897-1904
C-10269	Jedburgh, Scotland - Agent - Walter Easton. Bonus claims 1906-1914, 1919-1921
C-10311	Kelso-on-Tweed, Scotland - Agent - J. and J.H. Rutherford 1908-1921
C-10309	Kendal, England - Agent - M. Dehome and son 1907
C-10301	Leighton Buzzard, England - Agent - F.J. Hopkins. Bonus claims 1907-1914, 1917, 1920
C-10633	Letters from successful Scotch ploughmen 1908-1909, 1911
C-10408	London - Agent - A. Stanley Caesar 1907-1908
C-4746	London - East End Emigration Society 1892-1907
C-4747	London - East End Emigration Society 1892-1907
C-4747	London - East End Emigration Society 1907-1910
C-10621	Longside, Aberdeenshire, Scotland - Agent - W.G. Mailland 1908-1921
C-10605	Methodist Church. Religion of immigrants 1908-1910
C-10658	Naval and Military Emigration League - Overseas Settlement Scheme, London 1920
C-10311	Northumberland, England - Agent - William Gibson, Dudley 1907-1914
C-10269	Orkney, Scotland - Agent - J. Wood, Lyron, Rendall, Kirkwall. Bonus claims 1906-1921
C-7813	Overseas Settlement Committee - Training workers in England for farm employment 1925-1927
C-7813	Overseas Settlement Committee - Training workers in England for farm employment 1927
C-7814	Overseas Settlement Committee - Training workers in England for farm employment 1927
C-7814	Overseas Settlement Committee - Training workers in England for farm employment 1928-1929
C-10309	Penrith, England - Agent - J.W. Hodgson 1907-1914
C-10584	Presbyterian Immigration Society of Canada, Moose Jaw (British Settlement Society of Canada) 1927-1930
C-10584	Presbyterian Immigration Society of Canada, Moose Jaw (British Settlement Society of Canada) 1930-1931
C-4737	Rejections and Expulsions from United Kingdom 1909-1910

C-10605	Roman Catholic Church. Religion of immigrants 1909-1910, 1912
C-4769	Salvation Army - Lists and Correspondence 1926-1940
C-10268	Scotland - Group of 27 labourers sent from Leith, Scotland 1906
C-10275	Scotland - Party from Stornoway sent by the Queen Alexandra's Unemployed Fund 1906
C-10447	Scottish Immigrant Aid Society, Immigration and settlement of Hebrideans 1924-1925
C-4740	Self-Help Immigration Society, London 1901-1908
C-10264	Sir George Arthur, London, 200 families to be sent out by Lord Rothschild 1906
C-10439	Society for the Overseas Settlement of British Women 1938-1948
C-10440	Society for the Overseas Settlement of British Women 1938-1948
C-10318	Torrington, Devonshire, England - Agent - J. H. Stevens 1907-1914, 1921
C-4707	United British Women's Emigration Association 1890-1903
C-4708	United British Women's Emigration Association 1902-1906
C-7396	Western Canada Land Company (British Dominions Land Settlement) (Soldiers) 1924-1929
C-7833	Women's British Immigration League of Saskatchewan, Saskatoon 1926-1930

Empire Settlement Act

C-10254	Alberta Government agreement with Overseas Settlement Board for training 200 British Women 1928-1931
C-7845	British Columbia Boys Training Farm Agreement 1929-1932
C-7846	British Columbia Boys Training Farm Agreement 1929-1932
C-7370	British Dominion Emigration Society - Agreement with British Government (East End Emigration Fund) 1929-1930
C-7818	British Family Settlement Scheme 1926-1931
C-7380	British Public School Boys for Alberta 1924-1925
C-7380	British Public School Boys for Alberta 1925-1926
C-7819	British Public School Boys Training - Ontario (Vimy Ridge Farm Agreement) 1926-1927
C-7820	British Public School Boys Training - Ontario (Vimy Ridge Farm Agreement) 1926-1927
C-7820	British Public School Boys Training - Ontario (Vimy Ridge Farm Agreement) 1927-1931
C-10584	British Settlement Society of Canada (Presbyterian Immigration Society of Canada) 1931-1946
C-10585	British Settlement Society of Canada (Presbyterian Immigration Society of Canada) 1931-1946
C-7830	Cable advice on British Family Scheme and Bulk Nominations 1926
C-7831	Cable advice on British Family Scheme and Bulk Nominations 1926
C-10293	Calgary - Grant for the Calgary Women's Hostel 1923-1926
C-10293	Calgary - Grant for the Calgary Women's Hostel 1930-1933
C-10294	Calgary - Grant for the Calgary Women's Hostel 1930-1933
C-7821	Canadian Pacific Railway "After Care" Agreement 1925-1927
C-7821	Canadian Pacific Railway "After Care" Agreement 1925-1928
C-7822	Canadian Pacific Railway "After Care" Agreement 1925-1927
C-7822	Canadian Pacific Railway "After Care" Agreement 1927
C-7822	Canadian Pacific Railway "After Care" Agreement 1928-1930
C-7821	Canadian Pacific Railway "After Care" Agreement 1929-1930
C-7380	Canadian Pacific Railway - Domestics to Canada 1924-1925
C-7380	Canadian Pacific Railway - Domestics to Canada 1925-1937
C-10252	Canadian Pacific Railways Cottage Agreement 1928-1930
C-10261	Catholic Society of Canada for British Migration, Montreal 1929-1931
C-10271	Church Army, London 1906-1924
C-10271	Church Army, London 1925
C-10271	Church Army, London 1925-1927
C-10271	Church Army, London 1927-1928
C-10272	Church Army, London 1928-1929
C-10272	Church Army, London 1929-1933
C-10447	Clandonald Colonization Scheme (Scottish Immigrant Aid Society) (Hebrideans). 1930-1936, 1942
C-7360	Collections for 1925-1926
C-7359	Collections for 1925-1926
C-7368	Domestic Scheme 1923

NAME	DATE OF ADMISSION TO HOSPITAL	WHY HELD	REMARKS
Florence Relation	July 3	Inquiry	Awaiting decisi
D. Broche	May 17	Beaman	" ship
Peder Olsen	" 29	"	" "
Salvatore Picci	" 30	Deport	" "
Yum Yuer Nung	June 3	Inquiry	" decisi
Martin Welsh	" 8	Seaman	" ship
Arne Jensen	" 14	"	" "
Carl Randell	" 24	"	" "
Henry Glencross	" 25	"	" "
Hjalmer Molin	" 26		" "

A 1925 medical inspector's record of immigrants who were detained upon arrival at Montreal

C-10261	Fellowship of the Maple Leaf - Settlement of women doctors and social service workers in Western Canada 1929-1952
C-10646	G.C. Cossar, Glasgow, Scotland (Cossar Farm, Lower Gagetown, N.B.) 1909-1926
C-10646	G.C. Cossar, Glasgow, Scotland (Cossar Farm, Lower Gagetown, N.B.) 1926-1931
C-10647	G.C. Cossar, Glasgow, Scotland (Cossar Farm, Lower Gagetown, N.B.) 1926-1931
C-10647	G.C. Cossar, Glasgow, Scotland (Cossar Farm. Lower Gagetown, N.B.) 1931-1934
C-10236	Glasgow Training Scheme - Fifteen Parish trainees to Toronto. 1927-1938
C-10250	Hostel, London - Training of domestics 1929-1930
C-10250	Hostel, London - Training of domestics 1930-1931
C-7383	Land Settlement Service - Applications 1925-1926
C-7383	Land Settlement Service - Applications 1926-1927
C-7384	Land Settlement Service - Applications 1929
C-7385	Land Settlement Service - Applications 1929
C-7385	Land Settlement Service - Applications 1930
C-7383	Land Settlement Service - Applications for Farm Help 1925-1926
C-7383	Land Settlement Service - Applications for Farm Help 1926-1927
C-7383	Land Settlement Service - Applications for Farm Help 1927
C-7384	Land Settlement Service - Applications for Farm Help 1927
C-7384	Land Settlement Service - Applications for Farm Help 1929
C-7385	Land Settlement Service - Applications for Farm Help 1929
C-7385	Land Settlement Service - Applications for Farm Help 1929-1930
C-7385	Land Settlement Service - Applications for Farm Help 1930
C-7385	Land Settlement Service - Applications for Farm Help 1930-1936
C-7361	Lists of Passengers 1924
C-7361	Lists of Passengers 1924-1926
C-7361	Lists of Passengers 1926
C-7362	Lists of Passengers 1926
C-7362	Lists of Passengers 1926-1927
C-7362	Lists of Passengers 1927
C-7363	Lists of Passengers 1927-1928
C-7363	Lists of Passengers 1928
C-7364	Lists of Passengers 1928-1929

C-7364	Lists of Passengers 1929
C-7364	Lists of Passengers 1929-1930
C-7365	Lists of Passengers 1929-1930
C-7365	Lists of Passengers 1930
C-7368	Migration of female household workers 1923-1925
C-7368	Migration of female household workers 1925-1930
C-7369	Migration of female household workers 1929-1931
C-10252	National Boys Clubs, England 1928-1933
C-10243	Navy League of Canada. Settlement scheme 1928-1929
C-7839	New Brunswick Settlement Scheme 1929-1943
C-10237	Newcastle Training Scheme, Great Britain (Newcastle-on-Tyne Migration Committee) 1927-1932
C-10260	Provincial Boys Schemes 1929
C-7844	Public School Boys Training Farms, Manitoba 1929-1931
C-7845	Public School Boys Training Farms, Manitoba 1929-1931
C-7845	Public School Boys Training Farms, Manitoba 1931-1935, 1937-1938
C-7845	Saskatchewan Boys Training Farm Agreement 1922, 1927-1933
C-10447	Scottish Immigrant Aid Society. Hebrideans 1925-1930
C-7382	Settlers' Cottages, Prairie Provinces 1925-1928
C-7396	The 3000 British Families Settlement Scheme 1924-1925
C-7397	The 3000 British Families Settlement Scheme 1924-1925
C-7397	The 3000 British Families Settlement Scheme 1925
C-7397	The 3000 British Families Settlement Scheme 1925-1926
C-7397	The 3000 British Families Settlement Scheme 1927-1929
C-7397	The 3000 British Families Settlement Scheme 1929-1935
C-7398	The 3000 British Families Settlement Scheme 1929-1935
C-7398	The 3000 British Families Settlement Scheme 1935-1936
C-7398	The 3000 British Families Settlement Scheme 1936-1949
C-10241	United Church of Canada. Immigration 1929-1931

Juveniles

C-10667	Adoption of children 1913-1947
C-10316	British children evacuated to Canada 1940
C-10317	British children evacuated to Canada 1940
C-7846	British Immigration and Colonization Association 1924-1925
C-7847	British Immigration and Colonization Association 1924-1925
C-7847	British Immigration and Colonization Association 1925
C-7847	British Immigration and Colonization Association 1925-1926
C-7847	British Immigration and Colonization Association 1926-1927
C-7847	British Immigration and Colonization Association 1927-1928
C-7848	British Immigration and Colonization Association 1927-1928
C-7848	British Immigration and Colonization Association 1928
C-7381	British Public School Boys for Alberta 1925-1926
C-10648	C.E. Baring Young, Chipping Norton, Oxford, England. Farm School 1909-1940
C-7820	Canadian Pacific Railway. Admission of school boys to Macdonald College ("British Boys for Macdonald College" Scheme) 1926-1947
C-4747	Children's Aid Society, Shaftesbury Home 1892-1907
C-10430	Children's Allowance Board, Ottawa 1944-1947
C-10237	Children's Farm Home Association. (Ellinor Farm Home, Nauwigewauk, N.B.) 1904-1911
C-4745	Church of England Waifs and Strays Society 1893-1910
C-4745	Church of England Waifs and Strays Society 1910-1912
C-4746	Church of England Waifs and Strays Society 1910-1912
C-4746	Church of England Waifs and Strays Society 1912-1914
C-4746	Church of England Waifs and Strays Society 1923-1950
C-4746	Church of England Waifs and Strays Society 1927-1932

C-10398	Co-ordinating Council for Refugee and Evacuee Children 1940-1942
C-10398	Co-ordinating Council for Refugee and Evacuee Children 1942-1948, 1950
C-7833	Council for Social Service of the Church of England. Juvenile immigration 1926-1933
C-10435	Dakeyne Farm, Falmouth, Nova Scotia (Dakeyne Street Boys Brigade, Nottingham, England) 1918
C-7395	Delegation from Overseas Settlement Office 1924-1925
C-7396	Delegation from Overseas Settlement Office 1924-1925
C-4715	Dr. Barnardo's Homes - Training Home for Juvenile Immigrants 1873-1906
C-4716	Dr. Barnardo's Homes - Training Home for Juvenile Immigrants 1906-1913
C-4716	Dr. Barnardo's Homes - Training Home for Juvenile Immigrants 1913-1923
C-10399	Exemption from income tax for those supporting British children 1940-1946
C-10273	Fairbridge Farm School, Duncan, B.C. 1942-1945
C-10274	Fairbridge Farm School, Duncan, B.C. 1942-1945
C-10273	Fairbridge Farm School, Monte Creek, B.C. 1934-1936
C-4709	Fairknowe Home, Brockville, Ont. 1907-1914
C-4725	Fegen's Distribution Home, London, England 1892-1907
C-4726	Fegen's Distribution Home, London, England 1892-1907
C-4726	Fegen's Distribution Home, London, England 1907-1915
C-4726	Fegen's Distribution Home, London, England 1915-1922
C-4726	Fegen's Distribution Home, London, England 1922-1926
C-4726	Fegen's Distribution Home, London, England 1926-1932
C-7400	Fellowship of British Empire Exhibition - Training boys and girls to be farmers 1924-1926
C-7401	Fellowship of British Empire Exhibition - Training boys and girls to be farmers 1924-1926
C-15865	Girls Home of Welcome, Winnipeg (Canadian Women's Hostel) 1897-1906
C-4782	Glasgow Juvenile Delinquency Board - Girls Industrial School, Mary Hill, Glasgow - Children for Saint John, N.B.. 1895-1906
C-10612	Guardians of the Poor of the Parish of St. Mary, Islington, England. (Macpherson Home) 1908
C-7347	High Commissioner for Canada, London - Inspection of workhouse children 1898-1904
C-7348	High Commissioner for Canada, London - Inspection of workhouse children 1904-1913
C-7348	High Commissioner for Canada, London - Inspection of workhouse children 1913-1917
C-10318	Hurst House Training Home, South Craydon, Surrey, England 1907-1915
C-10237	Immigrant British children index 1905
C-4732	Immigration, W.J. Padt 1890-1908
C-10448	Inspection of British children from December, 1925, 1928-1930
C-10448	Inspection of British children from December, 1925, 1930-1933
C-10431	Inspection of British immigrant children 1915-1916
C-7380	Inspection of children 1900-1902
C-7814	Inspection of children 1902-1904
C-7815	Inspection of children 1902-1904
C-7836	Inspection of children 1903-1904
C-10237	Inspection of children 1904-1905
C-7836	Inspection of children 1904-1905
C-7837	Inspection of children 1904-1905
C-4734	Inspection of children 1904-1908
C-10251	Inspection of children 1905
C-10252	Inspection of children 1905
C-10237	Inspection of children 1905-1906
C-10270	Inspection of children 1906-1907
C-10251	Inspection of children 1906
C-10314	Inspection of children 1907-1909
C-10622	Inspection of children 1908-1909
C-4734	Inspection of children 1908-1911
C-4734	Inspection of children 1910-1915
C-4797	Inspection of Pauper Children 1896-1901
C-10285	Irish Catholic Immigration Society - Boys from the Boys Orphanage, Beacon Lane, Liverpool, brought out under its auspices and suffering from trachoma 1906
C-4691	Knowlton, Que. - Distributing Home 1907-1910

C-4691	Knowlton, Que. - Distributing Home 1910-1921
C-4735	Liverpool Catholic Children's Protection Society 1892-1902
C-7319	Liverpool Self Help Emigration Society - Children sent to Canada 1897-1917
C-4732	MacPherson Home - Reception and Placement 1893-1912
C-4732	MacPherson Home - Reception and Placement 1912-1923
C-4733	MacPherson Home - Reception and Placement 1912-1923
C-4733	MacPherson Home - Reception and Placement 1923-1925
C-10326	Medical inspection of British evacuee children 1940-1941
C-4731	Middlemore Homes, Halifax 1893-1903
C-4731	Middlemore Homes, Halifax 1903-1929
C-4732	Middlemore Homes, Halifax 1929-1945
C-4708	National Children's Home and Orphanage, London - Emigration of Children 1892-1903
C-4708	National Children's Home and Orphanage, London - Emigration of Children 1903-1907
C-4708	National Children's Home and Orphanage, London 1907-1912
C-4708	National Children's Home and Orphanage, London 1913-1921
C-10327	Ontario - Distribution of British evacuee children 1940-1943,1945
C-4709	Orphan Homes of Scotland, William Quarrie; Bridge of Weir and Fairknowe Home, Brockville, Ont. 1893-1907
C-7815	Pauper children 1898-1903
C-4768	Philanthropic Society Farm School, Redhill, Surrey, England 1898-1910
C-10627	Reports on children not from Union or Workhouse 1908-1909
C-10423	Return to Great Britain of Children's Overseas Reception Board 1944-1945
C-10424	Return to Great Britain of Children's Overseas Reception Board 1945
C-10425	Return to Great Britain of Children's Overseas Reception Board 1945
C-10425	Return to Great Britain of Children's Overseas Reception Board 1945-1951
C-10427	Salvation Army - Juvenile Immigration 1908-1922
C-10427	Salvation Army - Juvenile Immigration 1923
C-10428	Salvation Army - Juvenile Immigration 1923
C-10428	Salvation Army - Juvenile Immigration 1923-1925
C-10428	Salvation Army - Juvenile Immigration 1925
C-10428	Salvation Army - Juvenile Immigration 1927-1928
C-10428	Salvation Army - Juvenile Immigration 1928-1929
C-10429	Salvation Army - Juvenile Immigration 1928-1929
C-10327	Saskatchewan - Distribution of British evacuee children 1940-1945
C-4690	Sheltering-House, Liverpool, England 1892-1903
C-4690	Sheltering-House, Liverpool, England 1899-1903
C-10408	Southwark Rescue Society, London (Southwark Rescue Home, Prince Albert, Sask.) 1907, 1909
C-4786	Tiffield Reformatory, Tawcester, Northamptonshire - Boys sent out 1895-1900
C-10325	Transfer of English residential school students to Canadian schools 1940-1942
C-10326	Transfer of English residential school students to Canadian schools 1940-1942
C-10326	Transfer of English residential school students to Canadian schools 1942-1946
C-7367	Unaccompanied Juveniles 1923-1927
C-7368	Unaccompanied Juveniles 1923-1927
C-4794	Working Boys Home, 9 George Square, Liverpool 1896-1911

Europe

C-10277	Alien military personnel. Arrangements regarding entry to Canada 1946-1952
C-10313	Amsterdam, Netherlands - Agent - Hoyman and Schuurman's 1907-1915
C-10316	Antwerp, Belgium - Agent - G. Van Hersten, Union Ticket Office 1907-1921
C-10318	Antwerp, Belgium - Agent - P. Canon 1907-1914
C-10325	Antwerp, Belgium - Agent - Raydt and Bruynseels 1907-1921
C-7394	Antwerp, Belgium - Summary reports of admissions and rejections 1924-1926
C-7394	Antwerp, Belgium - Summary reports of admissions and rejections 1926-1927
C-7390	Association of German Canadian Catholics – Admission of 150 Refugees from Germany (Germans, Yugoslavs and Czechoslovaks) 1924-1926

C-7390	Association of German Canadian Catholics – Admission of 150 Refugees from Germany (Germans, Yugoslavs and Czechoslovaks) 1926-1927
C-10633	Belgium - Agent - August Van den Broeck 1908-1911
C-10407	Bergen, Norway - A. Litland, Bergen, Norway, booking agent 1907-1914
C-10265	Brittany, France - Agent - Rev. Father H. Peran 1906 and 1921
C-10418	Bulgaria - Allan Line. Party to be deported. 1907-1908
C-10418	Bulgaria - Deportation of Bulgarians from Toronto 1907-1908
C-10417	Bulgaria - Destitute in Toronto 1907-1908
C-10418	Bulgaria - Destitute in Toronto 1907-1908
C-10418	Bulgaria - Dominion Line Steamship Company. Party to be deported 1907-1908
C-10418	Bulgaria - Donaldson Steam Ship Line. Party to be deported 1908
C-10640	Bulgaria - H. and A. Allan, Montreal. Bulgarians rejected 1909
C-10589	Bulk labour from Europe 1947
C-10590	Bulk labour from Europe 1948
C-10590	Bulk labour from Europe 1948-1949
C-10590	Bulk labour from Europe 1949
C-10591	Bulk labour from Europe 1949-1950
C-10591	Bulk labour from Europe 1950-1952
C-10592	Canadian Christian Council for the Resettlement of Refugees 1947-1949
C-10592	Canadian Christian Council for the Resettlement of Refugees 1949-1950
C-10592	Canadian Christian Council for the Resettlement of Refugees 1952-1953
C-10612	Canadian Pacific Railway - Prepaid passenger business (passage loans and liens on homesteads) (Roumanians and Germans) 1908
C-10312	Christiana, Norway - Agent - Charles Bennett 1907-1914
C-7807	Continental Family Scheme - Cash deposited by families at ports of entry 1926-1943
C-10312	Copenhagen, Denmark - Agent - Joachim Prahl 1907-1915, 1923
C-10316	Copenhagen, Denmark - Agent - John Rath 1907-1921
C-10436	Czechoslovakia - 1939-1940
C-10597	Czechoslovakia - displaced persons 1948
C-7393	Danzig, Poland - Summary reports of admissions and rejections 1924-1927
C-7394	Danzig, Poland - Summary reports of admissions and rejections 1924-1927
C-7394	Danzig, Poland - Summary reports of admissions and rejections 1927-1929
C-7343	Denmark - Undesirable Immigrants from Scandinavia, Ex-Convicts 1898-1905
C-7344	Denmark - Undesirable Immigrants from Scandinavia, Ex-Convicts 1898-1905
C-10589	Doctors and nurses from refugee camps in Germany 1946-1950
C-7850	Domestics - Cabled advice on arrival of continental domestics 1927
C-7850	Domestics - Cabled advice on arrival of continental domestics 1927-1928
C-7851	Domestics - Cabled advice on arrival of continental domestics 1927-1928
C-7324	Domestics - Servants from Scandinavia - C.O. Swanson, Waterville, Que. - 1905-1910
C-7338	Doukhobors 1899-1902
C-7339	Doukhobors 1902
C-10322	Enemy Aliens 1939-1941
C-10322	Enemy Aliens and enemy alien seamen 1941, 1942
C-10322	Enemy Aliens and enemy alien seamen 1942-1947
C-10323	Enemy Aliens and enemy alien seamen 1942-1947
C-10327	Enemy aliens from Britain sent to Canada for internment 1940-1941
C-10327	Enemy aliens from Britain sent to Canada for internment 1941-1942
C-10327	Enemy aliens from Britain sent to Canada for internment 1942
C-10397	Enemy aliens from Britain sent to Canada for internment 1943-1946
C-10593	Estonia - Group of twenty-three Estonians may attempt landing 1947-1953
C-10598	Estonia - Refugees in Sweden 1946-1948
C-10598	Estonia - Refugees in Sweden 1949
C-10677	Farm labour from Europe 1953
C-7369	Finland - Activities of Finnish Agitators in Northern Ontario 1926-1942, 1946
C-10644	Finland - Donald Cable of Finland Steam Navigation Co. 1909-1912
C-10402	France - French subjects for enlistment with the forces of General Charles de Gaulle - admitted to

Canada 1940-1942

C-7334	Galician and other colonies in Western Canada 1898-1901
C-7334	Galician and other colonies in Western Canada 1901-1912
C-10621	Galicians - Request for an interpreter to get information from Galician prisoners in Toronto 1908
C-7814	German Catholic Settlement Society, Rosthern, Sask. 1902-1906
C-7833	Germans at Glace Bay, Cape Breton, wish to go to western Canada 1903-1906
C-10421	Germany - Return to Germany of undesirable German nationals 1943-1959
C-10588	Germany - Scientists and technicians 1948-1951
C-10677	Greece - Admission of 200 Greeks from China 1951-1952
C-10618	Hamburg-American Line - regulations as to admission of immigrants 1908-1933
C-10676	Holland - Artisans 1952
C-4699	Holland - immigration from 1947-1948
C-4700	Holland - immigration from 1948
C-4701	Holland - immigration from 1948-1949
C-4702	Holland - immigration from 1950
C-4702	Holland - immigration from 1951
C-10399	Holland - Netherlands Legion in Canada 1940-1941 1945
C-10400	Holland - Netherlands Legion in Canada 1940-1941 1945
C-10613	Holland - Reverend C.M. Van Aken, Zevenbergsche-Hoek, Holland. Settlers 1908-1909 1913
C-10646	Holland America Line 1933-1939
C-10422	Hungary - Alleged destitution amongst Hungarians, Touchwood Hills, Sask. 1907-1908
C-7343	Hungary - Zoltan Von Rajcs, Agent at Rosthern, Sask. 1903-1925
C-10262	Hutterite colonies in the United States and Canada 1929-1940
C-7307	Iceland - Bonuses 1909-1913
C-7307	Iceland - Immigration from 1897-1909
C-10676	Italy - Admission of 400 farm labourers 1950-1951
C-10677	Italy - Admission of 400 farm labourers 1950-1951
C-10602	Italy - Canadian Travel Agency, Montreal. Italian farmers 1949-1951
C-10603	Italy - Canadian Travel Agency, Montreal. Admission of farmers 1949-1951
C-10412	Jewish children from unoccupied France 1942-1947
C-10413	Jewish children from unoccupied France 1942-1947
C-10413	Jewish children from unoccupied France 1947-1948
C-10586	Latvia - Immigration from the Republic of Latvia 1920-1947
C-10586	Latvia - Immigration from the Republic of Latvia 1947-1948
C-10448	Lithuania - Immigration from 1919-1947
C-7389	Lutheran Immigration Board 1924-1927
C-7389	Lutheran Immigration Board 1927-1928
C-7390	Lutheran Immigration Board 1927-1928
C-10304	Malta - immigration from 1948
C-10304	Malta - immigration from 1950-1951
C-10304	Malta - immigration from 1951-1952
C-10305	Malta - immigration from 1951-1952
C-7349	Mennonites - Movements from South Russia 1921-1924
C-7350	Mennonites - Movements from South Russia 1921-1924
C-7350	Mennonites - Movements from South Russia 1924-1938 1946
C-7331	Mennonites 1930-1931
C-7331	Mennonites 1931-1940
C-7846	Norway - 500 families coming via Canadian Pacific Railway 1926-1928
C-10314	Paris, France - Agent - Hernie, Péron and Co. 1907-1920
C-7394	Paris, France - Summary reports of admissions and rejections 1924-1927
C-7394	Paris, France - Summary reports of admissions and rejections 1927-1929
C-7395	Paris, France - Summary reports of admissions and rejections 1927-1929
C-10314	Paris, France and Havre - Agent - Currie and Co. 1907-1924
C-10302	Persia - Immigrants brought in by Dr. Isaac Adams, Battleford (Nestorians from Persia) 1907-1909
C-10588	Poland - Admission of 4000 former Polish soldiers 1946-1947

C-10407	Poland - Admission of Polish technicians 1941-1942
C-10588	Poland - Department of Health and Welfare Committee to investigate health and welfare of Polish immigrants 1946
C-10445	Poland - Immigration from 1941-1942
C-10445	Poland - Immigration from 1942-1945
C-10446	Poland - Immigration from 1942-1945
C-10446	Poland - Immigration from 1945-1947
C-10674	Poland - Inspection of displaced persons in East Africa and Lebanon 1949-1951
C-10596	Poland - Orphan children from Europe 1948-1949
C-10446	Poland - Passports 1919-1926
C-10410	Poland - Polish Legation, Ottawa 1939-1948
C-10412	Poland - Proposal to move 50,000 women and children from Russia 1942-1949
C-7355	Portugal - Immigration from 1954
C-10667	Prisoners held for deportation 1911-1927
C-10435	Prisoners of War - Repatriated to Germany 1916-1919
C-10435	Prisoners of War - Repatriated to Germany 1919-1924
C-10602	Refugees - Admission of 261 refugee passengers from Sweden: Estonians, Latvians, Lithuanians, Finns, Austrians, Poles 1948-1949
C-10602	Refugees - Policy on uncleared Balts, Estonians and Latvians arriving by sea in 1948
C-7395	Rotterdam, Netherlands - Summary reports of admissions and rejections 1924-1927
C-10433	Russia - Passports and the deportation of Russian subjects 1915-1927
C-10433	Russia - Passports and the deportation of Russian subjects 1927-1931
C-7372	Russia - Refugees from the Far East 1923-1926
C-7372	Russia - Refugees from the Far East 1926-1927
C-7373	Russia - Refugees from the Far East 1926-1927
C-7373	Russia - Refugees from the Far East 1927-1933
C-10593	Russia - Surrendered Enemy Personnel - Ukrainian refugees from England 1946-1953
C-10315	Scandinavian and Finnish domestics brought forward by railways 1938-1939
C-10315	Scandinavian and Finnish domestics brought forward by railways 1939
C-10316	Scandinavian and Finnish domestics brought forward by railways 1939
C-10318	Spain - Refugees 1939-1943
C-10310	Spain - Repatriation of individuals who went to Spain for the Civil War 1937-1939
C-10310	Spain - Repatriation of individuals who went to Spain for the Civil War 1939
C-10311	Spain - Repatriation of individuals who went to Spain for the Civil War 1939
C-10598	Sweden - Refugees in Sweden 1950
C-10441	Switzerland - Emigration to Canada 1926-1938
C-10312	Syria - Complaint about alleged ill treatment of immigrants from Asia Minor 1905-1910, 1913
C-10313	Trondhejm, Norway - Agent - Oluf Rund 1907-1915, 1921

Asia

C-10410	Asiatics, Orientals (Japanese, Chinese, East Indians) 1907-1922
C-10305	China - Jin Wah Sing Theatre Company - Admission of actors 1944-1951, 1954
C-10662	China - Opium and Narcotic Drug Act 1923-1932
C-10281	India - Immigration from 1922-1935
C-10281	India - Immigration from 1939-1947
C-10282	India - Immigration from 1948-1949
C-4753	Japan - Immigration - Form file 1908-1909
C-4753	Japan - Immigration - Form file 1909-1910
C-4754	Japan - Immigration - Form file 1909-1910
C-4754	Japan - Immigration - Form file 1910-1912
C-4754	Japan - Immigration - Form file 1912-1913
C-4755	Japan - Immigration - Form file 1913-1914
C-4756	Japan - Immigration - Form file 1914
C-4756	Japan - Immigration - Form file 1914-1916
C-4757	Japan - Immigration - Form file 1916

C-4757	Japan - Immigration - Form file 1916-1918
C-4757	Japan - Immigration - Form file 1918
C-4758	Japan - Immigration - Form file 1918
C-4758	Japan - Immigration - Form file 1918-1920
C-4751	Japan - Immigration 1925-1930
C-10586	Japan - Repatriation of Japanese 1941-1943, 1945
C-10586	Japan - Repatriation of Japanese 1946-1947
C-10587	Japan - Repatriation of Japanese 1946-1947
C-10677	Jewish - Admission of Iraqi Jewish refugees from Shanghai, China 1950

United States

C-10268	Baltimore - Arrival of immigrants at Baltimore, Maryland, destined to Canada 1906,1910-1913
C-10301	Biddeford, Maine - Agent - J.B. Carbonneau 1907-1908
C-10301	Biddeford, Maine - Agent - J.B. Carbonneau 1908-1912
C-10301	Biddeford, Maine - Agent - J.B. Carbonneau 1912-1914
C-10302	Biddeford, Maine - Agent - J.B. Carbonneau 1912-1914
C-10302	Biddeford, Maine - Agent - J.B. Carbonneau 1914-1915
C-10652	Canadian Pacific Railway requests admission of coloured porters 1930-1943
C-10652	Canadian Pacific Railway requests admission of coloured porters 1943-1944
C-10653	Canadian Pacific Railway requests admission of coloured porters 1943-1944
C-10653	Canadian Pacific Railway requests admission of coloured porters 1944-1948
C-10664	Carnival shows from United States 1922-1926
C-7305	Chicago, Ill. - Agent - C.J. Broughton 1897-1905
C-15867	Chippewa Falls, Wisc. - Agent - H.C. McRae 1896-1918
C-10410	Coloured domestics from Guadeloupe 1910-1928
C-10613	Crookston, Minn. - Agent - William E. Black 1908-1911
C-10613	Crookston, Minn. - Agent - William E. Black 1912-1913, 1916
C-15867	Detroit, Mich. - Agent - M.W. McInnes 1897-1903
C-4798	Duluth, Minn. - Agent - J.H.M. Parker 1902-1904
C-4798	Duluth, Minn. - Agent - J.H.M. Parker 1904-1911
C-10323	Enlistments from the United States in the Canadian Military Forces 1939-1942
C-10409	Head tax on immigrants to Canada coming through United States 1904-1917
C-10667	Insane persons from United States to Province of Quebec 1914-1941
C-4738	Inspection of Immigrants by United States officials in Canada 1902-1903
C-4739	Inspection of Immigrants by United States officials in Canada 1902-1903
C-4740	Inspection of Immigrants by United States officials in Canada 1903-1916
C-7345	Mountain Lake, Minn. - Agent - J.C. Koehn 1898-1902
C-7345	Mountain Lake, Minn. - Agent - J.C. Koehn 1902-1909
C-7345	Mountain Lake, Minn. - Agent - J.C. Koehn 1909-1910
C-7346	Mountain Lake, Minn. - Agent - J.C. Koehn 1909-1910
C-7346	Mountain Lake, Minn. - Agent - J.C. Koehn 1912-1914
C-7346	Mountain Lake, Minn. - Agent - J.C. Koehn 1914-1919
C-7853	New York - Canadian medical inspection 1921-1923
C-10600	New York - Regulations regarding inspection of immigrants 1923-1927
C-7386	Omaha, Neb. - Agent - W.V. Bennett and S.S. Montgomery of Chaldron, Neb. 1901-1903
C-4783	Omaha, Neb. - Agent - W.V. Bennett 1895-1904
C-10664	Reciprocal arrangements between Canada and the United States for citizens from one country to work in the other 1937-1945, 1947
C-10262	Saginaw, Mich. - Agent - Romuald Laurier 1907-1912
C-7349	Salt Lake City, Utah - Agent - John W. Taylor (Mormons) 1903-1922
C-7381	St. Paul, Minn. Agent - Charles Pilling, also at Grand Forks, N.D. 1900-1912
C-10666	Theatrical organizations from the United States 1918-1936
C-7349	Utah - Lists of immigrants for 1903
C-7314	Watertown, S.D. - Agent - W.H. Rogers 1897-1903

Chapter 12
Naturalization and citizenship

Canada did not have any citizens of its own until 1947, when the federal Canadian Citizenship Act went into effect. Until then, even persons who had been born in the Dominion were not citizens – they were classed as British subjects or Canadian nationals.

New arrivals from elsewhere in the British Empire were also considered to be British subjects, and therefore were automatically equal, in terms of citizenship, to the people born in Canada.

However, the people who arrived from non-Commonwealth countries – such as the United States, Germany, or Russia – were considered to be "aliens," and had to be "naturalized" to gain status similar to that of a native-born person.

Several databases on the Internet will help a researcher find information about ancestors from non-Commonwealth countries.

Legislation relating to naturalization and citizenship changed several times over the years after the first Parliament of Lower Canada passed legislation in 1794 that was designed to screen aliens – primarily, in those days, people coming north from the new United States.

Under legislation passed in 1828 – the Act to Secure and Confer Upon Certain Inhabitants of this Province the Civil and Political Rights of Natural Born British Subjects – alien men who had been living in Upper Canada for seven years were expected to take an oath of allegiance before the county registrar and become British subjects.

The act was passed because of concerns that many settlers from the United States were not loyal to the British monarchy. After the union of Lower and Upper Canada, another Naturalization Act was passed in 1841. A third act, passed in 1845, reduced the required period of residence from seven years to five years.

Early naturalization records are spotty, but Library and Archives Canada holds two collections that might be of interest.

• The Upper Canada and Canada West Naturalization Records, dating from 1828 to 1850, contain 3,344 references for people in what is now Ontario. All entries include the name, residence, and date of registry.

ON THE INTERNET:
<www.collectionscanada.gc.ca/databases/naturalization/index-e.html>
These records are also available on microfilm – numbers C-15692 and C-15693.

• The Citizenship Registration Records for the Montreal Circuit Court, from 1851 to 1945, contain 8,432 references.

A typical file in this series will include the name, age, residence, former residence, place of birth, length of residence in Canada, occupation, and date of naturalization.

Naturalization or citizenship?
Naturalization is generally considered to be a step toward citizenship for someone born in another country. Citizenship confers the rights, duties, and privileges of a native-born person.

ON THE INTERNET:

<www.collectionscanada.gc.ca/databases/citizenship-montreal/index-e.html>

Legislation relating to naturalization and citizenship continued to evolve, with acts passed by Parliament to enable aliens to petition for naturalization. If successful, they would swear allegiance to the British sovereign and would be granted the rights of someone born within the British Empire.

These acts included:

• The Local Act, also known as the Law of Naturalization and Allegiance, implemented on May 22, 1868. A person could be naturalized after being in Canada for two years.

• The Naturalization and Aliens Act of 1881. This gave the Secretary of State authority to issue naturalization certificates to government employees. All other requests for naturalization were handled by provincial courts.

• The Naturalization Act of 1906. This act said aliens could become naturalized after spending three years in Canada. Naturalization declared the aliens to be British subjects – although they could only claim that status in Canada, not in England.

Applications were made to local judges of provincial courts. The application was presented on the first day of a court sitting, and if there were no objections during that sitting, the application would be granted.

After May 5, 1910, a person had to be in Canada for three years, rather than two, to be naturalized.

• The Naturalization Act of 1914. This act tightened the rules concerning naturalization – although the politicians eased the pain somewhat by delaying implementation of the new law. That allowed every alien who arrived before Jan. 1, 1915, to apply under the old rules. For a while, aliens could decide whether to be naturalized under the old, soft law, or the new, hard one. Not surprisingly, the old one was the most popular. In 1917, the last year for the old law, 9,029 aliens were naturalized under it. Only 135 used the new law.

The 1914 act marked a major departure from the old law, under which a naturalized person became a British subject in Canada only. The new law gave naturalized Canadians the same status as a natural-born British subject.

That meant the new law conferred Empire-wide naturalization, so many people who had been naturalized under the old law chose to be naturalized again under the new one.

The conditions and qualifications for naturalization were as follows:

1. Residence within His Majesty's Dominions for a period of not less than five years or service under the Crown for the same period within the past eight years before the application.

2. Residence in Canada for not less than one year immediately preceding the application and previous residence in Canada or in some other part of His Majesty's Dominions for four years within the last eight years before the application.

3. Good character.

4. An adequate knowledge of the English or French language.

5. An intention, if a Certificate of Naturalization is granted, either to reside in His Majesty's Dominions or to enter or continue in the service of the Crown.

The act gave full responsibility for the issuance of naturalization certificates to the federal Department of Immigration and Colonization.

• The Naturalization Act of 1919. This act, in force for just a year, was passed by the House of Commons in the belief that it would match one being passed in London.

The major change from the 1914 act was that "persons of former enemy alien nationality" could not be naturalized for 10 years. During the First World War, the government had refused to allow aliens from enemy nations to become naturalized Canadians.

The act also specified that a person had to be in Canada for five years in order to be naturalized. That requirement lasted until 1977.

• The Naturalization Act of 1920. In 1920, the legislators revised the law again, specifying that persons from former enemy countries could not be naturalized until July 7, 1929. Immigrants who had been in Canada for 10 years before the act was passed could, however, apply for naturalization.

The law was amended several times over the next 25 years. One of the early concerns was the status of women.

Until Jan. 15, 1932, women who were married to men being naturalized could be included in their husband's application. After that date, women had to make separate applications for naturalization, although children could still be included with a parent's application.

Female British subjects who married aliens before Jan. 15, 1932, lost their British subject status, even though the loss might have made them stateless. After that date, British women retained their British subject status unless they acquired their husband's nationality by marriage. Be warned, however, that that sounds simpler than it really was.

Women lost their British subject status if they married nationals of certain countries under certain conditions. For example, a British woman who married a man who was a citizen of France, Germany, or Switzerland would lose her British nationality, but not if she married an American. And a woman who was a British subject would lose British nationality if she married a Hungarian man – unless she was of Jewish origin. A woman marrying a Greek man would lose her status only if the ceremony took place in a Greek Orthodox church.

This odd system, which was made more complicated by the boundary changes in Europe in the 1940s, continued until Dec. 31, 1946.

In 1943, without a change to the law, the government began requiring aliens to fill out a declaration of intent at least one year before applying for naturalized status. This was similar to a policy that had been adopted by the United States.

• The Canadian Citizenship Act of 1946. With this act, which went into effect in 1947, Canada had citizens for the first time. The basic requirements for citizenship were carried over from the naturalization acts. For the first time, women were clearly viewed as individual persons.

• The Canadian Citizenship Act of 1977. This act made citizenship more widely available (among other ways, by reducing the period of residency required from five to three years), and eliminated the special treatment for British nationals and the remaining discrimination between men and women. The act also provided that Canadians could hold dual citizenship.

The citizenship indexes in the *Canada Gazette*, a weekly report of federal government activities, have several categories. These include aliens, British subjects, persons whose status is doubtful, and persons naturalized prior to the act of 1914.

Naturalization and citizenship came under the Department of the Secretary of State until November 1949. At that point, the responsibility was moved to the new Department of Citizenship and Immigration. That department was abolished in 1966, but re-established in 1993. In the interim, there was a department that looked after immigration and employment.

Records of naturalization and citizenship from 1854 are held by Citizenship and Immigration Canada. The originals of records created between 1854 and 1917 have been destroyed, although a nominal card index has survived. The index provides information compiled at the time of naturalization, such as present and former place of residence, former nationality, occupation, date of certification, name, and location of the responsible court. The index rarely contains any other genealogical information.

The Canada Gazette index includes the person's name, country of origin, occupation and address

In 1915, the government started its three-year introduction of new rules for naturalization. The new rules were more stringent than the ones they were replacing, and as a result many people opted to be naturalized under the earlier rules while they were still in effect.

THE NATURALIZATION ACTS, 1914 AND 1920.

LIST OF ALIENS to whom certificates of naturalization under the Naturalization Acts, 1914 and 1920, were granted by the Secretary of State of Canada during the month of May, 1925.

SERIES A.—Certificates granted to Aliens.
SERIES B.—Certificates granted to Aliens where names of children are included.
SERIES C.—Certificates granted to Minors.
SERIES D.—Certificates granted to persons with respect to whose nationality as British subjects a doubt exists.
SERIES E.—Certificates granted to persons naturalized previous to coming into force of above Acts.

Name	Country	Date of Certificate	Date of Oath of Allegiance	Occupation	Residence	Number and Series
Ackerman, Paul	Switzerland		May 9, 1925	Electrical engineer	Montreal, Que	36376 A.
Ackeman, Helen (Neuenschwander)	Wife					
Aesmont, Frances Mary	Poland		May 4, 1925	Housewife	Hamilton, Ont	11908 B.
Aesmont, Carl	Minor chlld					
Aesmont, Mary	Minor child					
Aesmont, William	Minor child					
Ahl, Joseph John	U.S.A		May 5, 1925	Farmer	Primate, Sask	36341 A.
Ahl, Mary Eva	Wife					
Akmakjian, Krekor	Turkey (Armenia)		May 7, 1925	Cook	Sandwich, Ont	36306 A.
Akmakjian, Ella	Wife					
Alessandrini, Enrico	Italy		May 14, 1925	Labourer	Sault Ste. Marie, Ont	36451 A.
Alessandrini, Assunta	Wife					
Alexander, Wilbert Howard	U.S.A		May 2, 1925	Farmer	Meadow Lake, Sask	11905 B.
Alexander, Edith Edna Cowan	Wife					
Alexander, Orlan James	Minor child					
Allen, Howard Miles	U.S.A		May 7, 1925	Farmer	Stettler, Alta	36366 A.
Allen, Uma Leticia	Wife					
Allen, Max	U.S.A	May 20, 1925		Theatre manager	Sandwich, Ont	9691 E.
Almagro, Edward	Italy		May 4, 1925	Motion picture operator.	Montreal, Que	36249 A.
Almagro, Dorothy (Mason)	Wife					
Aloff, Lody	Russia		May 21, 1925	Miner	Vancouver, B.C	36557 A.
Alonzo, Giuseppe	Italy		May 27, 1925	Bricklayer	Vancouver, B.C	36670 A.
Alonzo, Marie Errico	Wife					
Ander, Abe	Poland		May 29, 1925	Shoemaker	Toronto, Ont	11964 B.
Ander, Dora	Wife					
Ander, Annie	Minor child					
Ander, Louis	Minor child					

After 1917, only the new regulations could be followed.

Over the next three decades, hundreds of thousands of people followed them, gaining status as Canadians. By the early 1930s, an average of 26,000 people were being naturalized every year.

The records created after 1917 still exist. They include the surname, given name, date and place of birth, entry into Canada, and possibly the names of spouses and children. Files typically include the original petition for naturalization, a Royal Canadian Mounted Police report on the person, the oath of allegiance, and any other documents.

Once individuals were granted the status – weeks or months after the application date – their names, addresses, and countries of origin were published in annual reports produced by the Secretary of State until 1932, as well as in the *Canada Gazette* until 1951. Back issues of both publications are available in some large city libraries, as well as in many university libraries and archives.

The Secretary of State indexes from 1915 through 1932 have been digitized and placed on the Library and Archives Canada website, along with a searchable database of names. The resource is based on work done by the Jewish Genealogical Society of Montreal and the Jewish Genealogical Society of Ottawa.

ON THE INTERNET:
<www.collectionscanada.gc.ca/databases/naturalization-1915-1932/index-e.html>

The online naturalization database includes about 200,000 people who applied for and received status as naturalized Canadians from 1915 to March 31, 1932.

For April 1, 1932, and later, researchers will need to use the *Canada Gazette* indexes. These have also been digitized for posting on the Library and Archives Canada website. A finding aid to the lists, as published in the *Canada Gazette*, is on the following pages.

These indexes make it easier to track down missing ancestors and to confirm where people lived.

The indexes include the number of the certificate. They also indicate which certificates were granted with names of children included, which ones were granted to minors, which ones were granted to married women whose husbands were already naturalized, as well as the certificates in the basic category, the ones listed simply as having been granted to aliens.

Certificates were issued based on the category of naturalization. Each certificate had a letter denoting a series, as well as a number.

Series A: Certificates granted to aliens.

Series B: Certificates granted to aliens where names of minor children are included.

Series C: Certificates granted to minors.

Series D: Certificates granted to persons whose nationality as British subjects is in doubt.

Series E: Certificates granted to persons naturalized under prior acts.

Series F and G: Repatriations.

Certificates issued in French also include the letter F after the number.

The database might include references to people who were naturalized before

1917. If they interacted with the department in later years, those papers might still be available. Series E certificates, for example, were often issued to persons whose fathers or husbands had been naturalized earlier. The person was already naturalized through the naturalization of the father or husband – but if he or she later wanted a naturalization certificate, an application could be made. That application would have included much of the information that was on the father's/husband's pre-1914 papers, now destroyed.

Until 1947, immigrants from the British Isles were already British subjects and did not need to be naturalized to gain status in Canada. As a result, these records are primarily relevant to families who came from non-Commonwealth countries. This record series is one of the few Canadian resources of specific benefit to non-British immigrants.

A clue that naturalization records might be available will be found on ship passenger lists. If there is a handwritten date next to the person's name, that indicates when the person applied to be naturalized.

The naturalization indexes ended after the Canadian Citizenship Act came into force in 1947. Subsequently, citizenship indexes were published in the *Canada Gazette* until April 1951.

To obtain copies of records listed in these databases, contact Citizenship and Immigration Canada. Requests for copies of documents must be sent by mail to:

Citizenship and Immigration Canada
Public Rights Administration
360 Laurier Ave. W.
10th Floor
Ottawa, Ontario K1A 1L1

The request must be accompanied by a signed consent form from the person concerned or proof that he or she has been dead for 20 years or more. Proof of death can be a copy of a death certificate, a newspaper obituary, or a photograph of their gravestone showing name and death date.

The request should include the surname, given name, date and place of birth, and, if known, the number of the naturalization certificate including the alphabetic series identifier and the "F" suffix if the certificate was issued in French.

The fee is $5.00, payable to the Receiver General for Canada.

Each application must be submitted by a Canadian citizen or an individual living in Canada. The application must be on an Access to Information Request Form, available online.

ON THE INTERNET:
<www.tbs-sct.gc.ca/tbsf-fsct/350-57-eng.asp>

Naturalization documents might also be found in provincial archives. That is because the applications were normally heard in provincial courts. The British Columbia Archives in Victoria, for example, has a collection of naturalization indexes from courts throughout the province. Most of these cover the 19th century and the early years of the 20th century, although some are from after April 1951, the last month included in the indexes published in the *Canada Gazette*.

Naturalization Act

The indexes in the *Canada Gazette* identified the people who had been naturalized in a given period of time. This list of the indexes is in three columns – the first is the **time period** covered by the index; the second is the **date of the issue** of the *Canada Gazette*; and the third is the **page number** in the *Canada Gazette*.

1915				November	January 14, 1922	Page 2794
Entire year	January 8, 1916	Page 2179		December	February 18, 1922	Page 3384
				Supplementary	December 27, 1924	Page 1903
1916						
First half	July 15, 1916	Page 177		**1922**		
Third quarter	October 14, 1916	Page 1238		January	March 18, 1922	Page 3919
Fourth quarter	January 6, 1917	Page 2333		February	April 15, 1922	Page 4283
				March	May 13, 1922	Page 4765
1917				April	June 10, 1922	Page 5263
First quarter	April 21, 1917	Page 3674		May	July 8, 1922	Page 104
Second quarter	July 14, 1917	Page 105		June	August 19, 1922	Page 750
Third quarter	October 20, 1917	Page 1266		July	September 23, 1922	Page 1260
Fourth quarter	March 23, 1918	Page 3262		August	October 21, 1922	Page 1680
				September	November 18, 1922	Page 2132
1918				October	December 16, 1922	Page 2599
First quarter	April 13, 1918	Page 3587		November	January 27, 1923	Page 3195
Second quarter	August 24, 1918	Page 773		December	February 24, 1923	Page 3611
Second half	January 18, 1919	Page 2265		Supplementary	December 27, 1924	Page 1903
				Supplementary	January 24, 1925	Page 2165
1919						
First half	July 26, 1919	Page 281		**1923**		
Third quarter	December 20, 1919	Page 1851		January	March 24, 1923	Page 4031
Fourth quarter	January 31, 1920	Page 2376		February	March 31, 1923	Page 4147
				March	April 28, 1923	Page 4506
1920				April	May 26, 1923	Page 4867
January	March 6, 1920	Page 2936		May	June 30, 1923	Page 5270
February	April 3, 1920	Page 3341		June	July 28, 1923	Page 296
March	May 1, 1920	Page 3723		July	August 25, 1923	Page 598
April	June 5, 1920	Page 4249		August	September 29, 1923	Page 1043
May	July 24, 1920	Page 274		September	October 20, 1923	Page 1337
June	August 21, 1920	Page 668		October	December 1, 1923	Page 1792
July	October 2, 1920	Page 1251		November	December 29, 1923	Page 2159
August	October 16, 1920	Page 1446		December	February 2, 1924	Page 2647
September	October 23, 1920	Page 1569		Supplementary	January 24, 1925	Page 2165
October	December 4, 1920	Page 2183		Supplementary	March 28, 1925	Page 2884
November	January 15, 1921	Page 2866				
December	February 12, 1921	Page 3309		**1924**		
Supplementary	November 24, 1924	Page 1541		January	March 1, 1924	Page 3098
				February	March 29, 1924	Page 3534
1921				March	April 26, 1924	Page 3991
January	March 19, 1921	Page 3846		April	May 31, 1924	Page 4453
February	April 16, 1921	Page 4328		May	June 28, 1924	Page 4848
March	May 14, 1921	Page 4869		June	July 26, 1924	Page 296
April	June 25, 1921	Page 5556		July	August 30, 1924	Page 652
May	July 23, 1921	Page 314		August	September 27, 1924	Page 957
June	September 3, 1921	Page 937		September	October 25, 1924	Page 1267
July	September 10, 1921	Page 1041		October	November 22, 1924	Page 1533
August	October 15, 1921	Page 1609		Supplementary	November 22, 1924	Page 1541
September	November 5, 1921	Page 1907		November	December 27, 1924	Page 1894
October	December 10, 1921	Page 2364		Supplementary	December 27, 1924	Page 1903

Cowan, Helen I. *British Emigration to British North America.* Toronto: University of Toronto Press, 1961.

Danys, Milda. *DP: Lithuanian Immigration to Canada.* Toronto: Multicultural History Society of Ontario, 1986.

Dreisziger, N.F. *Struggle and Hope: The Hungarian-Canadian Experience.* Toronto: McClelland and Stewart, 1982.

Dunae, Patrick A. *Gentlemen Emigrants: From the British Public Schools to the Canadian Frontier.* Vancouver: Douglas and McIntyre, 1981.

Elliott, Bruce S. *Irish Migrants in the Canadas: A New Approach.* Montreal: McGill-Queen's University Press, 1988.

England, Robert. *The Central European Immigrant in Canada.* Toronto: Macmillan, 1929.

Epp, Frank H. *Mennonite Exodus: The Rescue and Resettlement of the Russian Mennonites Since the Communist Revolution.* Altona, Manitoba: Canadian Mennonite Relief and Immigration Council, 1976.

Errington, Elizabeth Jane. *Emigrant Worlds and Transatlantic Communities: Migration to Upper Canada in the First Half of the Nineteenth Century.* Montreal: McGill-Queen's University Press, 2007.

Gaida, Pr. , Kairys, S., Kardelis, J., Kardelis, Puzina, Rinkunas, J., Rinkunas, A., and Sungaila, J. *Lithuanians in Canada.* Ottawa: Lights Printing and Publishing, 1967.

Ganzevoort, Herman. *A Bittersweet Land: The Dutch Experience in Canada 1890-1980.* Toronto/Ottawa: McClelland and Stewart/Ministry of Supply and Services, 1988.

Gibbon, John Murray. *Displaced Persons.* Toronto: McClelland and Stewart, 1951.

Gilroy, Marion. *Loyalists and Land Settlement in Nova Scotia.* Halifax: Public Archives of Nova Scotia, 1937.

Glass, D.V. and Taylor, P.A.M. *Population and Emigration.* Dublin: Irish University Press, 1976.

Government of Ontario. *Emigration: The British Farmer's and Farm Labourer's Guide to Ontario the Premier Province of the Dominion of Canada.* 1880; reprint, Port Elgin, Ontario: Cumming Atlas Reprints, 1974.

Green, Alan G. *Immigration and the Postwar Canadian Economy.* Toronto: MacMillan of Canada, 1976.

Guillet, Edwin C. *The Great Migration: The Atlantic Crossing by Sailing-Ship 1770-1860.* 1937; reprint: Toronto: University of Toronto Press, 1963.

Harney, Robert and Troper, Harold. *Immigrants: A Portrait of the Urban Experience, 1890-1930.* Toronto: Van Nostrand Reinhold, 1975.

Harrison, Phyllis. *The Home Children.* Winnipeg: Watson and Dwyer Publishing, 1979.

Hawkins, Freda. *Canada and Immigration: Public Policy and Public Concern.* Toronto: McGill-Queen's University Press, 1972.

Hawkins, Freda. *Critical Years in Immigration: Canada and Australia Compared.* Kingston: McGill-Queen's University Press, 1989.

Hedges, James B. *Building the Canadian West.* New York: Macmillan, 1939.

Hibbert, Joyce, ed. *The War Brides.* Toronto: PMA Books, 1978.

Hollett, David. *Passage to the New World: Packet Ships and Irish Famine Emigrants 1845-1851.* Abergaveny, Gwent, Great Britain: P.M. Heaton Publishing, 1995.

Hoffman, Frances and Taylor, Ryan. *Across the Waters: Ontario Immigrants' Experiences, 1820-1850.* Milton, Ont.: Global Heritage Press, 1999.

Houston, Cecil J. and Smyth, William J. *Irish Emigration and Canadian Settlement: Patterns, Links and Letters.* Toronto: University of Toronto Press, 1990.

Iacovetta, Franca. *Such Hardworking People: Italian Immigrants in Postwar Toronto.* Montreal: McGill-Queen's University Press, 1992.

Irvine, Sherry and Obee, Dave. *Finding Your Canadian Ancestors: A Beginner's Guide.* Provo, Utah: Ancestry Publishing, 2007.

Israel, Charles E. *The Newcomers: Inhabiting a New Land.* Toronto: McClelland and Stewart, 1979.

Jackel, Susan (editor). *Flannel Shirt and Liberty: British Emigrant Gentlewomen in the Canadian West 1880-1914.* Vancouver: University of British Columbia Press, 1982.

Jarratt, Melynda. *War Brides: The Stories of the Women Who Left Everything Behind to Follow the Men They Loved.* Toronto: Dundurn, 2009.

Jensen, Joan M. *Passage From India: Asian Indian Immigrants in North America.* New Haven: Yale University Press, 1988.

Johnson, Peter. *Voyages of Hope: The Saga of the Bride Ships.* Victoria: Horsdal and Schubart, 2002.

Johnson, Stanley. *A History of Emigration From the United Kingdom to North America, 1763-1912.* London: George

December	January 24, 1925	Page 2158	July	September 1, 1928	Page 624
Supplementary	January 24, 1925	Page 2165	August	September 29, 1928	Page 965
Supplementary	March 28, 1925	Page 2884	September	October 27, 1928	Page 1309
			October	December 1, 1928	Page 1660
1925			November	January 5, 1929	Page 2081
January	February 21, 1925	Page 2477	December	January 26, 1929	Page 2367
February	March 28, 1925	Page 2876			
Supplementary	March 28, 1925	Page 2884	**1929**		
March	April 25, 1925	Page 3234	January	March 2, 1929	Page 2848
April	May 30, 1925	Page 3677	February	March 30, 1929	Page 3230
Supplementary	May 30, 1925	Page 3691	March	April 27, 1929	Page 3635
May	June 27, 1925	Page 3997	April	June 8, 1929	Page 4170
June	August 1, 1925	Page 297	May	July 6, 1929	Page 21
July	August 29, 1925	Page 542	June	August 10, 1929	Page 526
August	October 3, 1925	Page 881	July	September 21, 1929	Page 1048
September	October 24, 1925	Page 1079	August	October 5, 1929	Page 1237
October	November 28, 1925	Page 1359	September	October 26, 1929	Page 1557
November	December 25, 1925	Page 1653	October	December 7, 1929	Page 2036
December	January 30, 1926	Page 2021	November	February 1, 1930	Page 2736
			December	February 15, 1930	Page 2950
1926					
January	February 27, 1926	Page 2342	**1930**		
February	March 27, 1926	Page 2685	January	March 8, 1930	Page 3258
March	May 1, 1926	Page 2998	February	April 5, 1930	Page 3651
April	May 29, 1926	Page 3361	March	May 10, 1930	Page 4053
May	July 3, 1926	Page 15	April	June 7, 1930	Page 4436
June	July 31, 1926	Page 349	May	July 12, 1930	Page 103
July	September 4, 1926	Page 649	June	August 9, 1930	Page 400
August	October 2, 1926	Page 880	July	September 20, 1930	Page 831
September	October 30, 1926	Page 1144	August	September 27, 1930	Page 924
October	November 27, 1926	Page 1443	September	November 1, 1930	Page 1234
November	January 1, 1927	Page 1872	October	December 13, 1930	Page 1591
Supplementary	January 1, 1927	Page 1886	November	January 24, 1931	Page 2002
December	January 29, 1927	Page 2166	December	March 7, 1931	Page 2480
1927			**1931**		
January	February 26, 1927	Page 2520	January	April 4, 1931	Page 2769
February	March 26, 1927	Page 2862	February	April 18, 1931	Page 2907
March	April 30, 1927	Page 3254	March	May 16, 1931	Page 3185
April	May 21, 1927	Page 3518	April	June 6, 1931	Page 3390
May	July 9, 1927	Page 63	May	July 11, 1931	Page 67
June	July 30, 1927	Page 269	June	September 12, 1931	Page 621
July	August 27, 1927	Page 506	July	October 24, 1931	Page 994
August	October 1, 1927	Page 894	August	October 31, 1931	Page 1093
September	October 22, 1927	Page 1132	September	November 14, 1931	Page 1229
October	November 26, 1927	Page 1533	October	January 9, 1932	Page 1748
November	December 31, 1927	Page 1919	November	February 27, 1932	Page 2277
December	January 28, 1928	Page 2219	December	March 5, 1932	Page 2375
1928			**1932**		
January	March 3, 1928	Page 2706	January	March 12, 1932	Page 2460
February	March 31, 1928	Page 3120	February	April 23, 1932	Page 2878
March	April 28, 1928	Page 3436	March	May 21, 1932	Page 3124
April	May 26, 1928	Page 3785	April	June 11, 1932	Page 3312
May	June 30, 1928	Page 4152	May	July 16, 1932	Page 151
June	July 28, 1928	Page 265	June	August 20, 1932	Page 405

July	October 15, 1932	Page 875	July	November 7, 1936	Page 1206
August	November 12, 1932	Page 1122	August	December 5, 1936	Page 1431
September	December 3, 1932	Page 1292	September	January 23, 1937	Page 1865
October	December 31, 1932	Page 1524	October	February 27, 1937	Page 2165
November	January 21, 1933	Page 1693	November	April 10, 1937	Page 2521
December	February 11, 1933	Page 1868	December	May 22, 1937	Page 2958

1933   **1937**

January	March 11, 1933	Page 2084	January	June 19, 1937	Page 3219
February	March 25, 1933	Page 2195	February	July 3, 1937	Page 7
March	May 6, 1933	Page 2497	March	August 14, 1937	Page 380
April	June 10, 1933	Page 2747	April	October 2, 1937	Page 869
May	July 8, 1933	Page 61	May	October 20, 1937	Page 1140
June	August 12, 1933	Page 332	June	November 27, 1937	Page 1395
July	September 2, 1933	Page 496	July	December 25, 1937	Page 1613
August	October 7, 1933	Page 725	August	January 15, 1938	Page 1808
September	November 4, 1933	Page 922	September	February 19, 1938	Page 2072
October	November 25, 1933	Page 1076	October	March 19, 1938	Page 2286
November	December 23, 1933	Page 1263	November	April 9, 1938	Page 2454
December	January 27, 1934	Page 1564	December	April 23, 1938	Page 2603

1934   **1938**

January	March 3, 1934	Page 1763	January	May 21, 1938	Page 2937
February	March 31, 1934	Page 1929	February	May 28, 1938	Page 3018
March	April 28, 1934	Page 2108	March	June 18, 1938	Page 3212
April	June 9, 1934	Page 2395	April	July 30, 1938	Page 260
May	July 14, 1934	Page 51	May	August 20, 1938	Page 497
June	August 11, 1934	Page 264	June	October 1, 1938	Page 848
July	September 1, 1934	Page 427	July	October 15, 1938	Page 976
August	October 13, 1934	Page 830	August	November 26, 1938	Page 1332
September	October 27, 1934	Page 951	September	December 24, 1938	Page 1596
October	December 1, 1934	Page 1189	October	February 11, 1939	Page 1995
November	January 5, 1935	Page 1429	November	March 18, 1939	Page 2262
December	January 26, 1935	Page 1578	December	April 22, 1939	Page 2544

1935   **1939**

January	March 2, 1935	Page 1838	January	May 27, 1939	Page 2816
February	April 6, 1935	Page 2149	February	June 17, 1939	Page 2995
March	June 1, 1935	Page 2577	March	July 22, 1939	Page 203
April	June 22, 1935	Page 2744	April	August 12, 1939	Page 438
May	July 27, 1935	Page 178	May	August 19, 1939	Page 512
June	August 24, 1935	Page 481	June	September 30, 1939	Page 1005
July	September 28, 1935	Page 928	July	November 11, 1939	Page 1493
August	October 12, 1935	Page 1050	August	December 9, 1939	Page 1796
September	November 9, 1935	Page 1267	September	February 3, 1940	Page 2371
October	December 28, 1935	Page 1627	October	March 16, 1940	Page 2916
November	January 25, 1936	Page 1844	November	April 6, 1940	Page 3128
December	April 18, 1936	Page 2476	December	April 27, 1940	Page 3334

1936   **1940**

January	May 2, 1936	Page 2617	January	May 25, 1940	Page 3633
February	May 23, 1936	Page 2816	February	June 22, 1940	Page 3949
March	June 20, 1936	Page 3086	March	July 20, 1940	Page 113
April	August 1, 1936	Page 286	April	August 24, 1940	Page 566
May	August 29, 1936	Page 631	May	September 19, 1940	Page 814
June	October 3, 1936	Page 941	June	October 5, 1940	Page 1139

July	October 19, 1940	Page 1325	July	March 17, 1945	Page 1032
August	November 23, 1940	Page 1757	August	April 14, 1945	Page 1531
September	December 28, 1940	Page 2281	September	April 28, 1945	Page 1780
October	February 5, 1941	Page 2868	October	June 2, 1945	Page 2304
November	April 5, 1941	Page 3461	November	June 9, 1945	Page 2469
December	April 26, 1941	Page 3735	December	June 23, 1945	Page 2705

1941   **1945**

January	May 10, 1941	Page 3970	January	August 11, 1945	Page 3475
February	May 31, 1941	Page 4245	February	September 15, 1945	Page 3969
March	August 9, 1941	Page 408	March	September 15, 1945	Page 3978
April	October 18, 1941	Page 1226	April	October 13, 1945	Page 4581
May	November 1, 1941	Page 1374	May	November 17, 1945	Page 5084
June	December 13, 1941	Page 2037	June	January 5, 1946	Page 4
July	February 14, 1942	Page 2993	July	April 20, 1946	Page 2329
August	March 7, 1942	Page 3452	August	April 20, 1946	Page 2339
September	March 28, 1942	Page 3776	September	June 22, 1946	Page 3941
October	April 11, 1942	Page 4132	October	June 29, 1946	Page 4160
November	April 25, 1942	Page 4346	November	July 6, 1946	Page 4342
December	May 2, 1942	Page 4523	December	July 6, 1946	Page 4352

1942   **1946**

January	May 23, 1942	Page 4850	January	July 20, 1946	Page 4765
February	June 20, 1942	Page 5325	February	July 27, 1946	Page 4945
March	July 18, 1942	Page 244	March	August 3, 1946	Page 5149
April	August 15, 1942	Page 780	April	December 7, 1946	Page 7565
May	September 12, 1942	Page 1288	May	December 14, 1946	Page 7772
June	October 24, 1942	Page 1963	June	December 21, 1946	Page 7871
July	November 21, 1943	Page 2562	July	December 28, 1946	Page 7969
August	December 12, 1942	Page 3018	August	January 18, 1947	Page 199
September	January 2, 1943	Page 6	September	December 13, 1947	Page 4646
October	February 13, 1943	Page 610	October	December 20, 1947	Page 4854
November	March 13, 1943	Page 1070	November	January 10, 1948	Page 107
December	April 10, 1943	Page 1537	December	January 17, 1948	Page 239
			Supplementary	September 11, 1948	Page 3418
1943			Supplementary	April 16, 1949	Page 1386
January	April 24, 1943	Page 1697	Erratum	September 18, 1948	Page 3532
February	May 15, 1943	Page 2004
March	June 19, 1943	Page 2551
April	July 17, 1943	Page 2921
May	September 11, 1943	Page 3709
June	September 25, 1943	Page 3962
July	November 20, 1943	Page 4768
August	December 18, 1943	Page 5141
September	January 15, 1944	Page 168
October	March 4, 1944	Page 945
November	March 18, 1944	Page 1091
December	April 8, 1944	Page 1393

1944

January	April 29, 1944	Page 1757
February	June 17, 1944	Page 2462
March	July 15, 1944	Page 2895
April	September 16, 1944	Page 3801
May	December 9, 1944	Page 5110
June	February 24, 1945	Page 788

Canadian Citizenship Act

The Canadian Citizenship Act came into force on Jan. 1, 1947. The indexes published in the *Canada Gazette* from 1948 through 1951 identified people granted certificates under the new act.

This list is in three columns – the first is the **time period** covered by the index; the second is the **date of the issue** of the *Canada Gazette*; and the third is the **page number** in the *Canada Gazette*.

1947

January	January 24, 1948	Page 407
February	January 24, 1948	Page 415
March	January 24, 1948	Page 419
April	January 31, 1948	Page 558
May	January 31, 1948	Page 565
June	February 7, 1948	Page 662
July	February 14, 1948	Page 773
August	February 14, 1948	Page 779
September	February 21, 1948	Page 858
October	February 28, 1948	Page 925
November	April 3, 1948	Page 1363
December	May 1, 1948	Page 1740
Supplementary	September 18, 1948	Page 3532
Supplementary	July 23, 1949	Page 2951
Supplementary	December 10, 1949	Page 4673
Supplementary	March 25, 1950	Page 1041

1948

January	June 26, 1948	Page 2537
February	July 31, 1948	Page 2964
March	September 18, 1948	Page 3491
April	September 25, 1948	Page 3578
May	October 30, 1948	Page 4047
May erratum	November 13, 1948	Page 4264
June	November 13, 1948	Page 4244
July	December 11, 1948	Page 4625
July erratum	December 18, 1948	Page 4775
August	December 11, 1948	Page 4632
September	January 20, 1949	Page 312
October	February 5, 1949	Page 428
November	March 5, 1949	Page 788
December	April 16, 1949	Page 1367
Supplementary	September 24, 1949	Page 3664
Supplementary	March 25, 1950	Page 1041
Supplementary	May 13, 1950	Page 1674

1949

January	April 30, 1949	Page 1547
February	June 11, 1949	Page 2283
March	June 18, 1949	Page 2461
April	August 13, 1949	Page 3175
May	October 1, 1949	Page 3781
June	October 22, 1949	Page 4064
June erratum	January 21, 1950	Page 189
July	November 12, 1949	Page 4359
August	November 12, 1949	Page 4365
September	December 10, 1949	Page 4661
October	January 7, 1950	Page 18
November	February 18, 1950	Page 581
December	March 18, 1950	Page 951
Supplementary	March 25, 1950	Page 1042
Supplementary	May 6, 1950	Page 1581
Supplementary	May 13, 1950	Page 1674
Supplementary	December 16, 1950	Page 4339
Supplementary	May 5, 1951	Page 1279

1950

January	April 15, 1950	Page 1311
February	April 29, 1950	Page 1494
March	May 13, 1950	Page 1662
April	July 15, 1950	Page 2443
May	August 26, 1950	Page 2998
June	October 7, 1950	Page 3524
July	October 7, 1950	Page 3539
August	October 28, 1950	Page 3753
September	December 16, 1950	Page 4323
October	January 13, 1951	Page 105
November	February 10, 1951	Page 417
December	March 24, 1951	Page 875
Supplementary	May 13, 1950	Page 1674
Supplementary	December 16, 1950	Page 4339
Supplementary	February 10, 1951	Page 417
Supplementary	May 5, 1951	Page 1279

1951

January	May 5, 1951	Page 1264
January erratum	July 14, 1951	Page 1903
February	May 19, 1951	Page 1385
March	June 9, 1951	Page 1583
April	August 4, 1951	Page 2084

Chapter 13
Just passing through?

They were searching for new places to call home – and sometimes, their first choices were simply not good enough, so they moved on. While it's tempting to think that migration followed a simple one-way route, the reality is much more complex. Some Europeans have Canadian roots; William Coutts Keppel, one of the ancestors of Camilla, the Duchess of Cornwall, was premier of Canada West from 1854 to 1856.

Not everyone who came to Canada stayed here. Many people continued on to the United States after a few years or a few days. This was especially true in the latter half of the 19th century, when more people left Canada than arrived. Others came from the United States for a while, then headed south again.

Some arrivals from Europe remained in Canada long enough to get a sense of the place, or possibly to make more money than they could make at home, and then went back to Europe.

Sometimes it is hard to imagine why people would have gone back to their home countries, but it happened – there are records of people returning to the Soviet Union as well as to Nazi Germany. In some of these cases, men returned home so they could bring their families to Canada, but the borders were closed before they could return.

There are no records of people outbound from Canada, but there are inbound records from other countries that include information on people who moved there from Canada. Those records will be the only source to document the emigration from Canada – and in some cases, they will be the only evidence that the person was ever in Canada, because records of their arrival here might not be found.

United States

A variety of records are available for people who went to the United States from Canada. Some immigrants chose to use Canadian ports as they made their way to their intended destinations in the United States. The reason was generally either cost or convenience. They took whatever route would get them where they were going quickly and inexpensively.

Those routes might have been by land or by sea. Consider, for example, the American ports of Seattle and San Francisco. Seattle's passenger lists date from 1890; and San Francisco's from 1893. They include many ships arriving from Vancouver or Victoria. These lists are available on microfilm from the U.S. National Archives and Records Administration or from the Family History Library, as well as on the Ancestry.com website.

Also look for border crossings that might not be related to immigration. It is possible that your relatives were crossing for a vacation, or for business reasons, or to attend university. Every reference you can find will help to tell the story of that person. The databases available on the Internet make the research quick and easy.

Sometimes, immigrants took a route that would allow them to slip into the United States without scrutiny. In the 19th century, many people chose to use Canada as a way to enter the U.S. without going through the normal bureaucratic channels. The Canadian route was used so often – because European travel agents were promoting it – that the American government decided to act.

Under an agreement signed by the United States and Canada in 1894, immigrants destined for the U.S. were inspected and recorded by American immigrant inspectors at Canadian ports of entry. New arrivals in Canada who boarded trains for American destinations had to prove they were qualified to go.

Ship passenger manifests listing passengers who said they were going to the United States were filed in the Canadian Border District headquarters of the U.S. Immigration and Naturalization Service. This office was originally in Montreal, but later moved to St. Albans, Vermont.

Canadian ship passenger lists include pages identifying the passengers who stated their intention of going to the United States.

The information on these pages is not as complete as it is for the people planning to stay in Canada. The missing information can be found, however, in the records of their arrival on U.S. soil.

An extensive database of border crossings into the United States from 1895 to 1956 is on the Ancestry.com website.

San Francisco harbour during the California gold rush years in the 1850s

ON THE INTERNET:

<search.ancestry.com/iexec/?htx=List&dbid=1075>

The database is drawn from many different border crossings over six decades, so a wide variety of forms were used. The amount of information available for an individual in this database will vary. Generally, the database will include:

• Name
• Age
• Birth date
• Birthplace
• Gender
• Ethnicity/nationality
• Names of accompanying individuals
• Name of nearest relative or friend in former country
• Name of nearest relative or friend at destination

The database is linked to images of the manifests copied from National Archives and Records Administration microfilms. The original document might include additional information about an individual. Some records include a photograph of the individual or family.

It is also possible to use an index on microfilm, and the Soundex system of sorting names based on alphanumeric codes will make it relatively easy to find an entry.

The primary source for border entries from Canada is known as the St. Albans index, named for the district in Vermont that included, from 1895 to 1917, the entire Canadian border. From June 1917 to June 1927, the St. Albans district was reduced in size, covering only those crossing points east of the North Dakota-Montana state line. After July 1927, it included only those crossings east of Lake Ontario.

One St. Albans district index covers 1895 through 1924. It's on 401 rolls of microfilm, and is available through the U.S. National Archives and Records Administration and the Family History Library and its branches. A second St. Albans index, covering 1924 through 1952, is on 98 rolls of microfilm.

The U.S. archives, known as NARA, also has the passenger arrival records on 665 rolls of microfilm. Unlike regular passenger lists, which are arranged by port, date, and ship, these port records are arranged by month, port, and ship. As an example, to find a list for arrivals at Halifax in March 1910, first find the microfilm for 1910-March, then find Halifax within that month, then the ship within Halifax arrivals.

Each monthly collection of lists includes seaports and border ports on land.

Until about 1927, immigrant inspectors stationed at land border points of entry recorded each immigrant on a manifest list as they arrived at the port. At the end of each month, that list was forwarded to headquarters for filing.

Many people who arrived at Quebec City on their way to destinations in the United States took the train from their port of arrival to Windsor, Ontario. From there, they crossed into the U.S. at Detroit.

Researchers should look at the alphabetical card manifests of people arriving through Detroit. This collection covers the years 1906 through 1954 and is on 117 rolls of microfilm. It is available through the U.S. National Archives and Records Administration and the Family History Library. Another small collection – just six rolls of microfilm – covers ports on the Vermont border.

It is sometimes possible to use American resources to work back to an arrival in Canada. First, check for an American naturalization document, which will probably indicate a border crossing into the U.S. Then look for the border entry record, which, with luck, will indicate the port and date of arrival in Canada.

Be warned, though: Sometimes the naturalization record will list the port of arrival as Halifax or Quebec. That will not help you locate the border crossing from Canada.

United Kingdom

An extensive database of arrivals in the United Kingdom is on the Ancestry.co.uk website, part of the Ancestry.com network. It provides information on people from ports in Canada, as well as other ports outside of Europe, who entered the United Kingdom by ship from 1878 to 1960.

The database is an index to the Board of Trade's passenger lists and it is linked to colour images of the passenger lists from the collection of The National Archives. The lists date from 1878 to 1888 and 1890 to 1960, although many of the pre-1890 lists were destroyed in 1900 so coverage of the early years is not comprehensive.

There were separate lists for British (and Commonwealth) passengers and for alien passengers. Different form types were used over the years, so the amount of information collected for each passenger might not be consistent.

The index generally includes:
• Name of passenger
• Birth date or age
• Arrival date
• Port of departure
• Port of arrival (the final destination)
• Vessel name and shipping line

Some forms include the passenger's occupation and intended address in the United Kingdom, so always check the original passenger list. If the person was a tourist, the abbreviation T was used starting in the 1930s. (Of course, some people went to the United Kingdom as tourists before that – and you should check for their return to Canada as well.)

ON THE INTERNET:
<search.ancestry.co.uk/search/default.aspx?cat=40>

Chapter 14
Migration museums

I t is next to impossible to imagine life in an ancestral village without visiting that village, or one like it, and it is difficult to understand the immigration experience without visiting a port on either side of the water. At many migration ports, museums have been established to help provide a better sense of what it was like in the heady days when emigrants and immigrants were passing through.

These museums often have extensive collections of photographs that might help you see what it was like when your ancestor was there. Many have re-created shipboard accommodation to provide a better sense of life during the voyage. They also might have books about migration, documents and signs like those your ancestors would have seen, and original lists of people. Some museums have supporting material that explains how passengers were processed.

Many migration museums are members of an international organization, the Migration Museums Network.

ON THE INTERNET:

<www.migrationmuseums.org>

A visit to an immigration museum can be a key part of family history research. Here are some of the most important sites to consider.

Canada

Quebec City, Quebec

Grosse Île and the Irish Memorial National Historic Site of Canada commemorate the importance of immigration to Canada, particularly via the entry ports of Quebec City and Montreal, from the early 19th century to the First World War.

Grosse Île, in the middle of the St. Lawrence River, also marks the tragic events experienced by the Irish immigrants at this site, primarily during the typhoid epidemic of 1847. This national historic site is based on the role the island played from 1832 to 1937 as a quarantine station for the ports in Quebec, which were the main ports of arrival for immigrants to Canada.

Visitors may enjoy independent visits, guided tours, and walks along the forest trail.

Grosse Île is in the Île-aux-Grues archipelago, 48 kilometres east of Quebec City. Private ferry companies provide transport to Grosse Île for a fee. Ferries depart from the south shore of the St. Lawrence River near Quebec, from Quebec City, from Lévis, from Sainte-Anne-de-Beaupré, and from Île d'Orléans. Boat services are offered from mid-May to mid-October.

ON THE INTERNET:

<www.pc.gc.ca/eng/lhn-nhs/qc/grosseile/index.aspx>

Halifax, Nova Scotia

Immigrants arrived in Canada through Halifax for many years. The port's museum – Pier 21, Canada's Immigration Museum – has a special focus on the 20th century, to be more precise, on 1928 and later.

It is designed to celebrate and share the immigration experience by honouring the unique stories of immigration throughout history. It also pays tribute to 1.5 million immigrants, war brides, displaced people, evacuee children, and Canadian military personnel who passed through Pier 21 between its opening in 1928 and 1971.

With a goal of telling the story of all immigration to Canada, Pier 21 includes the broader story of nation-building. Plans are to showcase exhibits highlighting the early beginnings of Canada (including first contact) and immigration from 1867 to the present.

Pier 21 is the last Canadian immigration shed still standing.

Address:

1055 Marginal Rd.

Halifax, Nova Scotia B3H 4P6

Canada

ON THE INTERNET:

<www.pier21.ca>

A passenger liner at Pier 21 in Halifax, which is now home to Canada's most important immigration museum

Saint John, New Brunswick

The New Brunswick Museum (Musée de Nouveau-Brunswick) has an exhibit on Saint John's shipbuilding industry. Entitled Wind, Wood and Sail, it deals with the ships built during the 19th century. There is also a display on New Brunswick's marine industry.

Address:
Market Square
Saint John, New Brunswick E2L 4Z6
Canada
ON THE INTERNET:
<www.nbm-mnb.ca>

Vancouver, British Columbia
The Vancouver Maritime Museum is Canada's principal maritime museum on the Pacific Ocean, and is located in the heart of Canada's greatest ports at the gateway to the Pacific Rim. Its exhibits deal with maritime history, art, culture, industry, and technology. There is also an extensive library.
Address:
1905 Ogden Ave.
Vancouver, British Columbia V6J 1A3
Canada
ON THE INTERNET:
<www.vancouvermaritimemuseum.com>

Victoria, British Columbia
The Maritime Museum of British Columbia has exhibits dealing with exploration, pirates, shipbuilding, whaling and fishing, shipwrecks, and much more. There are also special temporary exhibits.
Address:
28 Bastion Square
Victoria, British Columbia V8W 1H9
Canada
ON THE INTERNET:
<mmbc.bc.ca>

United States

New York City
The Ellis Island Immigration Museum, on a small island in New York Harbor, is part of the Statue of Liberty National Monument and is one of the country's most popular historic sites. The American Family Immigration History Center at Ellis Island provides visitors with advanced computer and multimedia technology, printed materials, and professional assistance for investigating immigration history, family documentation, and for genealogical exploration.

From 1892 to 1954, more than 12 million immigrants entered the United States through Ellis Island. Through the years, this gateway to the new world was enlarged from its original 3.3 acres to 27.5 acres, mostly by landfill obtained from ships' ballast and possibly excess earth from the construction of the New York City subway system.

The Ellis Island Immigration Museum on Ellis Island and the Statue of Liberty on Liberty Island are in Lower New York Harbor, about two kilometres from Lower Manhattan. Liberty and Ellis Islands are accessible by ferry service only. Ferries are operated by Statue Cruises from New York and New Jersey. One round-trip ferry ticket includes visits to both islands.

ON THE INTERNET:
<www.nps.gov/elis/index.htm>

England

London

The National Maritime Museum at Greenwich is designed to illustrate the importance of the sea, ships, time, and the stars and their relationship with people. The museum was formally established by an Act of Parliament in 1934 and was opened to the public by King George VI in 1937. Its collections include about 2.5 million items, many on loan to museums elsewhere in Britain.

The public galleries display a thematically arranged selection and the remainder are accessible for public interest and research in various ways. Most of the museum's small-boat collection is on display at the National Maritime Museum, Cornwall, at Falmouth.

Address:
Romney Road, Greenwich
London SE10 9NF
England
ON THE INTERNET:
<www.nmm.ac.uk>

The museum called 19 Princelet Street in the Spitalfields district of London is an unrestored Huguenot master silk weaver's home. The frontage conceals a rare surviving synagogue built over its garden. The building is usually closed to the public so the charity that owns it can raise funds for repair work. The goal is to create Britain's first museum celebrating immigration and settlement. In the meantime, be sure to check for opening times.

Address:
19 Princelet St.
London E1 6QH
England
ON THE INTERNET:
<www.19princeletstreet.org.uk>

Liverpool

Merseyside Maritime Museum in Liverpool has a gallery that is designed to tell the story of the nine million people who left Europe through Liverpool between 1830 and 1930. At the time, it was the busiest emigration port in the world. Most of those who sailed from Liverpool were going to Canada, the United States, Australia, or New Zealand.

The gallery tells of the emigrants, the impact on Liverpool and the businesses

Naval reserve squadron of sloops moored alongside 'C' block of warehouses in the Albert Dock in the mid 1930s

Museum websites provide background information

that flourished as a result of the emigration, life on board the sailing vessels, the growth of major steamship companies, the great liners, and the waning years of the immigration era.

Address:
Albert Dock
Liverpool
L3 4AQ
England
ON THE INTERNET:
<www.liverpoolmuseums.org.uk/maritime>

Republic of Ireland

Cobh, County Cork

The Cobh Heritage Centre in County Cork traces the evolution of maritime traffic to and from Cobh – from the early coffin ships to the luxurious trans-Atlantic liners of today. The Deepwater Quay, beside the Cobh Heritage Centre, is the berthing dock for about 30 luxury liners every year.

It was also the departure point for millions of emigrants. From 1848 to 1950 more than six million adults and children emigrated from Ireland. More than 2.5 million departed from Cobh, making it the single most important port of emigration on the island.

Address:
Cobh, County Cork
Republic of Ireland
ON THE INTERNET:
<www.cobhheritage.com>

New Ross, County Wexford

The Dunbrody Visitor Experience offers insights into the Great Famine and the mass exodus of many people to America. It includes a nine-minute audio-visual presentation that gives the historic background to the famine and the emigration, as well as a chance to board a replica of one of the ships that carried the Irish across the Atlantic Ocean.

A ticket, issued as if it were 1849, allocates space and food rations for the voyage. The ship itself is fitted out exactly as it would be for a voyage. Visitors will encounter actors, playing the role of emigrants, in their cramped quarters with their meagre possessions.

The tour lasts about 50 minutes.

Address:
New Ross, County Wexford
Republic of Ireland
ON THE INTERNET:
<www.dunbrody.com>

Cannaghanally, County Sligo

Culkin's Emigration Museum in Cannaghanally, County Sligo, was built on the site of Daniel Culkin's Shipping and Emigration Agency, which was started in the 19th century and operated until the 1930s. The purpose-built museum houses a wide variety of artifacts as well as the original office, which has been restored and housed within the building.

Telephone +353 (0)96 47 152

Address:

Cannaghanally, Dromore West

County Sligo

Republic of Ireland

Strokestown, County Roscommon

The Famine Museum in Strokestown Park, County Roscommon, is designed to commemorate the history of the Great Famine of the 1840s. The famine contributed to a huge migration out of Ireland, with many of the emigrants heading to Canada.

More than two million people – almost one-quarter of the entire population – either died or emigrated.

The museum tells part of the story through documents discovered in the office that dealt with the administration of the estate during the tenure of the Mahon family.

This collection includes many haunting pleas from starving tenants on the estate and the responses they received.

Address:

Strokestown Park, Strokestown

County Roscommon

Republic of Ireland

ON THE INTERNET:

<www.strokestownpark.ie/museum.html>

Northern Ireland

Omagh, County Tyrone

Ulster American Folk Park in Omagh, County Tyrone, offers the story of Irish emigration from the thatched cottages of Ulster to a full-scale emigrant sailing ship to the log cabins of the North American frontier.

There is also an array of costumed characters with traditional crafts to show, tales to tell, and food to share.

Address:

2 Mellon Rd., Castletown, Omagh

County Tyrone BT78 5QU

Northern Ireland

ON THE INTERNET:

<www.nmni.com/uafp>

Rotterdam in 1847

The Netherlands

Rotterdam

The Maritime Museum Rotterdam (Maritiem Museum Rotterdam) is located in the heart of Rotterdam. Founded in 1874, it is the oldest maritime museum in the Netherlands and is considered to be one of the top museums of its kind in the entire world. It includes an extensive library with a wealth of information about the history of shipbuilding and shipping. The old Holland America Line (Holland Amerikalijn) piers are across the Erasmus Bridge from the museum.

Address:

Leuvehaven 1

3011 EA Rotterdam

The Netherlands

ON THE INTERNET:

<www.maritiemmuseum.nl>

France

Tourouvre

This community in Basse-Normandie is home to the Museum of French Emigration to Canada, part of Les Muséales de Tourouvre.

It has been estimated that about 80 families from this community went to New France in the 17th century, and the theory is that millions of North Americans could trace their roots to here. One notable Canadian with ancestry in Tourouvre is singer Céline Dion.

The Museum of French Emigration to Canada continues the work of the Perche Emigration Museum, a meeting point and place of Franco-Canadian genealogical research set up in 1987. It was created by the Communauté de Communes du Haut-Perche, with the help of the department of the Orne, the Basse-Normandie region, the French state, the European Union, and the Canadian government.

The museum is about two hours by car west of Paris.

Address:

15 Rue Mondrel

Tourouvre

France

ON THE INTERNET:

<www.musealesdetourouvre.com/en/the-french-emigration-to-canada-centre.html>

Norway

Åkershagan

The Norwegian Emigrant Museum -- Norsk Utvandrermuseum -- is located in Åkershagan, 2312 Ottestad, near Hamar, north of Oslo. It is an open-air museum designed to illustrate the life led by Norwegian emigrants to the American Midwest in the 1880s, the time of the greatest emigration from Norway. The buildings in the museum represent the first houses and barns put up by Norwegian emigrants in the United States.

Address:

Åkershagan, 2312 Ottestad

Norway

ON THE INTERNET:

<www.museumsnett.no/emigrantmuseum/index_en.html>

Germany

Bremerhaven

The German Emigration Centre Bremerhaven (Deutsches Auswandererhaus Bremerhaven) is designed to provide the visitor with the entire emigration experience, including departure at the crack of dawn, crossing the Atlantic on a steamship or ocean liner, and arriving at Ellis Island, New York.

Visitors start in a replica of the waiting hall where emigrants began their journey decades ago. Then they move to the wharf, where family members said their goodbyes. After that, they enter a vessel to see the accommodations offered to people making their way to the New World.

The final steps re-create the first experiences at Ellis Island.

Address:

Columbusstrasse 65

27568 Bremerhaven

Germany

ON THE INTERNET:

<www.dah-bremerhaven.de>

Hamburg

BallinStadt, the Emigration Museum Hamburg, is on the site of the emigration halls that were built a century ago. The museum is in three re-erected buildings on Veddel Island.

A century ago, the emigration halls in Hamburg were the last stop in Europe for many emigrants on their way to America. They became known as the "port of dreams," reflecting the optimism of the people leaving Europe.

The BallinStadt is named after Albert Ballin, the president of the shipping company HAPAG, one of the largest companies helping to move Europeans to North America.

A tour through BallinStadt begins with videos telling the story of emigration from 1850 until 1938.

The museum deals with the operation of the port and the emigration process, and tries to explain why people would have chosen to head halfway around the world to make a new home.

Address:
Veddeler Bogen 2
20539 Hamburg
Germany
ON THE INTERNET:
<www.ballinstadt.net>

The heritage village in Kommern, Germany, includes dozens of buildings from around the North Rhine region

Kommern

Many countries in Europe have outdoor heritage parks, with collections of old buildings and re-created streets.

One of note in Germany is the Rhineland Open-Air Museum (Rheinisches Freilichtmuseum) in Kommern, southwest of Cologne. It has a permanent exhibition entitled Brave New World: Rhinelanders Conquer America. The exhibition is based on the diaries of Johannes Herbergs of Wuppertal-Ronsdorf, who went to the New World in the 18th century.

It includes information on Germany in the 18th and 19th centuries, travel routes, and arrival in the United States. The exhibition includes a recreation of a Philadelphia street scene.

Address:
Auf dem Kahlenbusch
D-53894 Mechernich-Kommern
Germany
ON THE INTERNET:

Czech Republic

Kojákovice

The Kojákovice Peasant and Emigration Museum (Venkovské muzeum Kojákovice) in the southern part of the Czech Republic tells how people lived and worked in rural South Bohemia. All the displays are based upon the histories and stories of persons from Kojákovice and its surroundings.

Address:
Jílovice-Kojákovice 80
Kojákovice
Czech Republic
ON THE INTERNET:
<www.czechemigrationmuseum.com>

Italy

Gualdo Tadino

The Regional Museum of Emigration – Museo Regionale Dell'Emigrazione Pietro Conti – is in the Umbria region. It is arranged on three levels. One shows the arrivals abroad, the second the travels to reach foreign lands, and the third the historical reasons for emigration.

Address:
Palazzo del Podestà
06023 Gualdo Tadino
Perugia
Italy
ON THE INTERNET:
<www.emigrazione.it>

San Marino

The history of emigration from the tiny republic of San Marino is on display in the ancient Cloister of Santa Chiara house. The displays are in the Museum of the Emigrant and the Permanent Study Centre on Emigration.

Address:
Contrada Ombrelli, 24
San Marino Città
ON THE INTERNET:
<www.sanmarinosite.com/eng/museoemigrante.html>

Portugal

Fafe

The Museum of Emigration and the Communities – Museu da Emigração e das Comunidades – in Fafe, northern Portugal, deals with emigration but has a focus on Brazil and other European countries.

Address:

Rua Major Miguel Ferreira

P - 4820-276 Fafe

Portugal

ON THE INTERNET:

<www.museu-emigrantes.org>

Spain

Sant Adrià de Besòs

The Museum of the History of Immigration in Catalonia – Museo de Historia de la Inmigración de Cataluña – is in Sant Adrià de Besòs, a town on the mouth of the river Besòs, between the city of Barcelona and the towns of Santa Coloma de Gramenet and Badalona. It includes an old farmhouse as well as a new building that contains the museum.

Address:

Masia de Can Serra

Ctra. de Mataró, 124

08930 Sant Adrià de Besòs

Barcelona

Spain

ON THE INTERNET:

<www.mhic.net>

In the planning stage

Migration museums are being planned in several countries. Someday, if all goes well, we will see them in Zagreb, Croatia; Paris, France; Winterthur, Switzerland, and other centres. Some of these exist already on the Internet.

The Pacific Coast Immigration Museum in San Francisco deals with people arriving in the western United States. Some of the information might be applicable to Canada's West Coast.

Address:

ON THE INTERNET:

<pacificcoastimmigration.org>

The Scottish Emigration Museum is an ambitious museums, libraries, and archives partnership project that aims to provide the global community with a unique, authoritative, and inspirational collection of Scottish emigration-related material in partnership with key diaspora countries.

Address:

ON THE INTERNET:

Chapter 15
Additional sources

F amily historians should not think their search is complete when they find their relatives in ship passenger lists. There are other sources that should be consulted. Each additional source could help build understanding of the ancestor, and might confirm information that has been passed down through the years.

At times, something other than a passenger list might be the only source with the information you are looking for. Sometimes, information will not advance your research, but will be nice to have on hand.

Sources to check include the 1940 registration of Canadians, the Li-Ra-Ma collection of Russian documents, newspapers, printed passenger lists, and other miscellaneous documents. Items such as books and photographs might be found in libraries and archives.

1940 national registration

After the Second World War began in 1939, the Canadian government passed legislation requiring the registration of all persons aged 16 or older. The rules applied to everyone, whether born in Canada or elsewhere, whether naturalized or not.

The first such registration took place in 1940, under the authority of the National Resources Mobilization Act and the War Measures Act.

This series of registration forms is available to researchers through Statistics Canada, and may provide valuable information to help determine when a person came to Canada.

The forms include:
- Name
- Address
- Age
- Date of birth
- Conjugal status
- Dependents
- Country of birth (persons registered and parents only)
- Nationality
- Year of naturalization (if applicable)
- Year of immigration (if applicable)
- Racial origin
- Languages
- Education
- General health

- Class of occupation
- Occupation or craft
- Employment status
- Work experience by type
- Mechanical or other abilities
- Latent skills
- Wartime circumstances
- Previous military service

The National Registration File was continued annually until 1946, but only the one from 1940 is open to researchers.

These forms cannot be searched by individuals; that must be done by Statistics Canada personnel. They are filed geographically, by federal electoral district and polling division. That means a researcher must provide accurate information on where the person lived in 1940.

Also, information cannot be disclosed until the subject has been dead for 20 years, which means Statistics Canada will require proof of the death. A death certificate is preferable, but any document that indicates the date of death, for example an obituary notice, is acceptable.

The cost of the search is $45.00 (plus GST) payable to Statistics Canada. The money will be refunded if the search is not successful.

Send postal inquiries to:
Census Pension Searches Unit
Census Operations Division
Statistics Canada
B1E-34 Jean Talon Building
Tunney's Pasture
Ottawa, Ontario K1A 0T6
ON THE INTERNET:
<www.statcan.gc.ca/bsolc/olc-cel/olc-cel?catno=93C0006&lang=eng>

The Li-Ra-Ma collection of Russian documents

After the Communists took control of Russia in the revolution of 1917, the governments of Canada and the United States grabbed the files held by the Russian consuls here. The files were stored in the United States until about 1980, when they were microfilmed and made available to researchers.

There were three Russian consuls in Canada at the time of the revolution in 1917: Serge Likachev in Montreal, Constantine Ragosine in Vancouver, and Harry Mathers in Halifax. Their files have become known as the Li-Ra-Ma – short for Likachev-Ragosine-Mathers – collection.

The Li-Ra-Ma collection is available on the Library and Archives Canada website, as well as on 55 microfilm rolls plus a nominal index.

ON THE INTERNET:
<www.collectionscanada.gc.ca/databases/li-ra-ma/index-e.html>

For genealogists, the key element in the Li-Ra-Ma collection is the

Passport/Identity Papers series, which consists of about 11,400 files on Russian and East European immigrants who settled in Canada in the early years of the 20th century.

These files were compiled between 1898 and 1922. Most of the people in the files are Jews, but there are also forms filled out by Ukrainians, Poles, Finns, and Germans.

The files include documents such as passport applications, birth certificates, and background questionnaires. Most of the records are in Russian Cyrillic.

The National Archives and Records Administration holds the files for the seven consuls in the U.S. The file is known as Russian Consular Records. They are available on microfilm through the Family History Library.

An index is available on microfiche from:

Avotaynu
PO Box 99
Bergenfield, New Jersey 07621
United States
ON THE INTERNET:

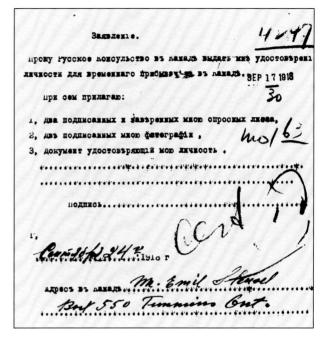

A sample from the Li-Ra-Ma forms

Newspapers

Daily newspapers published in port cities often carried reports on ship arrivals. These stories usually included the names of dignitaries and business people on board, but not immigrants.

They are still worth checking, however, because they might contain information about the voyage that would not be available otherwise. Besides, if a famous person was also on the ship that brought your family to North America, is that not worth a note in the family history?

If your relatives came to Canada before the start of passenger lists at that port, newspaper accounts might be the only source of information on the voyage. Be warned that coverage was not consistent, and in the 20th century, when ships were arriving every few days, the arrival of more immigrants was not deemed as newsworthy as it once had been.

Travellers were likely to be included in the report if they were business people, or entertainers, or diplomats, or Canadian residents returning from vacation. It was rare for a newspaper to make note of a person who did not speak English, or who was arriving in anything below cabin class. And even when a person is mentioned, the reference often includes nothing more than the name.

Newspapers will also contain valuable information about voyages that failed to reach their destinations. News reports on ships that sank often had the names of at least some of the people who died.

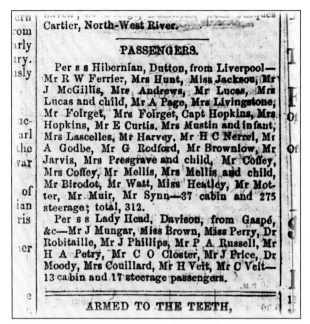

Cartier, North-West River.

PASSENGERS.

Per s s Hibernian, Dutton, from Liverpool— Mr R W Ferrier, Mrs Hunt, Miss Jackson, Mr J McGillis, Mrs Andrews, Mr Lucas, Mrs Lucas and child, Mr A Page, Mrs Livingstone, Mr Foirget, Mrs Foirget, Capt Hopkins, Mrs Hopkins, Mr E Curtis, Mrs Mustin and infant, Mrs Lascelles, Mr Harvey, Mr H C Nerrel, Mr A Godbe, Mr G Redford, Mr Brownlow, Mr Jarvis, Mrs Presgrave and child, Mr Coffey, Mrs Coffey, Mr Mellis, Mrs Mellis and child, Mr Birodot, Mr Watt, Miss Heatley, Mr Motter, Mr Muir, Mr Synn—37 cabin and 275 steerage; total, 312.

Per s s Lady Head, Davison, from Gaspé, &c—Mr J Mungar, Miss Brown, Miss Perry, Dr Robitaille, Mr J Phillips, Mr P A Russell, Mr H A Petry, Mr C O Closter, Mr J Price, Dr Moody, Mrs Couillard, Mr H Veit, Mr C Veit— 13 cabin and 17 steerage passengers.

ARMED TO THE TEETH,

Newspaper accounts, such as this one from Quebec City, provide information on ships and passengers

Using newspapers to complement immigration research is not a new idea. Historical researchers have been using them for years.

Newspapers from the 1840s offer eyewitness accounts of the horrors of the Grosse Île quarantine station, where thousands of new arrivals from Ireland died without ever setting foot on the Canadian mainland. These contemporary reports even help researchers understand the conditions faced by ancestors who made it through Grosse Île to start a new life in Canada.

Newspaper reports have been used to help re-create early San Francisco passenger lists, which were lost in a fire in 1940. Tens of thousands of names of arrivals at San Francisco have been gathered from newspapers from that city and throughout the United States. In the late 19th century, about half of the ships arriving at San Francisco were from Victoria, so there is a strong Canadian connection to those missing lists.

Every port city had newspapers that could be checked.

Quebec City newspapers included the *Daily Mercury*, the *Daily Telegraph*, the *Gazette* and the *Chronicle-Telegraph*, all in English. (The *Chronicle-Telegraph* can trace its roots to the Quebec City *Gazette* that was first published in 1864.) Also look for *Le Soleil*, in French.

In Montreal, the *Gazette* has been published continuously since 1778. It was started as a French-language newspaper, became bilingual, and was converted to English-only in 1822. Also look for the *Star* and the *Herald* (both in English) and *Le Devoir* and *Le Canadien* (both in French).

The first newspaper in Halifax was published in 1752, and dozens of titles have been published there over the years. Look for the *British Colonist*, the *Herald*, the *Chronicle*, the *Chronicle-Herald*, the *Daily Star*, the *Evening Mail*, the *Mail-Star*, and others.

Saint John, New Brunswick, also had a variety of newspapers to choose from, starting with the *Gazette* in 1783. Look for the *Daily Evening News*, the *Globe*, the *Morning Telegraph*, and the *Telegraph-Journal*.

In North Sydney, Nova Scotia, try the *Herald*.

Newspapers were published in British Columbia starting in 1858. Early newspapers in Victoria included the *Daily Colonist* and the *Victoria Daily Times*. They covered the arrival of passenger ships, and recorded the names of many of the passengers. In Vancouver, look for the *Daily News-Advertiser*, the *Province*, and the *Sun*.

Back issues of Victoria's *Daily Colonist* from 1858 to 1910 have been digitized and placed online. That project will make it easier to find arrivals in Victoria.

ON THE INTERNET:

<www.britishcolonist.ca>

Leona Taylor has extracted the names of ship passengers from 19th-century issues of the *Daily Colonist*. Her work is on the Victoria's Victoria website, which is run by the University of Victoria.

ON THE INTERNET:
<web.uvic.ca/vv>

Other old newspapers, including the Montreal *Gazette* and the Halifax *British Colonist*, are available on the Google news archive site. Search by keyword, and specify a likely source to get the most hits.

ON THE INTERNET:
<news.google.com/archivesearch>

Printed passenger lists and other documents

Once all of the normal sources of information have been exhausted, researchers can turn to the collector's marketplace to find items that might be of interest.

Printed passenger lists, for example, are available for many of the vessels that crossed the oceans in the 20th century. There's a catch, though – these lists generally include only passengers who were tourists or returning Canadians. Most immigrants travelled in steerage, which was usually third class.

The Canadian Pacific ship Montclare, which sailed from Antwerp to Quebec City in June 1927, is a good example. The printed passenger list has 171 people – only about 15 per cent of the number on board.

The cover of a Canadian Pacific passenger list

Beyond that, even when passengers are mentioned in these lists, all that was included was their names. As a result, they won't offer much information on a family.

There are times, though, when they can help. For post-1935 arrivals, a printed passenger list might confirm the date of arrival of an immigrant. And they can always provide a bit of colour, a tangible souvenir of a voyage.

It's also possible to find ship menus; again, these are for the better classes, not the ones used by the typical immigrant. They can, however, give a researcher a better sense of what it was like aboard a ship.

The easiest item to find will usually be a postcard, because these were not specific to a single voyage. Photographs of ships are a worthwhile addition to a family history project. Be careful, however, with the time frame; sometimes, ship lines used the same name for several vessels over the years, so there is a danger that you will find a postcard of the wrong one.

Also, look for guides to emigration or settlement. While these will not mention your ancestor by name, they will provide information that will make it easier for you to understand how he or she got from one place to another, the cost of the journey, and the conditions faced on arrival. Dozens of these guides were printed over the years. Some have been reprinted. An example is William Cattermole's *Emigration: The Advantages of Emigration to Canada*, which was first printed in 1831 in London, England, but reprinted in Toronto in 1970. Another, printed in Glasgow in 1821 and reprinted in Ottawa in 1978, has the delightful title *A Narrative of the Rise and Progress of Emigration, From the Counties of Lanark and Renfrew, to the New Settlements in Upper Canada, on Government Grant; Comprising the Proceedings of the Glasgow Committee for Directing the Affairs and Embarkation of the Societies*. That title was followed by a subtitle: *With a Map of the Townships, Designs for Cottages, and a Plan of the Ship Earl of Buckinghamshire, also, Interesting Letters From the Settlements.*

There were also guides printed in Canada that would help the new arrivals get to their destinations. Canadian Pacific timetables were published and can be found in original form and on microfiche in some libraries, as well as through antiquarian booksellers. Another publication of note is *Waghorn's Guide*, a comprehensive monthly reference to railway timetables, homestead information, and other items of interest to settlers. It was printed in Winnipeg.

A "public domain only" search for "emigrants guide" on Google Books will show several guides of interest, including an 1820 one by Charles Stuart and one from 1833 by Francis A. Evans.

Waghorn's Guide, published in Winnipeg, gave settlers valuable information

ON THE INTERNET:

<books.google.ca>

If you would like to buy your own copy of one of these items, the best sources include:

• eBay. The online auction site offers a steady supply of ship-related material, including everything from passenger lists and menus to ashtrays.

ON THE INTERNET:

<www.ebay.ca>

• Antiquarian bookstores. Several in Canada specialize in ephemera from the passenger-ship era. Again, check the Internet for sites such as Abebooks – Advanced Book Exchange.

ON THE INTERNET:

<www.abebooks.com>

• Collector organizations. An Internet search will probably help you determine the ones most likely to be of interest.

ON THE INTERNET:

<www.google.ca>

Dictionaries define "ephemera" as something without lasting significance, or a collectible with no lasting value, or printed matter of only passing interest. A genealogist, however, may find ephemera to be of great permanent value.

Libraries and archives

A vast amount of information is available on the immigration experience, primarily through hundreds of books that have been written about it in the past century and a half. These books cover just about every aspect of immigration – from the stories of individuals, to ships, to ports, to ethnic groups. A comprehensive bibliography is included in this book.

To find books of interest, start with public libraries, university libraries, and genealogical society libraries. Most of them have library catalogues online, so you can search by author, title, or keyword to find what you need.

Also search websites such as Abebooks and Amazon for titles that might help.

These books might provide context that will make it easier for you to understand the conditions and challenges faced by your ancestor. You might even find information that relates directly to your ancestor, such as a description of what it was like at the Grosse Île quarantine station.

One of the federal government's annual guides to encourage settlement on the Prairies

Archives will often have the key books relevant to that area, plus other documents relating to immigration and settlement of the region. Again, these references will make it easier for you to understand what your ancestor experienced.

The amount of information available has risen sharply in the past few years, and there is more on the way. Stay up to date! Check the top sources – Library and Archives Canada, FamilySearch, and Ancestry.ca – on a regular basis.

ON THE INTERNET:

<www.collectionscanada.gc.ca/databases/index-e.html>

<www.familysearch.org>

<www.ancestry.ca>

Other major sites might emerge in the years to come. The CanGenealogy website has up-to-date links that will lead to the best sources for your research.

ON THE INTERNET:

<www.cangenealogy.com>

More than just dates and names

Ultimately, whether your relatives arrived in Canada on a Tuesday or a Wednesday is probably not as important as the conditions that they faced in the old country, on the ship, and on arrival at a port in Canada. Learning more about the context will help you develop a more complete view of the forces that shaped your ancestor's life and decisions.

In other words – even if you have found your person in a passenger list, do not stop. There is more information to be uncovered!

Illustrations

Front cover: Liverpool landing stage, from a stereoscopic card, author's collection
Halifax arrival document, author's collection

Title page: Quebec *Mercury*, 1865

Page 1: *Illustrated London News*, July 6, 1850
Page 2: *Illustrated London News*, Dec. 22, 1849
Page 3: *Illustrated London News*, July 6, 1850
Page 4: *Times Colonist* collection, Victoria, B.C.
Page 6: *Times Colonist* collection, Victoria, B.C.
Page 7: *Times Colonist* collection, Victoria, B.C.
Page 8: Author's collection
Page 9: *Illustrated London News*, May 10, 1851
Page 10: *Illustrated London News*, May 10, 1851
Page 11: Postcard, author's collection
Page 12: London *Times*, May 24, 1910
Page 15: *Illustrated London News*, Jan. 30, 1847
Page 18: *Times Colonist* collection, Victoria, B.C.
Page 19: *Times Colonist* collection, Victoria, B.C.
Page 20: Author's collection
Page 21: Sherri Robinson collection
Page 22: *Times Colonist* collection, Victoria, B.C.
Page 23: Library and Archives Canada
microfilm T-6435
Page 24: <www.ancestry.ca>
Page 27: Library and Archives Canada microfilm T-481
Page 28: Postcard, author's collection
Page 29: Library and Archives Canada
microfilm T-15145
Page 30: Library and Archives Canada
microfilm T-14731
Page 31: Library and Archives Canada
microfilm T-14731
Page 33: *Illustrated London News*, May 1, 1869
Page 34: London *Times*, March 11, 1857
Page 37: *Illustrated London News*, Nov. 17, 1883
Page 39: *Illustrated London News*, May 1, 1869
Page 40: Map by the author
Page 41: Montreal *Gazette*, May 1865
Page 43: *Times Colonist* collection, Victoria, B.C.
Page 45: (top) *Canada Descriptive Atlas*, 1925
Page 45: (bottom) Halifax *Herald*, August 1880
Page 46: *Illustrated London News*, May 12, 1866

Page 47: Author's collection
Page 58: Map by the author
Page 59: *Times Colonist* collection, Victoria, B.C.
Page 60: *Times Colonist* collection, Victoria, B.C.
Page 61: *Times Colonist* collection, Victoria, B.C.
Page 62: *Times Colonist* collection, Victoria, B.C.
Page 63: Postcard, author's collection
Page 65: *Times Colonist* collection, Victoria, B.C.
Page 66: Map by the author
Page 67: *Times Colonist* collection, Victoria, B.C.
Page 69: Map by the author
Page 70: Map by the author
Page 80: *Times Colonist* collection, Victoria, B.C.
Page 81: *Times Colonist* collection, Victoria, B.C.
Page 83: Photograph by the author, 2008
Page 84: Map by the author
Page 86: <www.ancestorsonboard.com>;
image from The National Archives
Page 93: Postcard, author's collection
Page 96: Library and Archives Canada
microfilm C-10606
Page 103: *Times Colonist* collection, Victoria, B.C.
Page 107: Library and Archives Canada
microfilm C-7854
Page 118: *Canada Gazette*, June 27, 1925
Page 127: *Illustrated London News*, Nov. 17, 1849
Page 131: Pier 21 Museum, Halifax
Page 134: <www.liverpoolmuseums.org.uk/mar-
itime/albertdock/>
Page 136: *Illustrated London News*, April 10, 1847
Page 138: Photograph by the author, 2007
Page 143: Library and Archives Canada
microfilm M-7647
Page 144: Quebec *Mercury*, June 19, 1865
Page 145: Author's collection
Page 146: Author's collection
Page 147: Author's collection

Photo of the author: Debra Brash

Back cover: Bottom, author's collection
Top, used with permission of the
Pier 21 Museum, Halifax, Nova Scotia

Bibliography

Abella, Irving. *A Coat of Many Colours: Two Centuries of Jewish Life in Canada*. Toronto: Key Porter Books, 1999.

Abella, Irving and Troper, Harold. *None Is Too Many: Canada and the Jews of Europe 1933-1948*. Toronto: Random House, 1983.

Abu-Laban, Baha. *An Olive Branch on the Family Tree: The Arabs in Canada*. Toronto: McClelland and Stewart, 1980.

Adachi, Ken. *The Enemy That Never Was: A History of the Japanese Canadians*. Toronto: McClelland and Stewart, 1976.

Amstatter, Andrew. *Tomslake: History of Sudeten Germans in Canada*. Saanichton, B.C.: Hancock House, 1978.

Anuta, Michael J. *Ships of Our Ancestors*. Baltimore: Genealogical Publishing Co., 1999.

Avery, Donald. *Reluctant Host: Canada's Response to Immigrant Workers, 1896-1994*. Toronto: McClelland and Stewart, 1995.

Bagnell, Kenneth. *The Little Immigrants: The Orphans Who Came to Canada*. Toronto: Dundurn Press, 2001.

Baines, Dudley. *Emigration From Europe 1815-1930*. Cambridge, England: Cambridge University Press, 1991.

Basran, Gurcharn S. and Bolaria, B. Singh. *The Sikhs in Canada: Migration, Race, Class, and Gender*. Toronto: Oxford University Press, 2004.

Belkin, Simon. *Through Narrow Gates: A Review of Jewish Immigration, Colonization and Immigrant Aid Work in Canada (1840-1940)*. Toronto: Canadian Jewish Congress and Jewish Colonization Association, 1966.

Bender, Henninh. *Danish Emigration to Canada*. Aalborg: Danes Worldwide Archives, 1991.

Berton, Pierre. *The Promised Land: Settling the West 1896-1914*. Toronto: McClelland and Stewart, 1984.

Bowen, Lynne. *Muddling Through: The Remarkable Story of the Barr Colonists*. Vancouver: Greystone Books, 1992.

Broadfoot, Barry. *The Immigrant Years: From Europe to Canada 1945-1967*. Vancouver: Douglas and McIntyre, 1986.

Brown, Robert Craig and Cook, Ramsay. *Canada 1896-1921: A Nation Transformed*. Toronto: McClelland and Stewart, 1974.

Brye, David L., ed. *European Immigration and Ethnicity in the United States and Canada: A Historical Bibliography*. Santa Barbara, California: American Bibliographical Center, 1983.

Bumsted, J.M. *The Peoples of Canada*. Oxford: Oxford University Press, 1992.

Burnet, Jean and Palmer, Howard. *Coming Canadians: An Introduction to the History of Canada's Peoples*, Toronto: McClelland and Stewart, 1988.

Cameron, Ian Arthur. *Quarantine: What Is Old Is New: Halifax and the Lawlor's Island Quarantine Station 1866-1938*. Halifax: New World, 2007.

Cameron, Wendy and Maude, Mary McDougall. *Assisting Emigration to Upper Canada: The Petworth Project, 1832-1837*. Montreal: McGill-Queen's University Press, 2000.

Cameron, Wendy, Haines, Sheila and Maude, Mary McDougall. *English Immigrant Voices: Labourers' Letters From Upper Canada in the 1830s*. Montreal: McGill-Queen's University Press, 2001.

Campey, Lucille H. *A Very Fine Class of Immigrants: Prince Edward Island's Scottish Pioneers 1770-1850*. Toronto: Dundurn Press, 2007.

Campey, Lucille H. *An Unstoppable Force: The Scottish Exodus to Canada*. Toronto: Dundurn Press, 2008.

Canada Gazette. 1915-1951. Weekly publication of the Government of Canada, Ottawa.

Carrothers, W.A. *Emigration From the British Isles, With Special Reference to the Developments of the Overseas Dominions*. London: P.S. King and Son, Ltd., 1929.

Catermole, Wm. *Emigration: The Advantages of Emigration to Canada*. 1831; reprint, Toronto: Coles Canadian Collection, 1970.

Conrad, Margaret and Finkel, Alvin. *History of the Canadian Peoples: Beginnings to 1867, Vol. 1*. Toronto: Pearson Education Canada, 2008, fifth edition.

Conrad, Margaret and Finkel, Alvin. *History of the Canadian Peoples: 1867 to the Present, Vol. 2*. Toronto: Pearson Education Canada, 2008, fifth edition.

Copping, Arthur E. *The Golden Land: The True Story and Experiences of British Settlers in Canada*. Toronto: Musson, 1911.

Corbett, Gail H. *Nation Builders: Barnardo Children in Canada*. Toronto: Dundurn Press, 2002.

Routledge and Sons, 1913.

Johnston, Hugh. *The Voyage of the Komagata Maru: The Sikh Challenge to Canada's Colour Bar.* Bombay: Oxford University Press, 1979.

Kalbach, Warren. *The Impact of Immigration on Canada's Population: 1961 Census Monograph.* Ottawa: Queen's Printer, 1970.

Kelley, N. and Trebilcock, M. *The Making of the Mosaic: A History of Canadian Immigration Policy.* Toronto: University of Toronto, 1998.

Knowles, Valerie. *Strangers at Our Gates: Canadian Immigration and Immigration Policy, 1540-2006.* Toronto: Dundurn Press, 2007.

Knowles, Valerie. *Forging Our Legacy: Canadian Citizenship and Immigration, 1900-1977.* Ottawa: Citizenship and Immigration Canada, 2000.

Kobayashi, Audrey and Peake, Linda. *Urban Studies Research on Immigrants and Immigration in Canadian Cities.* Ottawa: Citizenship and Immigration, 1996.

Kohli, Marjorie. *The Golden Bridge: Young Immigrants to Canada, 1833-1939.* Toronto: Natural Heritage Books, 2003.

Kukushkin, Vadim. *From Peasants to Labourers: Ukrainian and Belarusan Immigration From the Russian Empire to Canada.* Montreal: McGill-Queen's University Press, 2007.

Lew, Byron. *European Immigration to Canada During the 1920's: The Impact of U.S. Quotas and Canadian Restrcitions.* Manuscript, 2000.

Lindal, W.J. *Canadian Citizenship and Our Wider Loyalties.* Winnipeg: Canada Press Club, 1946.

Lindal, W.J. *Icelanders in Canada.* Ottawa: National Publishers, 1967.

Lloyd's Maritime Atlas. London: Informa Publishing, 2009.

Ma, Ching. *Chinese Pioneers: Materials Concerning the Immigration of Chinese to Canada and Sino-Canadian Relations.* Vancouver: Versatile, 1979.

MacDonald, Norman. *Canada Immigration and Colonization 1841-1903.* Aberdeen, Scotland: Aberdeen University Press, 1966.

Mackay, Donald. *Flight From Famine: The Coming of the Irish to Canada.* Toronto: Dundurn Press, 2009.

Maheu, Robert. *Les Francophones du Canada, 1941-1991.* Montreal: Parti Pris, 1970.

Merriman, Brenda Dougall. *Genealogy in Ontario: Searching the Records.* Toronto: Ontario Genealogical Society, 2008.

Messamore, Barbara, ed. *Canadian Migration Patterns from Britain and North America.* Ottawa: University of Ottawa Press, 2004.

Mitic, Trudy Duivenvoorden. *People in Transition: Reflections on Becoming Canadian.* Markham, Ontario: Fitzhenry and Whiteside, 2001.

Mitic, Trudy D. and LeBlanc, J. P. *Pier 21: The Gateway That Changed Canada.* Halifax: Lancelot Press Nimbus, 1988.

Moore, Christopher. *The Loyalists: Revolution, Exile, Settlement.* Toronto: McClelland and Stewart, 1994.

Norris, John. *Strangers Entertained: A History of the Ethnic Groups of British Columbia.* Vancouver: Evergreen Press, 1971.

Norton, Wayne. *Help Us to a Better Land: Crofter Colonies in the Prairie West.* Regina: Canadian Plains Research Center, University of Regina, 1994.

Obee, Dave. *Western Canadian Directories on Microfilm and Microfiche.* Victoria, British Columbia: Dave Obee, 2003.

O'Driscoll, Robert and Reynolds, Lorna, eds. *The Untold Story: The Irish in Canada.* Toronto: Celtic Arts Of Canada 1988.

O'Gallagher, Marianna. *Grosse Île: Gateway to Canada 1832-1937.* Ste. Foy, Quebec: Livres Carraig Books, 2001.

Palmer, Howard. *Immigration and the Rise of Multiculturalism.* Toronto: Copp Clark, 1975.

Parr, Joy. *Labouring Children: British Immigrant Apprentices to Canada, 1869-1924.* Montreal: McGill-Queen's University Press, 1980.

Perin, Roberto and Sturino, Franc. *Arrangiarsi: The Italian Immigration Experience in Canada.* Toronto: Guernica Editions, 1989.

Public Archives of Canada. *Ships' Passenger Lists and Border Entry Lists in PAC RG 76 (Records of the Immigration Branch).* Ottawa: Public Archives of Canada, 1986.

Ramcharan, Subhas. *Racism: Non-Whites in Canada.* Scarborough, Ontario: Butterworths, 1982.

Ramirez, Bruno. *Crossing the 49th Parallel: Migration From Canada to the United States, 1900-1930.* Ithaca, New York: Cornell University Press, 2001.

Rees, Ronald. *New and Naked Land: Making the Prairies Home.* Saskatoon: Western Producer Prairie Books, 1988.

Reid, William D. *The Loyalists in Ontario: The Sons and Daughters of the American Loyalists of Upper Canada.* Lambertville, New Jersey.: Hunterdon Press, 1973.

Richmond, Anthony. *Post-War Immigrants in Canada.* Toronto: University of Toronto Press, 1967.

Roberts, Barbara. *Whence They Came: Deportation From Canada, 1900-1935.* Ottawa: University of Ottawa Press, 1988.

Robertson, Heather. *Salt of the Earth: The Story of the Homesteaders in Western Canada.* Toronto: James Lorimer, 1974.

Sadouski, John. *History of the Byelorussians in Canada.* Belleville, Ontario: Mika Publishing Company, 1981.

Secretary of State. *Annual Reports,* 1915-1932. Ottawa: Secretary of State.

Serge, Joe. *Canadian Citizenship Made Simple.* Toronto: Doubelday, 1993.

Shepperson, Wilbur S. *British Emigration to North America.* Oxford, England: Basil Blackwell, 1957.

Stechishin, Julian V. *A History of Ukrainian Settlement in Canada.* Saskatoon: Ukrainian Self-Reliance League. 1992.

Stratford-Devai, Fawne. *Getting From Here To There: Identifying Origins of Immigrants to Canada.* Milton, Ont.: Global Heritage Press, 2005.

Sturhahn, William J.H. *They Came From East and West: A History of Immigration to Canada.* Winnipeg: North American Baptist Immigration and Colonization Society, 1976.

Szabo, Frank. *Austrian Immigration to Canada.* Montreal: McGill-Queen's University Press, 1996.

Tanner, Helen Hornbeck, ed. *The Settling of North America.* New York City: Macmillan, 1995.

Thompson, Alexa and van de Wiel, Debi. *Pier 21, An Illustrated History of Canada's Gateway.* Halifax: Nimbus Publishing, 2002.

Troper, Harold. *Only Farmers Need Apply.* Toronto: Griffin Press, 1972.

United Empire Loyalists' Association of Canada, Heritage Branch. *The Loyalists of Quebec, 1774-1825.* Montreal: Heritage Branch of the United Empire Loyalists, 1989.

United Empire Loyalists' Association of Canada, Toronto Branch. *Loyalist Lineages of Canada 1783-1983.* Toronto: United Empire Loyalists' Association of Canada, Toronto Branch, 1983 and 1991.

VanderMey, Albert. *To All Our Children: The Story of the Postwar Dutch Immigration to Canada.* 1983. St. Catharines, Ontario: Paideia Press, 1903.

Verma, Archana B. *The Making of Little Punjab in Canada: Patterns of Immigration.* New Delhi: Sage Publications, 2002.

Walker, Barrington. *The History of Immigration and Racism in Canada: Essential Readings.* Toronto: Canadian Scholars' Press, 2008.

Wallace, Theresa. *The Role of Transportation in Canadian Immigration 1900-2000.* Ottawa: Canada Citizenship and Immigration, 2001.

Whetton, Cecilia. *The Promised Land: The Story of the Barr Colonists.* Lloydminster: Lloydminster Times, 1953.

Whyte, Donald. *Dictionary of Scottish Emigration to Canada Before Confederation.* Four volumes. Toronto: Ontario Genealogical Society, 1986-2005.

Winks, Robin W. *Blacks in Canada: A History.* Montreal: McGill-Queen's University Press, 1972.

Woodham-Smith, Cecil. *Great Hunger: Ireland, 1845-1849.* London: Penguin, 1992.

Woodsworth, James S. *Strangers Within Our Gates.* Toronto: University of Toronto Press, 1970 (first edition 1909).

Woycenko, Ol'ha. *The Ukrainians in Canada.* Winnipeg: Trident Press, 1968.

Wright, Esther Clark. *The Loyalists of New Brunswick.* Fredericton: the author, 1955.

Wright, Harold E. *The Diary of Nellie McGowan: Partridge Island Quarantine Station 1902.* Saint John, New Brunswick: Partridge Island Research Project, 1984.

Zuehlke, Mark. *Scoundrels, Dreamers, and Second Sons: British Remittance Men in the Canadian West.* North Vancouver: Whitecap Books, 1994.

Index

About the author

Dave Obee has been researching family history since 1978. He has given more than 300 presentations on genealogical research techniques at conferences in Canada and the United States, and is the author of several guides for genealogists.

Dave is the author of *Making the News*, published by the *Times Colonist* in Victoria, British Columbia, in 2008 to mark the 150th anniversary of the newspaper. He is also the co-author (with Sherry Irvine) of *Finding Your Canadian Ancestors: A Beginner's Guide*, published by Ancestry in 2007.

He served as president of the Federation of East European Family History Societies from 2004 through 2007 and runs CanGenealogy.com, an essential gateway to family history research in Canada.

Dave has been a newspaper reporter or editor for several different newspapers in British Columbia and Alberta since 1972. He is currently editorial page editor of the *Times Colonist*.

His other books of genealogical interest:
- *Making the News: A Times Colonist Look at 150 Years of History*
- *British Columbia 1871: A List of Residents Based on the Work of Edward Mallandaine*
- *Finding Your Canadian Ancestors: A Beginner's Guide* (with Sherry Irvine)
- *Back to the Land: A Genealogical Guide to Finding Farms on the Canadian Prairies*
- *Western Canadian Directories on Microfiche and Microfilm*
- *Royal Oak Burial Park: A History and Guide*
- *Federal Voters Lists in Western Canada 1935-1979*
- *Federal Voters Lists in Ontario 1935-1979*
- *Lethbridge 1891: A Settlement Becomes a Town*